CONTENTS

'Digo, paciencia y barajar!'
'I say, patience and shuffle the cards!'
(Miguel de Cervantes 1547–1616)

CHAPTER 1

BIRDS OF A FEATHER

The sky was blue. So was Ellie, and I knew how she felt. Mario Lanzarote had just died. He had been showing signs of dandruff. Nothing much to worry about in that, you might say. Perhaps not, except that Mario's dandruff had appeared between his toes.

'Athlete's foot,' I'd said to Ellie.

'Canaries aren't noted for their athleticism,' she'd pointed out. 'And anyway, Mario's feathers are starting to fall out, too.' She indicated the back of his head. 'A bald patch, see?'

I still hadn't felt the need to get too concerned. 'Probably just starting to moult . . . or a touch of athlete's head, maybe?'

Ellie was neither convinced nor amused. 'I think you should take him to the vet. Could be fowl pest. Bumble-foot, even.'

'*Bumble*-foot?' A little knowing snort of derision. 'Been reading the veterinary dictionary again, have you?'

'Well, there's nothing wrong with that. It's full of explanations about symptoms and things. Very useful, in fact.'

1

'Hmm, the same as *The Family Health Guide* is very useful. I know you. Every time you read about a nice juicy symptom – bingo! – you've got the disease. I mean, it's only a couple of months since you had that pimple on your top lip and thought you were developing bubonic plague. And now you're doing the same thing with the bloody canary, for heaven's sake!'

'But –'

'Forget it, Ellie. I am *not* walking into the vet's surgery toting a dinky gilded cage with Tweety's Mallorcan cousin here inside it. All those leathery old farmers sitting there with their macho hunting dogs and all, and I mince in with a balding canary. You're not on!'

'*Parásitos*,' said Señor Ramis the vet, smirking, I suspected, as he turned to write out a prescription. 'A not uncommon problem in caged birds, particularly in our Mediterranean climate. *Toma!* Take this mixture and administer it to the affected parts twice a day. *No problema.*'

I sauntered the gauntlet of the four inscrutable *campesinos* in the waiting room as strappingly as I could. '*Adiós*,' I baritoned.

'*Adéu*,' they mumbled in chorus.

Silence prevailed while I opened the door; dramatic moments of silence broken only by a sudden snorting snore from the piglet cradled in one of the old fellows' arms. Then one waggish old *compadre* smiled at me and added dryly,

2

'May your little hen soon be back on the lay, *señor*.'

They didn't laugh as I left. The titters would have been kept diplomatically on hold until they heard me starting the car; of that I was sure. A sign of the respect – face-to-face, at any rate – which we had come to appreciate from our farming neighbours around the little town of Andratx in south-west Mallorca, where we had settled some months earlier.

Ellie had elected to wait at home at Ca's Mayoral, our little orange farm in a valley amid the mountains away to the north of the town, while I made the reluctant trip to the vet with Mario. He'd been named Mario Lanzarote, incidentally, because he could sing, as could the late tenor Mario Lanza, and the 'rote' suffix had been added to make the Canary connection – Islands, that is.

'Too many things to do about the house,' Ellie had said. 'Anyway, you can explain things in Spanish much better than I can.'

She was busy watching a dubbed episode of *Neighbours* on TV when I got back.

'Spanish-ised tittle-tattle of the Melbourne suburbs easier to cope with than complicated words like *canario* for "canary" and *enfermo* for "infirm", is it?'

'No need to be sarcastic.' Her eyes never left the screen. 'Anyway, what did the vet say?'

'Talk about humiliation,' I muttered, hanging Mario's cage on its hook on the kitchen wall. 'I mean, I *do* bump into those old guys occasionally, you know. Down at the agricultural supplies store when I'm buying fertilizer or something. I was just beginning to get accepted by them, too.'

'Good. What did the vet say?'

'You know what I mean – I was finally getting round to talking to those old farmers about how we used to de-horn bullocks, castrate bull calves and snip the spare tits off heifers back in Scotland. That's the sort of stuff they understand. The only common denominators I've got with them. Then they catch me slinking out of the vet's with a poncy canary under my arm.'

'Mmm, good. Just a minute, I'm trying to catch this bit on the telly here.' With that, Ellie erupted into cascades of laughter. 'Priceless! Really priceless, this!' She glanced round fleetingly at me. 'Every bit as good in Spanish as it is in English.'

'But you don't understand anything they're saying.'

'Don't need to. Sh-h-h-h!'

I said amen to this unwittingly apt critique and started to prepare the anti-parasite mixture while Ellie revelled in the last few unintelligible minutes of her favourite soap. Bonny, our young boxer bitch, looked on intrigued as I clumsily tried to pluck the fluttering, panic-stricken Mario from his cage.

'Don't, you're frightening him!' Ellie chided, the feathered clamour having hauled her away from the rolling end-credits of *Neighbours*. 'Here, I'll do it.'

Sure enough, after a canary-soothing word or two, Mario was safely in her hand, dandruffy feet

4

sticking out one end, still reasonably-well-plumed head protruding out of the other.

Bonny licked her lips.

'So, what did the vet say?'

'Parasites. Dab on this mixture until the condition clears up. *No problema.*'

'Right, I'll hold. You dab.'

And so the twice-daily routine began. *No problema.*

Two weeks later Mario died. A shivering, sad, nocturnal death on the wall above Bonny's bed, my old straw hat placed on the roof of his cage to help keep out the draughts. But a tiny bird, stark naked except for a little tuft of feathers on the top his head, needs more than a straw hat to keep him warm at night – even in Mallorca. For several days Mario had looked like an oven-ready micro-chicken with a Mohican haircut, a pathetic-looking little fellow whose wretched state had prompted Ellie to start knitting him a pullover. He never got to wear it.

I buried Mario down among the almond trees which he'd looked out over when singing joyously from his sunny-day position on the balcony wall. I buried him in his cage.

'I notice you buried your favourite old straw hat with him as well,' Ellie sniffed when I got back to the house. She blew her nose and wiped her tear-filled eyes. 'That was a really touching thing to do – sending him off with the only thing of comfort he'd known recently. Just like a little Pharaoh.' She started to sob. 'Poor wee Mario.'

I snuggled her head to my shoulder, too ashamed to admit that the real reason I'd buried the hat with him was that I didn't fancy contracting avian leprosy, or any of the other nasty-sounding birdy ailments which I'd secretly identified in the veterinary dictionary since the onset of Mario's inevitable demise. Bumble-foot included.

Pep, our quirky old neighbour across the lane, had been right. '*Coño!*' he'd grunted the first time he saw Mario, 'it's the height of cruelty to keep a bird in a cage – unless you're going to eat him, *naturalmente.*'

Not that I'm suggesting that Pep ate canaries. He'd been alluding, I guess, to the little homemade wooden cage that always hung outside his front door and contained, one at a time, a short-lived succession of plump little red-legged partridges. Anyway, Pep's paradoxical qualification aside, I made a silent vow after burying Mario never to keep a caged bird again. Luck, in that respect, didn't seem to run in the family . . .

'You pay more attention to that budgie than you do to me,' my mother had told my father many years earlier, shortly after I'd first flown the family nest myself, leaving my parents to concentrate all their energies into getting on each other's nerves uninterrupted for the first time since my elder sister and I were born. 'You spoil it rotten.'

Ten minutes later, the budgie was dead. I was given the full account of his bizarre passing on my first visit back home to Scotland after moving to London to be a professional jazz musician a few months earlier. Chirpy, my mother related sadly, had been having his nightly spell of exercise, released from his cage to fly around the living room, working off a bellyful of seed from a new millet spray. After a few minutes, he'd tired of flying and settled in his customary position on my father's shoulder – all nice and cosy on an easy-chair by the fire, being tickled under his beak and making occasional short flips onto my father's hand to nibble pieces out of the edge of his newspaper. Every so often, he'd pause to undertake a head-bobbing show of breeding intentions to one of my father's fingernails. But Chirpy soon got fed up with that stretch-of-the-imagination routine as well. My father knew the sign. The excited little fellow had neatly dumped an attention-grabbing dropping on his thumb.

'Time to play oops-a-daisy, is it, Chirpy?' he said good-naturedly, putting down the newspaper and cupping the trusting little bird in the palm of his hand.

Chirpy knew what was coming, and he could hardly wait. 'Touch o' fine frost, wee man!' he croaked in animated budgie tones.

This statement was Chirpy's version of my father's usual greeting to him: 'Fine day, wee man. Touch of frost, though, eh?' But it was close enough to accuracy to have convinced my father long since that his little feathered pal was a verbal genius – potentially the first budgerigar poet ever. *And* it was a further sign that Chirpy was ready to play oops-a-daisy. So the nightly fun and games began – Chirpy being flung up in the air, squawking delightedly, then checking his swift upwards trajectory with a timely spreading of his wings, before fluttering back down to my father's hand to be launched on the next thrilling innerspace trip.

Whether it was over-enthusiasm on my father's part, a momentary lapse of concentration on Chirpy's, or simply just bad luck, we'll never know, but on the fourth fun flight, Chirpy, for the first time ever, hit the ceiling. Hard. As my parents looked on in anguish, he tumbled, wings motionless, bounced off a wall and disappeared behind the sideboard. Desperately, the heavy piece of furniture was hauled aside. Chirpy was lying against the skirting board, the only sign of life a feeble blinking of an eye as my distraught father kneeled to pick him up.

'Back's broken,' Dad said, his voice quivering. 'Paralysed.'

Chirpy had played his last game of oops-a-daisy. And so had my father.

My mother went straight into a flap over the plight of their flightless pet. 'He – he must be in terrible pain, the little chap,' she twittered, holding out a comforting finger towards the doomed budgie, but stopping short of actually touching him. 'What are you going to do, for Pete's sake!'

'Vet – I'll take him to the –'

'Don't be so stupid! That'll only prolong poor Chirpy's agony.'

'Wh-what am I going to do then?'

A state of panic was building up in the living room. What *was* he going to do?

'Gas,' my mother blurted out. 'Gas – budgies are like canaries – one whiff and he'll be gone. It's the kindest way.' She shoved my father towards the kitchen. 'Go on! Quickly, before he suffers any more.'

'But –'

'You've *got* to put him out of his misery. Now!'

His emotions in turmoil, my father stumbled to the gas hob, my mother goading him on. With a last whispered farewell to his beloved Chirpy, he held the little bird over one of the gas rings. Dad swallowed hard, fighting back the tears. Then, his hand shaking, he turned the knob. An instant hiss. The choking smell of gas. Chirpy trembled almost imperceptibly in my father's fingers, his little heart beating wildly.

'It's OK, wee man,' my father quavered. 'It'll soon be over now.'

Not quite.

What my father had forgotten in his distress was that the hob was equipped with auto-ignite.

'The sink!' my mother shrieked as my father juggled with the auto-ignited budgie blazing in his hands. 'Quick! Get him under the tap before he burns to death!'

Beyond thinking clearly now, my father did as

9

instructed. When the smoke from his singed feathers had cleared, Chirpy was at last dead. Very dead. Mugged, gassed, incinerated *and* drowned, with probably a heart attack thrown in at the end for good measure.

'I meant it for the best,' my father told me, his voice breaking emotionally while we stood over the tiny wooden cross that he'd placed at the head of Chirpy's grave in the back garden.

I couldn't think of an appropriate reply. Even Chirpy would have been hard pushed to do that, no matter how great a verbal genius my father thought his little feathered pal had been.

'You and your damned oops-a-daisy!' my mother berated, glaring at my father on her way past to bring in the washing. 'That's the last budgie *we'll* ever have!'

It was. And Mario Lanzarote would be the last canary *we'd* ever have.

Fortunately, it was September and there was much fruit-picking to do. Keeping busy, I was sure, would be the best cure for the dead-canary blues. So I coaxed Ellie out into the orchards the moment she'd shown signs of pulling herself together.

'Figs!' cried old Maria Bauzà, her twiggy little frame clad all in black as ever, her eyes glinting like tiny black olives beneath the shade of her straw hat as she glowered at me over the drystone wall that separated our two *fincas*. 'Look at all the figs on the ground!'

'Yes, well, no matter how often we pick them, there's always a few fallen ones every morning. Seems to be the way of –'

'*Hombre!* It is the way of the fig. That is why we Mallorcan farmers always keep a pig!'

Not again. I'd had a bellyful of Maria's well-meaning dissertations on the necessity of keeping a family pig on these little fruit farms. I'd actually bought one a while back, more to keep her happy than anything else, and had been instantly humiliated by the superiority-complexed piglet in return for my lack of . . . well, pig-headedness. The little porker escaped into the surrounding mountains before I'd even put him in his pen, and that, when all was said and done, had probably been the best possible outcome to the entire episode. No, second best, actually – the pig never showing up again being the ultimate reward as far as I was concerned. For, no matter how dispassionate we'd have tried to be, the pig would have been given a name, would have become more of a pet than a fallen-fruit recycler and, knowing Ellie, would never have been converted into chops, bacon and sausages. 'Porky', like Chirpy, would have been spoiled rotten, would have lived (unlike Chirpy) to a ripe old age – overfed, overweight and, given his arrogant mien, totally overbearing. A bloody nuisance, in fact.

But my worries today were unfounded. Maria wasn't about to resurrect past differences of opinion on the merits of keeping a pig. She turned her attention to Ellie, her impish features wrinkling into that distinctive little grin of hers, a mischievous smile that was still infectious, despite her trademark 'two-up-three-down' teeth being hidden behind a cupped hand on this occasion. It was a mannerism that I hadn't seen Maria employ before, and this was the second time she'd done so already today. Strange.

'As the Scottish *señor* does not have one,' she said to Ellie, while throwing me a dismissive glance, 'would *la señora escocesa* mind if I come onto your land to gather up the fallen figs every morning? For my own pig, you understand.'

We wouldn't mind at all, and Ellie told her so without hesitation. Letting Maria put to good use fruit that would otherwise go to waste was the least we could do in return for the generosity she'd shown us since our arrival in the valley; regular gifts of *finca*-fresh eggs, for instance, and even succulent cuts of meat from her own fig-fed pig (last year's model, of course).

It had struck me often enough how country ways and customs can change within a relatively short space of time. I well remember my own grandfather telling me how he'd always kept a pig or two – 'for the hooks on the kitchen ceiling, thoo kens' – on his own cattle farm back in the Orkney Islands between the two world wars. Even after moving to a farm in the south of Scotland in the late 'thirties, he'd thought nothing of butchering a sheep or even a small bullock for the families and neighbour's needs when the occasion arose. And here was I now, a mere two generations later, already too accustomed to the convenience of the supermarket, and, truth to tell, too chicken-hearted, to keep a pig for slaughter in a farming system that, as old Maria maintained, really did call out for it. I knew that Maria thought I was some kind of daft foreign wimp, a *loco extranjero*, who clearly didn't know his arse from his elbow when it came to making the most out of a little fruit farm like Ca's Mayoral. And she was right. Trouble is, though, when Maria's generation is gone, such age-old country customs as the *matances*, the party-throwing occasion of the annual killing and butchering of the family pig, will die out in Mallorca too. Tesco, Sainsbury and the food hygiene brigade have a lot to answer for – though the pigs probably won't notice the demise of the *matances* parties.

'*Sí*, you're, uhm-ah, very welcome, Maria,' Ellie bumbled in her customary Spanglish. '*Muy* welcome to the, ehm, *higados* on the ground.'

The fact that *higo* is the Spanish word for 'fig', and *higado* the word for 'liver', didn't seem to matter to Maria. She knew what Ellie was trying to say, and another hand-hidden grin showed that she didn't want to let Ellie see that she was tickled by yet another of *la Señora de Escocia*'s habitual linguistic clangers. Well, at least that's what I assumed had prompted the hand-to-mouth action this time.

But be that as it may, I was absolutely certain that, if Ellie had had the vocabulary, she would

13

have invited Maria to help herself to what figs were still on the trees as well. Figs and Ellie, you see, don't get on at all well. Or, rather, fig *leaves* and Ellie. For, despite their legendary dress usage as depicted on your typical ancient Greek statue, the large leaves of the fig tree can cause a skin irritation for some people – a fairly severe irritation in Ellie's case. They didn't bother me so much, although the slightly prickly feel that they have isn't particularly pleasant, often prompting me to ponder that the private parts of the characters of Greek mythology must have been as tough as old boots. And I can assure you that not even the most hardy of true Scotsmen would fancy wearing a kilt lined with fig leaves!

Fortunately, though, we didn't have too many fig trees at Ca's Mayoral. Orange trees mainly, row after regular row of the evergreen umbrellas stretching away over little walled fields lying snugly beneath the encircling green arms of the Tramuntana Mountains. There were lemons, too; and apricots, persimmons, quinces, loquats, almonds and carobs, plus several more exotic fruit and nut varieties that, coming from the cooler northern climes of Scotland, we'd had no experience of farming before settling in Mallorca. In fact, I was so ignorant of the subject that I'd even thought that 'navel' oranges were so called because they'd been fed to old-time seafarers to protect them from scurvy. It was only when Señor Jeronimo, our friendly Mallorcan fruit merchant from along the coast in Peguera, pointed out the distinctive belly button adorning the nether regions of this particular variety that I realised my knowledge of citrus fruit was about as derisory as my spelling prowess.

We'd been faced with a steep learning curve in our quest to adapt to and thrive in a way of farming so different from the barley-and-bullocks regime that we'd been accustomed to in Scotland, but we were getting there, thanks in no small measure to the support and advice so un-stintingly given by neighbours like Maria and old Pep. Although they'd never said so to us, there can be little doubt that they must have regarded us with some suspicion when we first arrived in their valley. To them, we'd probably have been just another example of what many of their rural compatriots looked upon as those 'more money than sense' foreigners who buy a Mallorcan farm only to make use of the house for loaf-about holidays, while allowing the land and trees to fall into disuse and ultimate ruination. *Coño*, what was the countryside of Mallorca coming to!

And it's a fact that more and more of these little farms throughout the island had already succumbed to precisely that fate as the older generation of country folk began to fade away. In many cases, their offspring had long since deserted their rustic roots to work in tourism-related jobs; often the bars, restaurants and hotels that for several decades now had sprung up like concrete mushrooms along previously unspoiled and pricelessly-beautiful stretches of the Mallorcan coastline. The lure of bright lights, 'easy' money and its material derivatives had been too much for those young country people to resist. Would any of us have reacted any differently anywhere else, given the same circumstances? For what was the alternative? A life, like that of their forebears, of manual work in the harsh summer heat of the fields, with little to look forward to but callused hands, a bad back, the fickle affections of your donkey, and the simple, home-cooked food gleaned from your land? Very likely. But that, on the face of it, was precisely the life that Ellie and I had chosen for ourselves and our two sons.

We, however, were foreigners (perhaps starry-eyed foreigners in many a Mallorcan pragmatist's view), and we visualised more to it all than merely the physical demands imposed by such a life. There was also the life*style* to appreciate – the *tranquilo* pace of working days spent in such wonderful surroundings and, just as importantly, in such a benign climate compared to the one we had left behind. Not that we were aiming to live as drop-outs or 'good-life' hippies, playing it cool in a rustic Mediterranean dreamland with the real world drifting hazily by. We couldn't have afforded to do that for a start, even if we'd wanted to, which we didn't. We were hands-on small farmers, we had a living to make for a family of four, and our aim (no matter how naively ambitious) was to develop this run-down *finca* in a way that would make such a living a viable one. And, in the process, we had no intention of stepping back in time any farther than was absolutely necessary. A donkey, for example, had never been on my shopping list!

But then, most of the local farmers, with the notable exception of 'there's nothing like the old days' diehards like Maria and Pep, had also switched allegiances from their four-legged friends to tractors long ago. Many of them, in eagerly yielding to 'progress', had even deserted their little honey-stone farmhouses to live in the all-mod-cons comfort of new apartments in Andratx town. Travelling the mile or two by moped or rattly 2CV van to their fields every day was a cheap price to pay for access to the best of both worlds – *plus*, the little farmhouse in the valley would always be there as a weekend retreat for departed young ones to return to with their own children when the old folks were dead and gone. And that, indeed, was already becoming the way of things for many Mallorcan country families. So it followed that our decision to try to reverse the trend had encouraged sympathetic reactions from incorrigible devotees of the old ways like Maria, once her inclination to regard us as crazy foreigners had subsided.

'What of your two sons?' she inquired, bending down to gather some fallen figs into her basket. 'Such strong young *chicos*. They will produce many fine grandchildren for you soon enough, mark my words, *Sí, claro.*'

'I bloody well hope not!' I said to myself, smiling politely at our old neighbour's well-intentioned remark. Hell's bells, having only just turned eighteen, Sandy needed a sprog even less than I needed a pig! And the thought of twelve-year-old Charlie putting some young *muchacha* up the spout didn't even bear thinking about!

'Well, Maria,' I replied, 'Charlie's back at school today, along at Sant Agustí near Palma. First day of the new term, you know. And Sandy – well, Sandy's still back in Scotland.'

Maria raised a critical eyebrow. 'It has been a long vacation for Señorito Sandee, no? Two weeks away from the *finca* of his parents is too long. *Madre mía*, he should be here helping you with the work! After all, one day the farm will be his, and with a wife and *muchos infantós* to support, he will have to –'

'Ehm, no, he's not on holiday,' I cut in, not wanting to be bombarded with any of Maria's hypothetical problems while I was still trying to cope with more than enough actual ones. 'He's actually gone back to work in the grain harvest. Just keeping his hand in at driving the big tractors he was used to and everything.'

'*Por qué?* Why? Bad enough to encourage him to work with the *small* tractor you have here. Stinking *máquina*! He should be learning how to work with a good Mallorcan donkey, and so should you!'

Maria's ensuing mutterings in her native *mallorquín* language spared me having to explain to her that the real reason for Sandy's return to Scotland was that, despite his initial enthusiasm for the move to Mallorca, after less than a year in the valley, he was unsure if this was really the life for him. A future working in a relatively antiquated style of farming, and in a fairly remote place that had already been deserted by so many native Mallorcans of his own generation, had gradually seemed less and less attractive. He missed the wide, open countryside of southern Scotland, the big, rolling East Lothian grain fields, the lush pastures, the modern farm machinery that was growing in size and sophistication to match a go-ahead young lad's aspirations. He missed 'home', and his returning for a spell had really been to find out for himself if his longing for it had merely been a fabrication of his being away, or if indeed he felt that his future lay back there, and not in the sleepy Sa Coma valley where his family had now put down roots. It was a dilemma, and the solution to it worried Ellie and me considerably. But it was a subject we had avoided mentioning to our venerable neighbours for fear of offending and even, perhaps, of disappointing them. Was the recent transfusion of much-needed young blood into the valley to start haemorrhaging so quickly? It was a question we hoped we wouldn't have to answer . . . not for a while yet, anyway.

'*Jesús, Maríay José!*' Maria gasped, her mouth

falling open to reveal a quartet of unnaturally white incisor teeth where the gap between her two yellowing upper-gum stalactites should have been. 'Talk about *excéntrica*, no?'

Struggling to tear our eyes away from the old woman's bizarre new dental attributes, we followed her pop-eyed gaze to the far side of our field, where Francisca Ferrer, the wily *mallorquina* woman who had sold us Ca's Mayoral, was walking along the headland of her own field with her customary attendant train of two mongrel dogs and a motley gang of half-wild cats. Her feet were hidden behind the low dividing wall, the steady, un-bobbing forward motion of her immacu-lately coiffured head giving the impression that she was somehow floating over the ground – or riding a motorised skateboard, as young Charlie preferred to ponder.

We'd had our share of tiffs with the petite and deceptively demure Francisca and her officious husband Tomás from time to time; nothing to come to blows about, just annoying little incidents that suggested the Ferrers were inclined to forget that Ca's Mayoral didn't belong to them any more. Having retained ownership of one field when selling us the rest of the farm, they'd since had a little mill that stood against the boundary with our land converted into a *casita fin de semana*, a small house in which they could spend weekends away from their smart apartment in Palma, where Tomàs held a prominent position in local government.

Francisca had grown up at Ca's Mayoral, the *finca* of her parents, and Tomàs had had a similar small-farm upbringing near the village of Felanitx on the other side of the island. The land and the country ways of Mallorca were in their blood, and despite the elevated social status they had attained since their move to the city many years ago, they still genuinely loved to return to the valley every weekend to till the soil and tend the trees on their field. Well, Tomàs did, while Francisca preferred to swan regally about their property with her entourage of scruffy cats and dogs in tow. But she adored those little creatures, and the feeling was clearly mutual. Besides, since resolving our differences with them, we'd found the Ferrers to be genial (albeit a mite reservedly), respectful and occasionally generous weekend neighbours. While we were never likely to become bosom buddies with them, a feeling of peaceful, if slightly strained, coexistence had built up, and that suited us fine. And if Francisca's devotion to her raggle-taggle menagerie of cats and dogs seemed a tad eccentric, then far be it from us to question or criticise. As newcomers to the valley, we wanted to be on as good terms as possible with *all* of our neighbours, after all.

Not so old Maria. She couldn't stand Francisca Ferrer, and it had become obvious that the sentiment was reciprocated. We had heard a few rumoured reasons for the patent ill-feeling that existed between the two women. Everything had

21

been mooted, from inherited wrangles about water rights to decades-old jealousies involving a mutual romantic suitor. The former we could understand, because shared wells and the inevitable hassles over equal access to their precious water (the very lifeblood of agriculture in a Mediterranean climate) had already featured on our list of Mallorcan lessons learned the hard way. The latter was a much less credible vindication of the feud, however – particularly when Pep, the cantankerous old shepherd with the *finca* across the lane from ours, was whispered to have been the Romeo at the centre of all the fuss. There were three reasons for doubting that this could have been the case. Firstly, Pep could have been anything upwards of fifteen years older than Francesca, and secondly, Maria (over ninety and past counting!) was probably at least twenty years Pep's senior. That's not to say that such age differences would have mattered that much if the object of the two women's desires had been, well . . . desirable. But old Pep? Scraggy old *Pep*, the tasty hunk of beefcake in a sandwich of squabbled-over love? It seemed unlikely, and this for the third reason that here was a man who appeared, nowadays at least, more of a mule-mounted Don Quixote than even a threadbare, beret-and-bomber-jacket version of Don Juan. In truth, we'd probably never find out the real reason for Maria's loathing of Francisca, but the evidence of its existence was never disguised.

Maria's expression was a mix of disbelief and utter glee. 'So!' she smirked, nodding towards the gliding figure of Señora Ferrer, 'Queen Cleopatra has truly lost her needles at last! *Magnífico!*'

And indeed it did look as if Francisca had, perhaps, passed over the narrow divide between gentle eccentricity and full-blown loopiness. Having now led her procession of diminutive disciples into the open, it was possible for us to see clearly what Maria had obviously caught a glimpse of when Francisca had traversed a gap in the wall a moment or two before. Leading the entourage immediately behind her heels was not a hairy creature as usual, but a feathered one. Not a pet hen, though, not a tame duck, not even a peripatetic goose, nor any other common farmyard fowl. No, the bird waddling along happily behind its mistress today was –

'A parrot!' I gasped.

'A green one!' Ellie noted, slack-jawed.

'*Lunática!*' Maria grunted, screwing a gnarled forefinger into her temple. '*Totalmente loca!* I always knew the woman was a few oranges short of the kilo!' Her bony old shoulders shook as she wheezed a delighted little titter into her cupped hand.

'A perambulating parrot?' I muttered, still struggling to believe what I was seeing.

'But why doesn't it just fly away?' Ellie asked, transfixed.

'Must've clipped the poor bugger's wings.'

'But why don't the cats and dogs go for it?'

'They would, quicker than it could say "Pretty Polly", if it wasn't for Saint Francisca there and her strange influence over them.'

'Hmm, she does have an uncanny way with animals.' Ellie scratched her head. 'Imagine that,' she sighed, 'a parrot leading a parade of cats and dogs. Who'd have believed it?'

'*Una bruja!*' Maria growled. 'A witch! Always thought so – now it's proved!' She crossed herself and raised her eyes heavenward, mumbling in Latin now.

A few hours later the parrot was dead, though not as a result of Maria's invocations, I'm sure. It was simply that, whatever bewitching powers Francisca may have had over domesticated creatures, they turned out not to extend to their wild cousins. Perhaps carried away a little by the thrill of the inaugural stroll through the orchard with her new parrot, Francisca had decided to treat Princessa, as she called the trusting bird, to a bracing walk along the seafront at Sant Elm, the little fishing village turned holiday resort just a few miles beyond Andratx. A small crowd had gathered on the rocky foreshore, fascinated by the sight of this middle-aged woman ambling regally along with a parrot walking and squawking in her footsteps just a few paces behind. Francisca was delighted, Princessa was delighted, the onlookers were delighted. The resident Sant Elm seagulls, however, were most definitely not. Furious at the audacity of this weird green alien tresspassing on their territory, a squadron of them swooped down on the flightless Princessa and proceeded to maul her mercilessly. Francisca was distraught, the onlookers were aghast, and Princessa was summarily dispatched – to join Chirpy and Mario Lanzarote in birdie heaven, as Ellie put it.

Dewy-eyed, she savoured the thought as we climbed into bed that night. 'I do believe in after-birth, you know – even for birds and things.'

'I think you mean the afterlife,' I yawned.

'That's what I said.'

'Hmm, yeah, OK, Ellie,' I muttered, pulling the covers over my ears. 'Goodnight, eh.'

A few moments' pensive silence.

'I wonder if Mario will have all his feathers back.'

'Mmm-hmm . . .'

More silence.

'He'll be singing to them.' Ellie's voice was crumbling into an emotion-hit yodle now. 'He'll be (*sniff!*) whistling his nice wee songs again.'

'Mmm, right enough . . .'

'Singing his wee heart out to (*bubble!*) Chirpy and Princessa.'

'Yeah, and Chirpy and Princessa will be reciting poetry to him in return.' It had been a long day and I needed sleep – badly. 'Verses from Rabbie Burns in Chirpy's case,' I snapped, 'and the Spanish parrot will be doing readings from the works of Fredrico bloody Lorca. Now go to sleep!'

More sniffles and sobs, a gulp, a shuddering

sigh, then the sound of Ellie's nose being resolutely blown. She tucked herself into her customary foetal ball. In the ensuing silence, the soporific chirping of nocturnal crickets drifted in through the open window on the balmy, citrus-scented air. Then, just as I was finally nodding off, Ellie kneed me in the backside and pronounced:

'And you know, there's something *very* strange about those new teeth of old Maria's. They're just not . . . normal!'

Yes, I thought to myself, and there's nothing like an excuse for a bit of female cattiness to finally cure the dead canary blues.

CHAPTER 2

WHEN MAÑANA MEANS *TODAY!*

Getting the long-neglected fruit trees back into good health and shape had been our top priority since arriving at Ca's Mayoral and, as autumn approached, the clusters of still-green but plump and shiny oranges on the trees promised a good harvest to come. Pepe Suau, the local tree-pruning maestro, had done a good job for us back in the early part of the year, despite our initial fears that his savage-looking surgery may have been too much for some of his 'patients' to survive. Drastic treatment was what Pepe had said was required, and the passing months had proved him absolutely right. But with all the attention we had been paying to improving the farming aspect of Ca's Mayoral, precious little time had been left to tackle the work that needed to be done in and around the house. Ellie had definite plans in mind, and with the weather set to become a little cooler soon, I knew that the days were numbered for all those *mañana*-based excuses I'd used to great effect during the stifling heat of summer. Getting the hang of slipping effortlessly into the good old Spanish procrastination syndrome hadn't been easy for a northern promptitude freak like me, but I'd managed it, and what's more, had come to enjoy it.

'Cracks in the plasterwork,' Ellie said, pointing to a series of hairline fissures running down and across the inside walls of the *almacén*, the big workroom-cum-store that occupied a good three-quarters of the ground floor of the house.

'Yes – common problem in this climate, they say. All to do with the stonework heating up in summer and cooling down again in winter. Expansion and contraction, you know. You'll never cure it in these houses.'

'I'm not asking you to cure it, just fill up the summer cracks before the winter ones come along and join them. The way things are going, these walls are going to look like a bunch of sketches for a Picasso still life before long. I mean, just look at that lot of squiggly lines beside the window there – a dead ringer for a nude woman with an eyeball staring out of her armpit.'

'Uh-huh, I *think* I see what you mean,' I said, tilting my head this way and that while squinting at the collection of cracks in question. 'But a nude isn't strictly speaking a still life, you know. Mmm, and I don't think it's her armpit the eyeball's looking out of either.' I stepped over to the wall, pointing. 'See, *that's* her arm there. What you're talking about is definitely a leg.'

'Faff about as much as you want with your smutty suggestions. It won't do you any good.

You promised to fix these cracks in April, it's now September, and we need to see to them to*day!*'

Ellie was good at using 'we' when she meant 'you'. In this case 'you' meant 'me', and I knew she also meant business.

'OK, fair enough, I'll make a start just as soon as we've finished harvesting the almonds.'

'No deal! We've only got half a dozen almond trees. It isn't even a day's work to knock the nuts off them, so that job can wait until the weekend when Charlie's around to lend a hand.'

The laid-back outlook of the Mallorcan country folk really had infected me, despite my initial attempts, no matter how futile, to resist the powerful forces of *tranquilo*ness. Back in Scotland, I'd have tackled such routine building-maintenance chores immediately and without giving it a second thought, no matter how busy we were on the land. But now, with almost a year's exposure to the *mañana* approach to life behind me, the inclination to put off anything, with the exception of farm work, that was less than absolute life and death was almost as natural as breathing.

Ellie handed me the car keys. 'Proplast is what the crack-filling stuff's called. You'll get it at the hardware store in Andratx.'

The Ferreteria Ca'n Mateu (*ferretería* meaning literally an ironmonger's, but in this case an Aladdin's Cave crammed with everything from plastic clothes pegs to rubber buckets and complete horticultural irrigation systems) is situated in the upper part of old Andratx town, on the Calle General Bernat Riera, a narrow street that eventually becomes the road to Sant Elm. It's a street that was built for nothing much wider than a couple of donkeys and carts to squeeze past on, the proximity of the facing buildings all part of the traditional Spanish way of providing maximum summer shade for the street and its inhabitants. Since becoming part of Andratx's mesmerising one-way system, the Calle General Bernat Riera can now cope easily (in theory!) with normal car and small van traffic, although scrape marks on the walls on either side are testament to how tight it is for trucks and buses to negotiate the narrower, more twisty sections. A strict no-parking rule, both to facilitate the smooth flow of vehicles along the street and for the safety of pedestrians on the narrow sidewalks, is imposed at all times, of course.

I drove in to be confronted with a scene of utter chaos. This morning, as every morning, a line of light vans was parked outside the *ferretería*, each little Citroën, Seat or Renault *furgoneta* abandoned with two wheels on the pavement and two wheels on the street, thus effecting the maximum inconvenience for driver and pedestrian alike. A builder's tipper truck, bulky, battered and belching diesel smoke, was slowly edging its way through the space left between the vans and the opposite building – a gap which looked hopelessly inadequate to me.

But then, I wasn't the Spanish driver of a Mallorcan builder's truck.

He had his elbow and head leaning out of the driver's window, the ubiquitous stubby cigar wedged in the corner of his mouth beneath the overhang of a bushy black moustache. He winked at a young mother waiting patiently with her baby's pushchair at the far end of the row of vans, her way ahead totally blocked now. She smiled coyly, her eyes lowered, lashes batting. Her baby wailed and thrashed his arms and legs about in an impatient tantrum. The young woman was soon joined by a trio of black-clad village matrons, replete with shopping baskets and gathering brows. What did the inconsiderate *tonto* of a driver think he was up to? one of the old ladies warbled at him in tones and dudgeon of equal height. *'Imbécil!'*

'Con calma, yaya!' The driver grinned. 'Take it easy, granny! Hey, don't heat your water, eh!'

'Hijo de puta barcelonesa!' another matron piped up in solidarity with her affronted companion. 'Son of a Barcelona whore!' (It should be noted that many Mallorcans like to maintain that they aren't too keen on their Catalonian cousins just over the water on the mainland. It's a bit like the attitude that some English people have towards the French, except that, in the Mallorcans' case, the distaste, in extreme examples, has been known to apply to their near neighbours' wine too, excellent wine though it may be!)

31

The driver showed the irate *vieja* an erect middle finger and sounded his truck's horn to add an extra touch of drama to the proceedings. The third old woman hobbled forward and walloped the front of the truck with her handbag, prompting further mischievous insults from the guffawing trucker. At that, the shutters of two first-floor windows on either side of the street flew open simultaneously.

'*Silencio!*' a woman screamed from one of them, her hair in curlers, one cigarette-toting hand clasping her dressing gown to her throat, the other raised in a fist. 'Some of us are trying to watch *televisión* in here! *Madre de Dios!*'

'*Cállate, guapa!*' a bleary-eyed youth, naked from the waist up, bellowed at her from the window opposite. 'Stick a pie in it, will you! *Jesucristo*, it's not even nine o'clock in the morning – middle of the goddam night!'

The crunch and tinkle of a disintegrating wing mirror accompanied the ensuing vocal pandemonium as the driver edged his truck determinedly forward. Glancing down at the newly de-mirrored van alongside, he pulled a one-shouldered shrug of insouciance and revved a billow of diesel smoke from the exhaust pipe of his constrained steed. Then another blast on the horn for good measure.

Animated whistle-blowing heralded the arrival of an officer of the *policía local*, the blue-uniformed lawmen who are expert at dealing with such everyday traffic problems in the narrow streets and alleys that are a universal feature of Mallorcan country towns. Swaggering matador-style towards the front of the truck, he weighed up the situation instantly and, with assertive blasts on his whistle and some text-book hand-signalling, proceeded to direct the driver slowly but confidently towards him. Another van's wing mirror shattered and clattered to the ground, and a howl of protest rose from a hidden householder on the far side of the truck as its protruding metal bits gouged a chunk of stone out of his window sill.

'But why doesn't the policeman just go into the hardware shop and ask the owners of the vans to move them?' I asked an elderly man who was standing beside me watching the ongoing entertainment.

'*Hombre!* Where would be the fun in that?' he scoffed. Why, he had two brothers and five cousins who had been policemen, so he knew full well how to make the most of such situations in order to liven up a boring day. '*Mira, amigo.* Just observe this, my friend.'

He tottered off to the rear corner of the truck and made his presence known to the driver by banging on the metal tailgate with his walking stick.

'Oy! Back up a bit, *tío!*'

Trusting, in a blasé sort of way, the driver obliged.

'*Excellente.* Now left hand down – keep coming – now right a bit – steady as you go – that's it.

Perfecto!' The old boy glanced round at me and smirked, while the sad sound of crushing sheet metal emanated from the point of contact between the *camión*'s huge front tyre and a little van's door.

Augmenting this pageant of unbridled mayhem, the impatient drivers of a long line of vehicles already forming behind the blockage struck up an impromptu recital of mass horn blowing. At the front of the truck, meanwhile, the *policía local* officer, who was now being harangued by the three old ladies, the young mother and the two opposing upper-floor residents, blew his whistle with renewed gusto, waved his arms, and the whole performance started all over again.

Inside the shop, a chattering congregation of half a dozen farmers and tradesmen, the actual owners of the vans that were being audibly bashed about outside, were patently unconcerned. What was another dent here and there, or another ripped-off wing mirror? That appeared to be their attitude. *Coño*, if you wanted the convenience of shop-front parking in the town centre, you had to expect a little *in*convenience as well, *sí?*

They were standing in a huddle between the door and the counter, their conversation a noisy mix of slagging off Barcelona's football team and discussions about the outlook for Mallorcan farming in the European Economic Community, which Spain was soon to join – albeit only as a provisional member. More likely only as a *temporary* member, was their unanimous view. Once those political ponces in Madrid had seen the folly of their ways, they'd soon haul the country out of the EEC again. It would bring money rolling into Spain, the politicians had said in all their build-up propaganda. Bullshit! It would ruin everything for everyone, except for the faceless administrators, that is. Bureaucrats were hungry cats to feed, one man reminded the others. Ah *sí*, another agreed, and they multiplied quicker than rabbits. And who would pay their obscenely gross salaries? 'We will!' was the unanimous reply. Taxes! Higher taxes, more taxes, dearer alcohol, dearer tobacco was what they'd be saddled with – just like those poor sods in Britain.

And that observation was a fair expression of the stalwart Spaniard's natural attraction to reducing any tax-paying liability for himself, or, if at all possible, to paying no taxes at all. It was a delightfully-rebellious attitude that had successfully permeated many a government-imposed levy, whether derived from 'declared' income or the 'officially-agreed' value of your house. And, curiously enough, it was a trait that had long been tacitly accepted by officialdom in a country where the administrators of government decrees had traditionally been known as past masters of paper-chasing, and sticklers for rubber-stamping everything that moved. Indeed, the lax attitude to taxes in Spain had attracted many 'doing-a-runner' foreigners to the country's flashier *costas* over the years, each runner arriving with a suitcase full of folding money, of course. And no questions asked.

35

There would be no shortage of people, both native and foreign, who would lament that good old fiscal lenience being eroded by Spain 'joining Europe'.

'Common Market?' the *ferretería* customers asked rhetorically. '*Vate a la mierda, amigo!* Piss right off, pal!'

Motion carried.

I had to admit to having pangs of disquiet myself about Spain becoming part of this expanding free-trade union. Britain's joining hadn't done her small farmers much good. I knew that from personal experience, and I harboured worries about how little *fincas* like Ca's Mayoral would fare once Spain's import doors were fully opened to competition from other Mediterranean fruit-growing countries. Incomes were liable to fall, and as Mallorcan farmers were already earning little more for a kilo of oranges than the cost of one orange in Britain, margins were already extremely tight. Could it be that we'd soon be facing the same 'only the biggest will survive' scenario that we'd so recently encountered to our cost in Scotland? Almost without thinking, I blurted out my feelings on the matter to the nearest *campesino* in the group, picking my words carefully, stringing them together falteringly in 'standard' Castilian Spanish.

The man, in his sixties, stocky and with the leathery skin of someone who'd spent his life in the sunny outdoors, turned his head, pushed his

36

cap back from his forehead and squinted at me, a slightly suspicious look to his expression.

'*Británico?*' he probed. 'You British?'

'Ehm, well, Scottish actually. *Sí, escocés.*'

'Ah,' he smiled, giving me a hearty slap on the shoulder, 'Scandinavian, eh! *Muy bien.* That's good.'

He and his companions then launched themselves into an enthusiastic exchange of views on the upper-body attributes of *chicas* from Denmark and the free-sex habits of those raunchy Swedish *muchachas*. These guys knew all about this stuff. They'd seen the movies, they boasted – not that their wives knew anything about that, of course! Much suggestive chortling, phallic arm movements and back-slapping followed, then the conversation returned to the topic of the threat posed to Mallorcan farmers by all this new *Comunidad Económica Europea* business. And it wasn't that they had anything against the *Británicos*, one of them stressed, hedging his bets on the geographical location of Scotland. No, it was just that the dogged refusal of 'one of those Scandinavian countries' to join this dodgy political club appealed more to their Mallorcan sense of independence than the half-baked, failed resistance of the Brits.

So, whether I liked it or not, I was included in the debate now too. But as the proceedings were being conducted in the *mallorquín* language, of which I still knew little, and not in 'mainland'

Spanish, which I could now get by in not *too* badly, my contribution to the discussion consisted mainly of the words '*sí*', when asked something in a positive sort of way, and '*no*', when the questioner's expression seemed to warrant it. For all that, as part of a typically raucous confab in which everyone talked at once anyway, my negligible input probably lent as much to the substance of the debate as any of the more verbose offerings.

Five minutes soon became ten, and ten drifted into fifteen – a mere blink of the eye in *mañana* terms, but a quarter of an hour wasted in the clock-watching eyes of my northern European taskmistress back at Ca's Mayoral. I stopped saying '*sí*' and '*no*' for a moment and looked anxiously towards the counter, where a chap in a cement-caked boiler suit had been mulling over the respective pros and cons of two identical-looking bricklayer's trowels since I'd come in. At last, the brickie lifted his elbows from the counter, stood up, pinged the blade of first one trowel then the other with his fingernail, listening intently to the ringing tone of each, the way a musician would to a tuning fork. He repeated the process a few times, then dropped the corners of his mouth and shook his head. No, he told the patiently waiting shopkeeper, he'd stick with his trusty old trowel out in the van, *gracias* all the same. Unperturbed, the shopkeeper dropped the corners of *his* mouth and raised a slow, 'suit yourself' shrug. There'd be plenty other days and plenty other bricklayers. *No problema.* He took the trowels and replaced them on their shelf in the back corner of the store.

'*Quién sigue?*' he shouted when back behind the counter. 'Who's next?'

My five debating society friends were all ahead of me, but not one of them budged, stopped talking, or even glanced round at the shopkeeper.

'*Quién sigue?*' he repeated wearily. '*Hey, hombres, a quién toca, eh?*'

Still no response from the debating society.

Well, I thought, if no one else was in any hurry to be served, there was no point in me standing about waiting any longer. I'd already indulged in enough *mañana*ness for one morning. 'Two large packs of Proplast, *por favor*,' I said, approaching the counter.

'*No es posible, señor,*' the shopkeeper replied, deadpan. 'The Proplast we now only stock in our suburban branch.'

Suburban branch? The only place on the island big enough to have proper suburbs was Palma, for crying out loud, and that was over half an hour's drive away. My face fell in sympathy with my spirits. Silence had suddenly fallen inside the shop, too. The shopkeeper was the first to start laughing, quickly followed by my erstwhile debating companions.

'Do not worry, *amigo mío*,' one of them shouted to me, 'he only means his other Andratx shop.'

'His *other* Andratx shop?'

'*Pues sí* – you know, the one on the other side of the street, right opposite this one.'

My shoulders stung under the onslaught of good-natured punches and slaps that rained down on them as I exited the store. So much for falling an easy victim to the droll Mallorcan sense of humour, and so much for my powers of observation. For all the times I'd been in the Ferretería Ca'n Mateu since arriving in the area, I'd never once noticed the existence of the so-called 'suburban' branch opposite. But, true enough, there it was facing me across the street, cunningly disguised as a private dwelling. For, like so many village shops in Mallorca, the Ca'n Mateu's other branch lurked behind a plain façade, with no hanging sign or telltale window dressing to give a clue to its true identity. Until you become familiar with what's what and who's where in towns like Andratx, you can very easily walk into a cobbler's when you really want a watchmaker, or sit in a corridor waiting for a haircut when what's being provided in the back room is dental treatment.

The drama involving the builder's truck had now passed (as had the truck, albeit minus a layer or two of paint left on the fronts of buildings here and there), and the street had resumed its usual calm atmosphere, its inhabitants their normal unhurried pace. Inside Ca'n Mateu 2, the scene that I'd just left in Ca'n Mateu 1 was being re-enacted almost exactly, except that the customer

40

at the counter was a farmer weighing up the pros and cons of a petrol-engined water pump, rolls of hosepipe, bundles of drip-irrigation nozzles and a selection of liquid fertilizer cans. And the gathering of fellow customers (also discussing Spain's impending entry into the EEC, as it happens) were in no more of a hurry to be about their respective businesses than their counterparts across the street had been. Not wishing to risk stumbling into another *sí* and *no* interlude, I turned tail and headed back along the street to Plaça Pou, the little 'Square of the Well', around which an irresistible aroma of fresh coffee had been drifting as I'd driven through earlier.

The purchase of Proplast crack-filler was clearly fated to take some time, so why not do the waiting in the congenial surroundings of a bar? After all, by the time the early morning 'rush' had subsided at the hardware shop, I'd eventually accomplish the mission in relative speed anyway. In the meantime, best just to adopt the 'when in Rome' attitude and be *tranquilo*. Plenty of time is needed for embarking on such everyday errands in rural Mallorca, and plenty of time is what everyone seems to have. And even if you do happen to run out of hours today, then 'There's Always Tomorrow' – the enviable motto of *Mañana*land.

The Bar Cubano is located at one side of the Plaça Pou, at the hub of the old town and right at the top of the Avenida Juan Carlos Primero, the long main street that bisects the town from south to north. The bar's name is a reminder of Andratx's long-standing links with Cuba, local men once having gone there in large numbers to seek their fortune in the sponge-fishing trade. That was in the days when Mallorcan country towns like Andratx offered little in the way of lucrative work, and the Caribbean island enjoyed much greater prosperity than it has of late. Recent renovations had transformed the interior of the once dingy old bar into a snappy modern establishment, boasting generous expanses of shiny plastic and finishings of gleaming chrome, all glittering beneath the mandatory illumination of fluorescent strip lights. A bit like an alcohol-serving ice cream parlour, in fact, but with a strictly all-male clientele (as is the norm in such Spanish watering holes), and with a distinct absence of ice cream – and sponges!

The acrid smell of cigar smoke and beer mingled with the inviting whiff of coffee and anise, while the sound of communal laughter rose above the mechanical ping-pong music of a fruit machine. I quickly noticed that the butt of all the hilarity was a colour poster pinned to the wall opposite the bar, and I recognised the voice leading the outpourings of ridicule.

Today, Jordi Beltran had clearly moved from his regular hangout at a pavement table outside the Bar Nuevo in Plaza de España, the main square of Andratx. But, then, Jordi liked to give all of the local bars (and there are many of them) a bit of trade from time to time. His contribution to the redistribution of wealth, would be Jordi's description of his gregarious social habits, although it's fair to say that whatever wealth Jordi was blessed with was certainly not of the material kind. Slightly built, as wiry as a terrier, ever cheery and always with plenty to say on any subject you cared to mention, Jordi was a native Mallorcan, born in the village of Santanyí over on the other side of the island, but an Andratx resident for many years, and a local card known to one and all. Originally a carpenter by trade, he'd spent sixteen years working in large car-manufacturing plants in the Midlands of England during the period when mass tourism was just starting to burgeon in Mallorca. It followed that he'd missed out on the boom time when so many of his fellow construction workers on the island established their own businesses and set themselves up for life with the rich pickings so readily available. But Jordi wasn't one to waste time feeling bitter about lost opportunities. The wanderlust that had taken him all over Europe may have denied him the lucky breaks grabbed by his less adventurous contemporaries, but he'd been happy just to return eventually to his native soil, working – when the urge took him – on his tiny *finca* on a mountain pass out by the road to Peguera, picking up a bit of casual boat-repair work from visiting yachties down at the Port of Andratx during the summer months, and generally enjoying an uncomplicated life in which he really was master of his own time and destiny. Too many of those 'self-made' Mallorcan *compadres* of his had already died of heart attacks, Jordi had been known to sagaciously observe.

Though he could lay no claim to sartorial elegance, his wardrobe being as limited as his means were modest, Jordi did have a certain style about him. Even in his scruffy working clothes he had 'presence', an eye-catching appearance – debonair almost – generated by lean, well-lived-in features smiling out from under a thick shock of greying hair. And his demeanour, whether tootling along the country roads on his faithful old *Mobylette* moped, or sitting cross-legged and smoking a cigarette while 'holding court' at his favourite table outside the Bar Nuevo, somehow suggested that Jordi could well have been suited to a station in life more gentrified than the humble one he clearly occupied. But he was content with his given lot, and genuinely appeared to envy no one anything. A thoroughly likeable character, Jordi Beltran had been an invaluable source of advice, contacts and local know-how for us since befriending him after a chance meeting in the Port d'Andratx newspaper shop when we were still rookie residents of the island.

'Hey, bloody 'ell, man!' he shouted out to me across the bar room. 'You been being see the damn baster pissters the bloody gubbermint been stick up? Is bloody ridickliss!'

Jordi was very proud of his command of the

English language. He spoke it in an accent that blended the linguistic nuances of Karachi and Coventry, having lived for so long in an Asian community in the latter city, and he owed his range of much-used swearwords to the coarse banter of the factory floor. What Jordi lacked in width of English vocabulary he more than made up for in enthusiasm for its use, and with a confidence in improvisation that saw him never stuck for a word. He'd once told me, while seated opposite him outside the Bar Nuevo one market-day morning, how difficult it had been for him, when first arriving in Coventry, to get used to the ways and customs of the Asian family in whose house he'd taken lodgings. Evening meals were included in the rent he paid for his room, but after the uncomplicated attitude to food that had been a feature of his Mallorcan country upbringing, he found it strange dining with a family whose religious beliefs dictated that a slightly more 'defined' gastronomic regime be observed. It was bad enough that they'd regarded as absolutely taboo his liking for, as he put it, 'the English slim stew stuff being cook from the damn bugger mudguard of the cow's arse', which I took to mean Oxtail Soup, but there was an even weirder culinary idiosyncrasy that Jordi had had to cope with . . .

'I being tell you, man,' he revealed, 'they never even been eat the whole baster chicken!'

'That a fact?'

45

'Bloody 'ell, Jordi being tell the truth, I tell you. Oh yes!' He'd then leaned closer, glancing about to make sure that no potential offendee was within earshot. 'I tell you, man . . .' He paused, leaned even closer, then eagerly whispered in confidence, ' . . . when they been being eat the bloody chicken, they no being eat his baster wheels!'

It was my turn to pause, thinking carefully. 'Wheels?' I checked. 'You said the chicken's . . . *wheels?*'

Typically, Jordi sat back in his chair and stared at me, aghast. 'Crice sake, man! You no being understand plain bloody English? *WHEELS!*' he shouted, suddenly unconcerned about the risk of potentially-umbraged eavesdroppers. Then, realising from my still-mystified expression that a mimed back-up to the word was required to get the message into my thick head, he bent his arms, raised his elbows, and proceeded to flap them up and down while making loud 'puck-puck-puckee' sounds. '*WHEELS!*' he reiterated. 'The damn baster *WHEELS* of the chicken!'

'Oh,' I laughed, the penny finally dropping, 'you mean the chicken's *wings!*' I was instantly concerned that my instinctive correction may have offended Jordi. But I needn't have worried. He was not to be put down by someone so obviously ignorant of the finer points of the English language.

'Bloody 'ell!' he retorted, 'that being exackly what Jordi been damn bugger tell you.' He leaned towards me over the table again. '*RINGS!*' he

46

loudly declared, staring me straight in the eye. 'Wheels, rings – all the baster same, OK!'

Touché! He'd had the last word as usual, and I knew he'd have been the prevailing voice of authority in this morning's Bar Cubano poster-mocking session as well. He beckoned me over, gesturing at the offending notice as his companions dispersed to continue their animated discussions at tables of their choice. The subject of the poster, I immediately noticed, was notification to all growers that in future, in accordance with EEC regulations, all oranges would have to be of a certain 'quality', *and* they would have to be presented for sale arranged neatly on shallow trays in the manner depicted in the poster's explanatory colour illustrations.

'Damn gubbermint shit,' Jordi sniggered, pointing to the official heading on the notice. 'You being look at all this crap already, man? Baster pissters been being stick up in all Andratx bars today, oh yes!'

I hadn't seen them before, I confessed, eliciting an incredulous look from Jordi by admitting that this was the first bar I'd been into today, being not quite nine-thirty in the morning yet. I'd never seen Jordi the worse for drink, and he probably drank no more during all of his frequent bar visits throughout the day than the average British office worker does in desperate dashes into the pub between the end of work and catching the train back home every evening. But Jordi was a devotee of the Mallorcan working men's custom of starting the day by stopping off at a favourite bar en route to *finca* or workshop to enjoy a relaxed 'breakfast' of a *rebentat* – a small, strong coffee fortified with a 'splash' of liquor. That's the time-honoured Spanish way of kick-starting the metabolism in the morning, and it seems to do the participants no harm. Besides, it gives them an opportunity to continue the previous night's conversations with their friends, while also exchanging views on the morning's news.

It's also a ritual that some repeat before lunch, after the afternoon siesta and before the evening meal as well. Of course, detractors of the custom say, quite correctly too, that alcohol is never out of the bloodstream of such fellows. But so what? Their physical systems are attuned to it, and their well-spaced, low-volume tippling doesn't result in the unsavoury sight of mass public drunkenness so prevalent in the binge-culture countries of the north. 'What about the Breathalyser?' you might ask. Well, let's just say that some Mallorcan traffic cops, before even getting round to kick-starting their motorbikes in the morning, aren't averse to a little kick-start for their own metabolisms either. Yes, there's a lot to be said for the Spanish attitude towards bar frequenting – laid-back, male-bonding and essentially sociable as it is. It's just that, when not too busy (which was usually), Jordi liked to repeat the routine even more often than most throughout the day. That was his *estilo de vida* – his chosen way of life – and no one who knew him well begrudged him it.

His wife, whom he'd met and married while working in Coventry, had returned permanently to England with their two children a year or so after coming to the island with Jordi, citing as her reasons a dislike of the Mallorcan summer temperatures and the need to go 'home' to look after her recently-widowed father. Beneath his outward show of devil-may-care bluster and exuberance, Jordi was at heart a very sensitive person, and, although he'd never admit it, essentially a lonely one at that. He missed his wife and kids, and frequenting the bars in the Andratx area was simply his way of compensating for the family companionship he craved.

He nodded towards the poster and let rip with a chesty chuckle. Had I ever seen such nonsense? he asked, tapping the notice contemptuously with the back of his fingers. 'Hey, man, you be looking at this!' he said, drawing my attention to one line in the list of new regulations. 'The oranges must to being of uniform shape, they being say here. *Uniform* shape? Bugger Jordi for a game of dominoes! Who the bloody 'ell ever been seeing a square damn orange?'

The government had gone too far this time, he pronounced. Did they think Mallorcan farmers were idiots? Had they forgotten that oranges had been grown and sold on the island for a thousand years or more? Yes, for a thousand years before

49

those bureaucrats in Brussels had heard of Mallorca, or even learned how to suck a damn orange. Jordi had been to Belgium, he declared, so he bloody well knew.

'Baster Eurapeein' Onion?' he barked. 'Is bloody ridickliss! They can going stuff it right up Jordi's forking assholes!'

With that, he ripped the poster off the wall and, to loud cheers of encouragement from his watching friends, crumpled it into a ball and drop-kicked it straight out of the door. I had a feeling that this wouldn't have been the first or, indeed, would be the last copy of the poster to meet with a similar fate that day. And with considerable justification on the various perpetrators' part at that. Jordi was right – Mallorcans had been growing and selling oranges for aeons, and, as he went on to point out, the inherited skills of the island's farmers and merchants amounted to a knowledge of the business that no distant, desk-bound maker of rules and regulations could hold a candle to. Mutterings of agreement from the nearest table helped Jordi warm to his theme. For instance, he asked in a voice that everyone in the bar could hear, had the French merchants in Marseilles, who for centuries had imported boat-loads of oranges from the little Mallorcan port of Sóller each year, ever complained about how they were shaped, graded or packed? Never! Nor would they in the future. Jordi was adamant about that, and for one simple reason: because he and his fellow orange growers would continue to present their oranges for sale exactly as they did right now. What need was there to fiddle about laying them side-by-side, one-deep in silly trays, each orange hand-selected to look like an exact clone of its neighbour? None! The oranges would be sold just as they were at present, and that was in the way most convenient for grower and merchant alike – heaped into nice deep plastic crates, with a leaf or two still attached to the stem of each orange to prove that it was Mallorcan, and *fresh*. Case dismissed!

The fact that Jordi didn't actually have even one orange tree of his own was conveniently ignored. It was the principle that mattered, and Jordi had stated that dynamically enough to prompt shouts of approval from all present.

'*Sí, sí, sí,*' Jordi grinned in acknowledgement of the accolades, his arms raised, paradoxically enough, in the manner typical of his despised politicians on an election campaign trail, '*Y VIVA MALLORCA, EH!*'

Those damn baster political gangsters would never put Mallorca under the EEC yoke, he told me while shepherding me over to the bar, his sense of social importance rising rapidly on the echoes of his chums' playful plaudits, his euphoria already floating dangerously close to cloud seven. Mallorca had been invaded many times in its long history, he reminded me. Phoenicians, Greeks, Romans, Moors, Barbary pirates and even

Catalanes from mainland Spain had imposed their presence. But never their will! The spirit of the true Mallorcan had always prevailed; the independent spirit of an island race with the guile to accept the presence of the invader, while also exploiting him to the hilt. Just take the modern invasion, for example . . .

'Baster tourists!' he grinned, tapping the side of his nose. 'Hey, be saying no more, man!'

I bowed to Jordi's knowledge of Mallorcan history, and I equally admired his patriotism. The truth, though, is that, in common with peoples all over the 'Old World', the diversity of blood that has been injected into the indigenous population of Mallorca through the ages is actually the very stuff of its individuality. And it truly is an individuality much to be admired. But I doubted whether even that strong spirit of independence would be enough to allow Mallorcan farmers to stave off the spidery fingers of the form-filling, control-creeping officialdom that would invade them soon. I worried again for the future of little family farms like our own.

'Drink?' Jordi asked.

'Just a small coffee, thanks. *Café solo.*'

'*Rebentat,*' he said to the barman, ignoring my request for a 'straight' coffee and asking for a 'spiked' one instead. '*Sí, un rebentat para mí amigo.*' Then he turned to me. 'What you be wanting in it? *Coñac, anís,* gin? Hey, maybe whisky, eh?' Inspired, and not bothering to await my reply,

Jordi addressed the barman again. '*Si, un café con whisky para el* Scotchman!' He dug me in the ribs with his elbow and winked: 'Mac*Rebentat*, eh?' His shoulders shook with silent laughter. Jordi was in fine fettle.

I fancied drinking a whisky-charged coffee at that early hour about as much as I'd have fancied taking curry sauce with my porridge, but knowing Jordi as I did, to refuse would have been futile. In this ebullient mood, Jordi took a bit of stopping when it came to ordering drinks, and he was never shy of paying his way either, despite his ostensibly modest means. Rumour had it that Jordi was, in fact, in receipt of some obscure new Spanish state pension for having suffered 'industrial injuries' that prevented him from seeking gainful employment, although it was plain for all to see that he was as fit as a butcher's dog. Clearly, the years he'd lived under the umbrella of the British social security system had not been spent with his eyes and ears closed!

As had happened earlier in the hardware store, five minutes soon became ten, and ten drifted into fifteen. By the time Jordi had ordered up my third *rebentat*, I was rapidly approaching the stage when I was no more concerned about the passage of time than he was – or rather, than I *thought* he was.

'Jordi must to going,' he suddenly said, downing his drink in one gulp. 'Busy day for Jordi up the *finca*. Many baster potatoes for the lifting, oh yes.'

Then, having given me the customary slap on

the shoulder, he was out of the door in uncharacteristic haste. It was only after the sound of his moped's little engine had buzzed off into the distance that I noticed the reason for Jordi's sharp exit. There, at the other end of the bar, was the same policeman who had been orchestrating the traffic chaos earlier. He was interrogating the barman while holding up the very poster, uncrumpled now but ruined, that Jordi had dispatched into the street over half an hour ago. The lawman would have gleaned as much information had he directed his questions to a stone wall. After a few more moments of wresting nothing but a series of silent shrugs from the barman, he re-crumpled the poster, dropped it on the floor and ordered himself a coffee. No, on second thoughts, he told the barman, he'd better make that a *rebentat*. '*Sí, un café con coñac, gracias!*' Here was one policeman who was nothing if not a realist, and he wore his priorities on his sleeve like a corporal's stripes – a rank which he was highly unlikely ever to attain, if his performances this morning were anything to go by.

Back at Ca'n Mateu 2, the early morning 'rush' had indeed fizzled out. The shop was totally devoid of customers, and the assistant was sitting behind his counter, happily reading a newspaper, sipping coffee and smoking a cigarette.

'Two large packs of Proplast, *por favor*,' I said, glancing uneasily at my watch. I'd been away from the house so long now that I feared Ellie would have had time to watch even more Picasso sketches draw themselves on the walls of the *almacén*.

'*Lo siento, señor*,' the assistant replied with an apologetic shake of his head, 'but I sold the last pack only five minutes ago. Come back *mañana*, eh?' Noticing my look of despair, he thought a moment, then flashed me an inspiration-induced smile. 'But, hey, you could always try our other branch across the street!'

When I eventually got back to Ca's Mayoral, I found Ellie in what we called the 'middle' field, the orchard second farthest from the house, and one that contained more non-orange fruit trees than the others. She was sitting on an upturned fruit crate, her back against the trunk of an apricot tree, her face lifted to the warm September sunshine. Bonny the boxer was sleeping at her feet.

'Don't tell me,' she muttered without opening her eyes. 'You've come back without the Proplast, haven't you?'

'Yes, well, it's a long story. You see, first there was a –'

'Save your breath. In fact, your breath's saying it all for you. Whisky! You met Jordi, didn't you?'

'Tomorrow,' I blurted out, attempting a deft change of subject. 'Yeah, they were sold right out of it today, but the hardware guy said they'd have more Proplast in stock tomorrow.'

'Hmm, *mañana* as usual.' Ellie yawned and blinked one eye at me. 'Just as well, as it happens.'

She was good at making a conundrum out of a simple statement if she thought she had you on your back foot – a teasing little torture reserved for inflicting on me when she suspected that my senses and defences were alcohol-weakened. Rare occasions, I must stress!

'But you said you wanted those cracks in the plaster fixed today.' Drinking three wee *rebentats* hadn't made me *that* befuddled, so I decided to assert myself. 'And it isn't a problem. I only just remembered that a new hardware store opened along in Peguera recently. The Ferreteria Capri, it's called. Big shop – nice guy who owns it – local bloke called Gabriel – met him in the bar at the Restaurante El Piano when I was delivering fruit there the other day. I mean, I could have driven along to his place before coming home just now, but I knew you'd be worried, so I reckoned it'd be more thoughtful of me just to –'

'You haven't got time to be thoughtful.'

I had become *tranquilo* enough by now not to agree with Ellie on that score, but to argue would have been pointless. Besides, she'd managed to find time to sit down and peacefully bask under an apricot tree while I'd been embroiled in the hurly-burly of town life Andratx-style for the past hour and a half. I reckoned Ellie had the right idea, no matter what she said to the contrary, so I made myself comfortable on the ground beside her and adopted the same eyes-closed, sun-worshipping pose.

Ah, the bliss of it! This is what we'd come to Mallorca for; the Mediterranean sun in a cloudless blue sky, caressing your upturned face through a comforting dapple of apricot leaves, with all around the intoxicating smells and muted sounds of orchard and mountain lulling your senses and soothing away your worldly cares. Heaven.

A ripe fig dropped from a nearby tree and plopped softly onto the earth like a fat, syrupy raindrop. Without even bothering to lift her head, Bonny gave a little grunt of awareness of the momentous event, heaved a great sigh, smacked her lips in that contented way that sleepy dogs do, then resumed her dreams.

For endless moments nothing stirred in the valley, and not a sound assailed our ears, save for the faint, distant crow of a cockerel affirming his territorial rights on one of the *fincas* that cling to the topmost slopes of the Sierra Garrafa – little farms hidden snugly away behind the great mountain's cloak of evergreen oak and sweet-smelling pine. A passing breeze, gentle as the waft of an angel's wings, as they say in these parts, rustled the canopy of leaves above our heads, and left in its wake a hundred scents of the approaching autumn.

'It reminds me of one of those old poems we had to learn at school,' I muttered, lyricism

57

melding with my drowsiness as the narcotic spell of nature helped the effect of the three *rebentats* finally to kick in. 'Never really appreciated what it meant until now. Mmm, Keats, wasn't it? Or maybe it was Wordsworth. One of them, anyway.'

Ellie said nothing.

Bonny broke wind . . . softly.

I was drifting away. 'Yeah, Keats it was. Then again, it could have been Tennyson. I remember it as if it was yesterday. How'd it go again? Oh yeah, that was it . . . *Season of mists and mellow fruitfulness, Close bosom friend of the maturing sun* . . . Hmm, magic line that, *Close bosom friend of the maturing sun*.'

'Close *boozing* friend of the maturing Jordi, more like!' Ellie sprung to her feet like a jack-in-the-box. Before I could even focus on what was happening, she clattered me on the head with the plastic crate, and Bonny pounced on me, not understanding what the sudden fun was all about, but making sure she was in on it anyway. 'That's enough of your poetic musings for one day,' said Ellie, giving me a firm nudge with the toe of her shoe, 'so rise and shine, sonny boy, and make it smartish!'

'You've got absolutely no appreciation of the arts, Ellie, that's your trouble.' I tutted in exasperation as I struggled to fend off a slobbery face-washing from Bonny. 'Hell's teeth, what's all the hurry about anyway?'

'Well, I don't suppose Keats, or whatever artistic

layabout it was, ever had an order for a kaki in his entire puff. But you have. Two dozen kakis, in fact!' Anticipating my response, she held up a silencing hand. 'And they have to be delivered to*day!*'

CHAPTER 3

FROM FINCA TO INCA

The kaki was another fruit I knew nothing of until being given Francisca Ferrer's sales-pitch tour of the Ca's Mayoral orchards prior to buying the *finca* from her. Before that I'd thought that 'kaki' was just a misspelling of the colour of the cloth that army uniforms are made of. However, the appearance of the kaki fruit, or persimmon to give it its posh name, is the very antithesis of that drab military hue so reminiscent of freshly-laid cow dung. A striking golden colour when immature, kakis develop into orange-red fruits that look uncannily like big, plump tomatoes when ripe. But, unlike tomatoes, they grow on trees; decoratively-shaped and extremely handsome trees that are native to Japan and China. According to our Andratx tree maestro Pepe Suau, the persimmon is a type of ebony, and its timber, although relatively rare, was tradition-ally prized by golf club manufacturers for making the heads of drivers and other such 'woods' before the real thing was challenged by more readily available synthetic alternatives.

There were only four kaki trees on Ca's Mayoral,

dotted randomly within regular ranks of citrus, peach, pomegranate and quince, and looking at their most attractive now that their glossy summer leaves were taking on the soft shades of autumn. Soon, all their foliage would fall, leaving the remaining fruit hanging like clusters of little blushing pumpkins on the slender, naked limbs. Despite its beauty, however, the kaki is a fruit that conceals a wicked surprise for the unenlightened. To those with a sweet tooth, biting into the yielding, succulent flesh of a fully ripe kaki is arguably about as close as you'll get to sampling the mythical nectar of the gods. Bite into a kaki before it reaches that state of perfect ripeness, though, and you won't ever do so again. In my ignorance, I had already found that out the hard way. One eager mouthful of a deceptively mature-looking kaki plucked straight from the tree was so cheek-puckeringly, sphincter-shrinkingly bitter as to be painful. I'm not exaggerating when I say that my taste buds felt as though they'd been subjected to a battery-acid mouthwash, while my brain sent out red-alert signals to my teeth that their fillings were about to dissolve. Never, ever again!

And that's the trouble with kakis as far as the fruit farmer is concerned. When truly ready to eat, kakis are as soft (in the words of old Pep) as a fat nun's boobs, and their skin will burst and release a lava flow of gooey pulp if the fruit isn't handled extremely delicately – a wasteful and messy problem for both picker and customer alike. Naturally, fruit merchants aren't too interested in buying mature kakis, unless they have a specific order for them, and that often turns out to be for a quantity so small as to make all the effort involved for the grower unprofitable. The alternative is to pick them while still firm and hope that a bulk purchaser can be found who's prepared to gamble on being able to sell them on before they ripen and become too squelchy to handle.

So far, we hadn't found kakis easy to market, and according to Pepe Suau, our four trees – even in their 'recovering from surgery' state – could well yield a total of something like a ton of fruit. That's a lot of kakis. So, rather than let the ripe ones fall from the trees and go to waste, we'd been using them as complimentary 'sweeteners' when buying supplies from storekeepers, or negotiating prices with tradesmen. The fact of the matter is, I suppose, that the freebie kakis made precious little difference to what we were charged by the recipients, but being canny Scots, we liked to think that it did. Anyway, if nothing else, those modest gestures of generosity did our reputation no harm locally, and knowing the proudly-reciprocal side of the Mallorcan character as we already did, it was always likely that we'd be repaid in kind some day.

'Inca? You've accepted an order to deliver a measly two dozen kakis to *Inca*?' Logically enough, I'd thought that the phone order Ellie had taken while I was on my abortive trip to buy Proplast would have been from someone no farther away than Andratx, and preferably from someone prepared to come to Ca's Mayoral and collect the kakis himself. 'Do you know how far away Inca is?' I grouched, laying the trays of gently picked ripe kakis on the old worktable in the *almacén*.

'Not that far.' Ellie was nonchalance personified.

'*Not that far?*' My voice was already ascending to boy-soprano pitch. 'Typical! That's your trouble, Ellie – you have absolutely no idea of distance. God! I remember asking you when you were talking about coming out here to live how far you thought Mallorca was from Scotland. And do you remember what you said? No? Well, I'll tell you. Instead of answering fifteen hundred miles or whatever, you blandly came out with, "Oh, not far – only about an hour or so from Edinburgh airport"!'

Ellie remained her exasperatingly detached self. 'Here, take some tissue paper and help me wrap each kaki carefully. We don't want them to get bruised or burst, do we?'

'*Bruised? Burst?* Ellie, that is the least of our worries! Let's face it, we're already struggling to make ends meet here, and you walk blithely into a deal that only the petrol station will make anything out of!' I was in full flow now, getting right into my ranting stride. 'I mean, you agree to deliver a relatively worthless amount of bloody kakis all the way to Inca – thirty-five miles each way if it's an inch – and all you're concerned about is not hurting the fruit! What about our bank balance, for crying out loud?'

Ellie smiled demurely while giving the back of my hand a calming pat. 'I'll answer that in just three little words.'

'Let me guess! Stark, raving and mad, right?'

'Nope.' She shook her head, the coy little smile broadening into a mischievous smirk. 'What would you say if I told you . . . Celler, Ca'n and Amer?'

My rising blood pressure instantly morphed into a pleasant feeling of heightening anticipation, my scowl into a delighted grin. 'Hey,' I enthused, 'I'd say let's get these kakis nicely wrapped, loaded into the car, and we'll be on our way to Inca. But *rápidamente!*'

The town of Inca sits in the lee of the eastern foothills of the mighty Tramuntana Mountains, on the edge of *Es Pla*, Mallorca's broad and windmill-dotted central plain, midway between Palma city and the northern town of Alcúdia, the old Roman capital of the island. Nowadays, a fast *autopista* highway links the present-day capital to Inca, but if you'd rather drive at a more leisurely pace, giving yourself a chance to appreciate the scenery en route, then, like us, you'll take the old road.

Once clear of Palma's northern suburbs, overflowing with a sprawl of industrial estates, hypermarkets and nofrills apartment blocks so typical of burgeoning urbanisations everywhere, you soon find yourself once more in a world far removed from the hustle and bustle that has been accepted as the dowry of 'progress' by those once pastoral flanks of the city. Like the other towns and villages on the way to Inca, the main street of Santa María was subjected, in pre-*autopista* days, to the noise, fumes and dust raised by relentless convoys of trucks and coaches passing through on their way between Palma and the resort-ports of Pollença and Alcúdia on the north coast. Now, though, the rumble of traffic has faded to a comfortably-distant murmur, and the old agricultural town of Santa María has rediscovered the peaceful ambience that it enjoyed for centuries before the advent of mass tourism. Once again you can wander across the pretty town square without fear of ending up in the bay of Alcúdia spreadeagled on the front of a speeding truck; once again you can sit at a pavement table outside the Bar Ca'n Calet, sipping a refreshing drink in the shade of a pepper tree without risk of being suffocated by diesel fumes; once again you can park your car right on the main street while retreating into the coolness of the town centre's old *bodega*, within whose stout stone walls hearty country wines can be bought for unbelievably low prices. 'Bring your own flagon for even bigger bargains!' is the advice of those in the know. Careful, though, because a taste for some of the more robust examples on offer can definitely be defined as acquired. Watch how even seasoned Mallorcans, weaned on such muscular vintages, take the precaution of 'cutting' their *vino peleón* with *gaseosa de limón*, the sparkling lemonade of Spain. Look and learn, and do your stomach lining a favour. It's not that different, after all, from how the more prudent Scotsman, balancing a keen appreciation of his national drink with a healthy regard for the preservation of his bodily filters, will choose to temper even the choicest single malt with 'a wee skoosh o' thinners'. 'Nah, nah, it isna sacrilege, laddie,' he'd say to any shocked whisky-purist, 'it's bloody survival, so just pass the water jug, eh!'

The existence of that old wine store in Santa María gives a clue to the landscape that's about to unfold as you continue northwards, and it also hints, though indirectly, at the reason for our enthusiasm to undertake this unprofitable business trip to Inca. Almond orchards and sheep pastures yield increasingly to vineyards as you approach Consell, for you are now entering the cradle of Mallorca's reborn and thriving wine-producing industry. Not so long ago, while being swept along in a stream of dust-billowing vehicles, all you were likely to see of this unpretentious little town was a blur of forlorn beige buildings lining either side of a main street that seemed to go on forever. It appeared that Consell had fallen victim to two of the worst urban blights – the unrestrained strip development of old and the modern ravages of exhaust pollution. Now that the traffic siege of Consell has been lifted, however, it's worth making a point of stopping for a while, if for no other reason than to seek out a little eatery that serves up a version of a classic Mallorcan country dish that's unlikely to be bettered anywhere on the island.

The Bar-Restaurante Los Pinos is tucked away behind its eponymous pine trees at one side of the Plaçeta des Pau, the Little Square of the Well, that commonly-occurring place name evocative of an age when a piped supply of mains water to individual homes was undreamed-of by the populations of country towns and villages. Consell's municipal well is still there, in the middle of the little square that takes its name; and it's still working, albeit that its ancient *sínia* water wheel is now driven by electricity instead of mule-power.

We had stumbled upon this restaurant one chilly evening during the previous winter, when returning home after buying a second-hand car from an 'honest dealer' contact of our friend Jock 'Mr Fixit' Burns in the northern coastal town of Ca'n Picafort. The little white Ford Fiesta looked good, sounded healthy, drove well, and came at a fair price. The point that it also came without any documentation was so insignificant as to be unworthy of a moment's concern, according to Jock, a long-time Scottish resident of the island and a serial go-getter who, in such matters, believed in asking questions only if he reckoned he was going to like the answers. As his car-dealer pal Enrique had said, the papers would be in the post 'one of those *mañanas*', so I should just be *tranquilo* like him in the meantime and think myself lucky to have a legitimate excuse for not coughing up the *ridículo* car tax to those robbers at the town hall.

'No papers, no can pay the tax, *amigo!*' A manly slap on the back, a hearty '*Hey-y-y, no problema, hombre!*', and all, Enrique assured me, would be well in my world.

How prophetic. Twenty minutes out of Ca'n Picafort, the temperature gauge on the little Ford's dash warned me that Enrique had been a mite *tranquilo* about keeping its radiator topped up with water recently, too. Which was our reason for making an unscheduled pit stop at Consell's Little Square of the Well. Intending only to ask the genial *dueño* of the restaurant for the use of a jug, the look and smell of a dish being carried to one of the tables as we waited inside the door instantly had us drooling . . . and silently wondering.

'*Escaldums de Gallina*,' Jock informed us without waiting to be asked. 'The best o' Mallorcan grub, by the way. Magic!'

'Esky-whats *de* which?' Ellie inquired, nostrils twitching.

'*Escaldums* o' chicken, hen. Aye, ye cannae whack it!'

Ellie was clearly convinced, but still curious. 'But what's esky-thingies?' she probed. 'Esky – does that mean they're frozen? Never too happy about frozen chicken, me, unless you know it's been properly defrosted and everything.'

'Nah, nothin' to do wi' frozen anything, darlin',' Jock muttered distractedly. He had a love of food that would easily have qualified him for representing Scotland in the Eating Olympics, and his *escaldum*-hit senses had already fired the starting pistol. '*Una mesa para tres*,' he called to the returning waiter, any thought of consulting us first having been left at the starting line. '*Sí*, a table for three as soon as there's one available, *por favor*.'

While waiting at the bar, we ran our eyes over a mouthwatering array of *tapas* in the glazed display shelf under the counter. The selection comprised several traditional Spanish titbits, ranging from spicy diced potatoes to chopped calves' brains and meatballs.

'Fancy some Franks?' Jock asked me, his resistance instantly showing the white flag to temptation.

'Franks?'

'Aye, ye know – Frank Zappas – *tapas*. Rhymin' slang, ye see.' He licked his lips, eyeing up what was on offer. 'Mmm, Ah could fairly murder some o' them Carnegies. Fancy a few, son?'

'Carnegies? Sorry, Jock, you've lost me.'

'Carnegies, man! Come on – use the heid!' Being a schoolteacher was one of many strings that Jock had to his busy bow, and he was now glowering as if about to order me to go and stand in the corner for half an hour, my back to the class. It worked.

'Oh, yeah, I see what you mean now. The, uhm, Carnegie Halls, right?'

'Aye, ye've got it.'

'Well, the meatballs *are* tempting all right, Jock, but no thanks. No, I think I'll save myself for the *escaldums*.'

'Me too,' said Ellie. 'The esky-thingies look great, so I don't want to spoil my appetite.'

'Aye, well . . . maybe ye're right,' Jock grunted, his words in conflict with the expression on his face. Before you could say 'calorie count', his hand shot out and grabbed a fistful of shiny black olives that were heaped in a large bowl on top of the bar. 'Better just have a wee nibble to keep ma strength up, though, eh?'

Jock's 'wee nibble' turned out to be about half a kilo of plump pickled olives, consumed in just five minutes flat. But that didn't deter him from ordering a portion of *chipirones a la plancha*, baby squid seared on a wood-fired hotplate, when we were eventually shown to our table. 'Just for somethin' to pick at while we're waitin' for the *escaldums*, like,' he informed us in a casual sort of way. As the waiter was writing down the order, Jock touched his elbow and added as a multiple afterthought, '*Sí*, and eh, some olives, bread – toasted – and a bowl of *all-i-oli* garlic mayonnaise, *por favor*. Uhm-ah, *sí*, and some tomatoes with the bread, *naturalmente*, and better throw in a few *gambas* on the *plancha* with the squid – and I mean your *biggest* prawns, right?' Then, pointing towards the bar, Jock told the furiously-scribbling *camarero*: '*Sí*, and a plate of your *albóndigas* – those

70

nice big meatballs under the counter there.' Obviously misinterpreting the looks of wonderment on our faces, Jock flashed an almost-guilty little smile at Ellie and me and said, 'Aw, sorry – should've asked first. Any starters for you guys?'

But, strange as it may seem, it wasn't Jock's medal-deserving performance with his fingers and fork that made the biggest impression on us that evening. It was the much-lauded and eagerly-anticipated *escaldums de gallina* themselves. Each of us was presented with a whole breast and leg of chicken, simmered slowly in a golden fricassee of ground almonds, egg yolk, saffron and olive oil, with just a hint of garlic and a liberal sprinkling of fresh herbs. Served with chunky roast potatoes in individual *greixoneras*, the distinctive earthenware casseroles of Mallorca, the *escaldums* turned out to be a prime example of the island's deceptively simple country cookery at its very best. As Jock had said – magic!

'*Chupitos?*' he smiled in a schoolteacherly way to the waiter when he brought us our coffees. Jock made tippling movements with his forefinger and thumb, reminding the waiter (just in case he had forgotten) of the customary end-of-meal gesture of appreciation shown by proprietors of Mallorcan country restaurants to their clients, particularly to those who had praised the food as highly as we had his.

'*Naturalmente, señor,*' the *camarero* replied, his accompanying stiff but courteous nod of the head giving the impression that, although Jock's reminder had been received and understood, it hadn't really been necessary. He duly returned with not just one bottle of liqueur, but three, inviting us to help ourselves to whichever we preferred.

'They're no what they seem, mind,' Jock advised us. 'They maybe look like bottles o' Cointreau and Tía María or whatever, but if ye check the labels, ye'll see the names are different.'

'Certainly tastes like Cointreau to me,' I remarked, taking a tentative sip of my chosen snifter.

'And I'd have sworn this was Tía María,' Ellie concurred, sniffing, as was her wont, instead of sipping.

'Aye, it's good stuff, right enough,' said Jock, already pouring his second glass of a clear anisette, which he assured us was a dead ringer for Marie Brizard. 'Made at a wee distillery down the road there outside Santa María,' he informed us. They produce taste-alike versions of several famous liqueurs, he went on, and all cheaper to buy than the originals. For all that, their most popular line was *Hierbas*, Mallorca's own anise-flavoured green liqueur, infused with a variety of herbs, including juniper, rosemary, myrtle and a secret fusion of other 'aromatic wild plants of the Mallorcan countryside'.

'That reminds me,' Jock declared, pouring himself a shot of pseudo-Cointreau, 'I havenae had a snort from the green, green glass o' home for ages.' He hailed the waiter by making that same tippling movement with his hand as before. '*Hierbas, amigo?*'

72

If Jock's uninhibited 'helping himself' to copious nips of gratis liqueur from the four bottles which eventually graced our table abused the spirit of the landlord's gesture of goodwill, neither the landlord nor his inscrutably-obliging waiter showed the slightest sign of it. Even if they'd now be making an earlier-than-expected phone call to the distillery for fresh supplies of *chupitos*, their only concern when bidding us goodnight was to be reassured that we had enjoyed their speciality of the house, their *escaldums de gallina*.

So good had the *escaldums* been, in fact, that I promised there and then to make a return visit to the same little restaurant the next time we were in the area. But that, in common with the car's still-absent registration papers, would have to wait for another *mañana*. Today we had an urgent appointment to keep in Inca, and we knew that there, with luck, an even rarer treat awaited us.

As you approach Binissalem, the next little town on the Inca road, you know you're really in wine country. On all sides, the perspectives of endless rows of carefully tended vines taper into a mellow infinity of green-turning-gold. Beneath those russet September leaves, the grapes that have been kissed all summer by *el bon sol*, the sun-god of Mallorcan farmers, hang pendulous, purple and plump for the picking.

The name Binissalem, as the look of it suggests, is a legacy of the ancient Moorish occupation of

Spain, where, in parts of the mainland, Arab rule lasted for up to six hundred years. *Bini* is a derivation of the Arabic term for 'son of', and is a prefix seen in many place names of Mallorca and the neighbouring Balearic Island of Menorca. That Binissalem should be the centre of wine production in Mallorca could be regarded as all the more curious, therefore, since the drinking of alcohol was forbidden under the strict religious laws of the Moors. For all that, history tells us that the art of wine-making, said to have been introduced to the island by the Romans (Pliny described Mallorcan wines as the best in the Mediterranean), not only survived but actually flourished in Mallorca under Moorish rule, which lasted from the tenth to the thirteenth century. So, although the Koran prohibited the drinking of it, there must have been *some* demand for wine during that era, otherwise why go to all the trouble of perfecting its production? Intriguingly, it was one of Islam's most lyrical sons, Omar Khayyám himself, who said:

All the riches of the world for a chalice of wine,
All the books and wisdom of man for the perfume
of wine,
All the poems of love for the sound of wine that
flows.

But, of course, the great man doesn't actually admit to drinking *vino*, only to looking at, smelling and listening to it. Yeah, pull the other one, Omar.

Perhaps the popularity of Mallorcan wine under the Moors' law of temperance was but a forerunner to the burgeoning booze business that would emerge during America's prohibition period in the 1920s. Certainly, the sweet Malvasia wines of Mallorca, produced on the awe-inspiring mountain terraces constructed by the Arabs around the village of Banyalbufar (in Arabic, *Buniola al-bahar*, the Little Vineyard by the Sea), were said to match the finest in the world. So, quality had clearly been maintained since the Roman times of which Pliny wrote, and wine production continued to flourish and develop after the Christian reconquest of the island by King Jaume I of Catalonia and Aragon in 1229. The fame and popularity of Malvasia wine, otherwise known as Malmsey, or (in Mallorca) Albufar, eventually spread as far as England, where the Duke of Clarence was said to have drowned in the stuff in 1478. Consequently, with apologies to the Good Book, it could be said that greater love hath no man for his wine than to lay down his life while swimming in it. The Malvasia of that era *must* have been good.

Production of wine – not just the sweet sort – expanded dramatically in the following centuries. Quality improved apace, so that by the 1800s, six times as much Mallorcan wine compared to today was being made. Moreover, it was so highly valued that much of it was actually exported to France. Then, in the latter part of that century, phylloxera,

75

the dreaded plague of viniculture, spread from France – a cruel irony – and the prized vineyards of the island were totally destroyed. It proved a long and slow process to re-establish wine production of any volume and merit. But, happily, that has now changed, and dedicated Mallorcan oenologists such as Miguel Oliver, Francisco Servera, Jaume Mesquida, the Macià Batle family and Benissalem's own José Ferrer are making wines of excellent quality, using the most modern techniques. Yet the method of harvesting the grapes has remained virtually unchanged since Roman times. Save for the occasional tractor having replaced a mule for hauling the grape-laden carts from vineyard to press, the scenes which we drove past on our journey that day could have come from a bygone age. Groups of workers, their bent backs beaten by the still-fierce sun of September, were hand-picking grapes and filling their baskets in the time honoured way – a labour of urgency dictated by the need to complete the harvest while the crop is in optimum condition.

As bustling autumn vineyards give way once more to sleepy almond groves, the far-off roofs of Inca, Mallorca's third-largest town, serrate the northern skyline. To the left, your gaze wanders upwards to the towering Tramuntanas, where vultures, kites and kestrels wheel and hover in a cloudless sky over craggy peaks that rise majestically above the wooded foothills. Already, the sweet, musty smell of ripe grapes and withering vine leaves has been left behind, and the drifting aromas of a myriad of wild herbs and flowers fill the warm air streaming through the car's open windows. The temptation to pull over and succumb to the siesta-inducing tranquillity is strong.

Rising above the horizon ahead, the outskirts of Inca shimmer in the sunshine. From this distance, the town's profile seems more evocative of a village by a desert oasis than of a country town in the heart of a fertile Mediterranean island. But it's only an illusion, a trick played on the eye by the heat haze floating over the tarmac surface of the road. The cube-like buildings that occupy the fringes of Inca aren't, in fact, little adobe houses, relics of a Moorish past. They are modern apartment blocks, a testament to Inca's commercial importance, not so much as the hub of the area's agricultural trade, but rather as the leather capital of the island. The manufacture of quality footwear and clothes is the town's speciality, with much of the production traditionally exported to northern Europe and America. However, thrifty members of the public are always made welcome at the factories, where you can buy, for considerably less money, exactly the same leather wares that are on display in the smart shops of Paris, Hamburg or New York. You can even have the garment or shoes of your choice made to measure, and you don't have to be a millionaire to indulge yourself either.

Inca's other claims to fame include the biggest weekly street market on the island, held every

Thursday morning, when, particularly in summer, the town is invaded by swarms of bargain-hunters and idle browsers from all over Mallorca. Inca also boasts the island's largest annual agricultural fair, *Dijous Bo*, which takes place in November and sees the town centre streets and *plazas* crammed with thousands of people, the agriculturally-enlightened thronging to see the impressive displays of livestock and farm equipment, but most folk there simply to soak up the wonderful carnival atmosphere that pervades the entire town.

For Ellie and me, though, the main attraction that Inca has to offer was not to be found *on* its streets, but, strange as it may seem, *under* them. Reminders of Inca's former status as the core of the area's wine-making industry are the town's old cellars, most dating from the seventeenth century, and some said to have links that can be traced as far back as Moorish times. But the ravages wreaked by phylloxera on the surrounding vine-yards put an abrupt end to Inca's association with wine over a century ago. Faced with impending ruin, some enterprising *cellerers* then converted their unique underground properties into restaurants, and none more distinctive or successful than the Celler Ca'n Amer, the destination of the loss-making little cargo of kaki fruits that we had transported carefully all the way from Andratx.

As if finding a way through the maze of narrow, twisting streets that forms Inca's heart isn't difficult enough for the unpractised visitor to cope with, the local council have added a devilish (though doubtless necessary) one-way traffic system to the puzzle, thereby making it simpler to park your car on the perimeter of the old town and use shank's pony instead. Having visited Ca'n Amer only once before, all I could remember about its location was that it was near the big indoor food market, right in the centre of town. However, Inca happens to be one of those not-too-big towns where, if you allow your sense of direction to lead you to where you *think* the centre should be, the chances are that you won't go far wrong. That said, I still had to ask directions several times before we eventually emerged into the market square. It was deserted now, but a scatter of discarded vegetable leaves, squashed tomatoes and broken bits of wooden fruit trays littering the steps of the market building itself were evidence of a brisk morning's trade having been done. The debris would be swept up in good time, no doubt, but not until those responsible had attended to their first priority. It was hot, and it *was* siesta time, after all.

Calle Pou, the Street of the (ubiquitous) Well, leads off the market square, and it's there you'll find the surprisingly unprepossessing entrance to one of the most remarkable eating places in Mallorca. For, although the concept of the *bodega-*turned-restaurant has been much imitated throughout the island over the years, the Celler Ca'n Amer is the genuine article, and its unmistakable air of authenticity hits you the moment you walk through the door. But you're in for a surprise if you assume that, because you're entering an old wine cellar, you'll be descending step by hesitant step into some dark, dank and claustrophobic chamber, with vaulted stonework sprouting cobweb-draped fungus in an atmosphere dominated by the whiff of dry rot and mouse droppings. Instead, an elegant stairway leads you down into a large, refreshingly cool and airy room, with high ceilings supported by age-darkened wooden beams, from which traditional 'lantern' chandeliers hang on chains to illuminate the wide expanse of floor, laid with polished terracotta tiles as mellow in hue as the place is old.

'*Fundado en el año 1700*', the sign at the entrance says, proudly proclaiming the establishment's three hundred year history. Naturally, the paraphernalia of wine-making has long been removed to make way for ranks of tables, each covered in crisp, chequered cloths that compliment the rustic tone of the dark wood furnishings. And throughout, the décor has been sympathetically chosen to harmonize with the aged oak of the huge wine vats that still protrude from the surrounding whitewashed walls. All of that would be merely cosmetic, however, if the cuisine of Ca'n Amer failed to pay equal homage to the traditions of Mallorca. But it does, and in a manner that elevates it into a class of its own.

'*Ah, muy buenos tardes, señores,*' beamed the petite

and affable Antònia Cantallops, greeting us at the foot of the stairs. '*Oo-ooh, los caquis!*' she enthused, running an appraising hand over the delicate fruits, but taking care not to touch them. '*Qué estupendos!*' She beckoned two waiters, resplendent in long aprons of starched white, to come and relieve us of the fruit trays. Señora Antònia, her greying hair as immaculate as her attire (but, significantly, always with her sleeves rolled up), is not only the proprietor of Ca'n Amer, but is also the culinary talent on which its deserved reputation for excellence has been built. Her unassuming demeanour belies the impressive list of international awards she has to her credit, as does the unpretentious atmosphere that is the hallmark of her restaurant.

Her husband Josep is also her maître d', though that's probably a description he'd regard as much too ostentatious for his own liking. Tall, slim and casually elegant in shirtsleeves and cravat, he has that rare knack of being welcoming, genial and attentive towards his clients without ever being intrusive. Here is a natural gentleman who knows that the output of his wife's kitchen will always be the star of the show, allowing him to carry out his front-of-house duties with quiet confidence and without any need for the camouflage of false swagger.

'You have saved our reputation, *señores*,' he smiled, striding toward us as if keen to renew acquaintances with old friends, instead of meeting for only the second time just two of hundreds of other guests who had enjoyed his hospitality during the six months that had passed since we first visited Ca'n Amer. A fruit merchant at the Inca market had let them down this morning, he told us, despite having promised faithfully to supply two dozen fully ripe kakis to allow his wife to create a dish specially requested by a party who had booked the restaurant for a large family celebration that same evening. 'Fortunately,' Señor Josep went on, 'I remembered that you told me when last here that you had some kaki trees on your *finca*, and as I had kept a note of your telephone number . . .' He smiled a smile that combined a look of relief with a little smirk of self-satisfaction. '. . . Roberto is my uncle, as you say in *Gran Bretaña*, no? But come – you have driven a long way, and you must eat before making the return journey to Andratx.'

Looking forward to something too much can all too often result in disappointment, but one glance at Antònia's bill of fare told us that our sense of expectation on this occasion was likely to be well justified. In keeping with her insistence on using Mallorcan produce of the best quality, while allowing her flare for culinary inventiveness to create the most wonderful recipes from deceptively simple ingredients, the menu which Señora Cantallops had prepared for lunch today offered a tantalising selection of main courses:

Barrels of Pork Fillet wrapped in Bacon,
with a Grape Sauce, Hot Grapes and
Crispy Potato Straws
★
Rabbit with Prawns in a Salsa Picante
★
Partridge in a Savoury Lentil Stew
★
Sliced Leg of Baby Lamb in an Orange
and Honey Sauce

We were completely spoiled for choice, and our patent indecision was remedied by an observant Señor Josep, who discreetly suggested that sharing 'modest' portions of each of the four dishes might be appropriate. He spoke the truth in all but the use of the word 'modest', but the excellence of his wife's creations was endorsed (if it ever needed endorsing) by the sight of four empty serving *greixoneras* and two full stomachs a little over half an hour later. But even at that, we didn't take much persuasion to agree to his recommendation of some cinnamon ice cream and a grape-must sorbet to refresh our palates.

Truly, this had been food to die for, and my only fear was that the bill, when it came, might well trigger such a response. Despite Ellie's half-hearted attempts to sing the praises of restraint when first appraising the menu, I hadn't shown any at all – not even when Señor Josep had suggested an excellent and rare bottle of José

Ferrer Gran Reserva to compliment the meats 'so carefully chosen for today's humble offering', as he put it. Since Ellie had allowed herself only one glassful, my solo consumption of the rest of the wine would at least, I now reasoned, help soften the financial blow about to be delivered.

'*La cuenta?*' Josep inquired when I mimed the act of signing the tab. 'The bill? But you have eaten at *my* invitation, *señor. And* you have travelled a long way to fulfil our last-minute order for kakis today. It is *I* who must pay *you!*'

'The price of two dozen kakis wouldn't even amount to a fair tip for your waiters,' I assured him, reaching for my wallet.

But Señor Josep's restraining hand on my shoulder and his reassuring smile prevented me from doing even that. 'It has been our staff's pleasure to be of service to you today, and my wife and I have been honoured to have you as our guests.'

I knew that to insist further would only serve to offend him more, so I accepted his wishes without undue ceremony. We had just experienced a glowing example of the proudly reciprocal side of the Mallorcan nature. Our comparatively insignificant act of supplying a couple of trays of fruit that was about to fall from the trees anyway hadn't just been repaid in kind, it had been rewarded by a gesture of unstinting generosity. Feeling distinctly mellow in the afterglow of the fine José Ferrer *vino*, as well as savouring the feeling of well-being in my wallet, I repeated that thought to Ellie as she drove us back down the Palma road.

'I know,' she replied, 'but I still think you spoiled it all when you said your goodbyes, then shouted back at Señora Cantallops that she shouldn't hesitate to get in touch again soon if she needed a few quinces or pomegranates in a hurry. Subtle as an earthquake!'

There was no answer to that, so I sat back duly rebuked and settled down for a long-overdue siesta. 'Drive carefully, Ellie,' I muttered. 'You've got a valuable cargo on board.'

'Don't flatter yourself,' she retorted, stepping on the gas. 'We left the kakis in Inca, remember!'

CHAPTER 4

CHARLIE GOES TO 'HOLLYWOOD'

'What do you miss most about home?' That was the question invariably asked by people dropping by to pay us a visit at Ca's Mayoral during their holidays on the island. The honest answer to that was 'family and friends', although members of that small but close circle had helped counter any such negative feelings by flying out from Scotland to stay with us for a week or two from time to time. And, our growing sense of 'belonging' in Mallorca aside, we were always delighted to see them. On the other hand, those just 'dropping by' were, more often than not, merely casual acquaintances we hadn't clapped eyes on for years, and their numbers had increased as our first summer in the valley had progressed.

'Just thought you'd like to see a friendly face from back home,' they'd say, arriving at the gate unannounced. 'We were just passing,' they'd usually add. What they conveniently neglected to admit, however, was that they'd probably spent the previous evening in their hotel pouring over maps in search of clues that would lead them to the location of Ca's Mayoral. Then, armed with what little information they had managed to glean, they'd embark on a determined expedition of discovery through the tangle of country lanes of south-west Mallorca. To be 'just passing' had usually taken a lot of time and curiosity-driven effort. But, to be fair, they *had* made the effort, and being sociable folk, we always tried to make such casual visitors welcome. At the same time, there were occasions when, after spending the best part of a day entertaining them, we'd finally bid farewell to 'friendly faces from back home' without even being sure who they were.

'Oh aye, this is the life for me,' one such nameless face enthused while reclining on a deck chair in front of the house. 'The stuff of dreams, this is. Yer endless sunshine, fabulous scenery, quaint old peasants for neighbours, yer cheap fags and booze, and bags o' time to lap it all up. Yeah, a place like this would suit me just fine. Shangrila.' He showed me his empty wine glass, and, with a little twitch of the head, grinned expectantly: 'Tide's out, squire, eh!'

Booze, I could have told him, would never come any cheaper for *him* than the stuff he was being plied with by a put-upon and increasingly irked host who'd had to part with his own hard-earned pesetas to buy it. I could also have informed him that the reality of life in this particular Shangri-la was far removed from the layabout one he purported to crave. And I probably *should* have

87

pointed out that every hour Ellie and I spent forcing ourselves to be nice to his 'friendly face' was an hour wasted for us. Like all 'peasants', our home was also our workplace, and, its idyllic location on a Mediterranean holiday island aside, Ca's Mayoral belonged as much in that category as any wind-swept, rain-lashed spread on a cold Scottish hillside. And you don't get many 'just passing' visitors in places like that. But I said nothing to this particular uninvited guest. What would have been the point? He *had* said he was an old friend of the family, after all, and, vague though it was, I did have a recollection of having met him *some* where before.

'Hey, I'm gonna make sure I don't leave it so long before I visit you again,' he announced when he finally decided to leave. 'Now that I know how to find this place, just try keeping me away, eh! Yeah, I come across to Mallorca at *least* a couple o' times a year.' Ellie and I cringed in unison. 'Next time I'll bring the wife and kids,' he added with a smile that did nothing to quell the rush of dismay that instantly had us raking our minds for polite ways of discouraging him from carrying out his threat. 'Bunch o' wee tearaways, the sprogs,' he chuckled, flicking our frantic deliberations into overdrive. 'Tornadoes with squeaky voices, I call 'em. Oh aye, but they'd love this place, though. Orchards – all those trees to climb and everything. Plenty fruit to scoff and all. Typical kids, eh? Always stuffing their faces.' He slapped me on the back – a tad too enthusiastically, I reckoned. Then he winked at Ellie – a tad too familiarly, she reckoned. 'Just like all those calves you used to rear back home, darlin', eh?'

It was his ensuing forced laugh that jogged my memory; that and the reference to calves. Now I knew who this time-wasting freeloader was. He was the smarmy salesman who, all of ten years previously, had called at our farm in Scotland offering to sell us cut-price cattle-feed pellets made from 'purified' poultry droppings, or *henpen* as it was euphemistically called 'in the trade'.

'Two-thirds the price o' yer regular high-protein calf mixes being flogged by the big feed compounders,' he'd said with that wink of his – an almost masonic one on that particular occasion. 'Terrible waster o' protein, yer average hen, squire. Craps something like ten per cent o' the protein it eats right back out its arsehole again. Scientific fact that. So ye see, my contacts in the trade just collect up tons o' hen shite from battery-cage houses all over the country, put it through this secret purifying process – dead scientific – developed in the Middle East – big lack o' plant-type protein in yer average desert – and wallop! ye've got yer unlimited supply o' high-protein cattle feed for – pun intended – shitpence. Recycling, it's called in the trade. Waste not, want not, squire.'

His last pronouncement made him sound, in a perverse kind of way, a bit like old Maria in full advice-flow. But that's where any similarity between the two ended. Maria's 'old-ways' assertion that we should buy a pig to make good use of fallen fruit was a helluva lot more wholesome than being told that modern science had devised ways of fooling herbivorous animals into eating 'treated' poultry dung and, equally unnaturally and ultimately more lethal, into wolfing down reconstituted body parts of their own species. No one ever heard of an incurable disease being transmitted to humans by fig-eating pigs, after all. That said, just don't let your wholesome 'Porky' get near a dead cow, poultry-droppings-fed or otherwise, because he'll gladly eat it. Isn't nature fickle?

I had been glad to see the back of the pushy *henpen* rep back in Scotland, and I was no less pleased to see him leave Ca's Mayoral. I'd hoped, mistakenly as it now transpired, that we'd left brazen sales creeps like him back in the UK, and I'd certainly never had a visit from anything like a Mallorcan equivalent since we settled in the valley. The closest parallel, I suppose, was an estate agent from Palma who telephoned shortly after we'd moved in, demanding a commission of a hefty percentage of the price we'd paid to the Ferrers when we bought the place. My first earful of abusive Spanish was my reward for telling him that, as we'd bought the *finca* in a private agreement between ourselves and the vendors without any estate agent being involved, his asking for a commission was totally unjustified. I was in Spain now, he reminded me in less than hospitable tones, and – for my own good – I'd better learn to do things the Spanish way, but fast. The farm of Ca's Mayoral had been put on his firm's books by the Ferrers, he claimed, and he was entitled to his slice of the sale price, whether we had used his services or not.

'If you made a deal with the Ferrers,' I told him, 'it's up to you to get your commission from them, not from me.'

'That may be the way where you come from, *amigo*, but it is not how we do such things here. You owe me my cut, and I intend to get it – one way or another!'

After several such threatening phone demands, each one getting the same response from me, the agent finally gave up, but not without having advised me – with a liberal spattering of expletives in English – that I would regret having crossed him. If indeed anyone had crossed him, it was the Ferrers. But even if they had, I knew from our own dealings with the canny couple that there would be as much chance of his getting a commission out of them as there would be of old Maria's pig sprouting wings. No doubt he knew that himself, and that's probably why he'd tried to bully us into coughing up for what he maintained he was entitled to, having gone to the expense, allegedly, of advertising the property in the press for some considerable time. Did I think, he asked, that he'd spent so much time during the past year travelling out from Palma to show prospective buyers round Ca's Mayoral just for the good of his health?

What we had almost stumbled into here, we later discovered, was a classic situation in which property owners could put the selling of their place in the hands of one estate agent (or more), on the understanding that the agent's commission would be added to the price paid by the purchaser. Naturally, to comply with even the most basic of ethics, this condition would have to be pointed out to prospective purchasers at the time of their approach to the agent. As we had come across Ca's Mayoral and its 'For Sale' sign purely by accident after getting lost during a holiday drive in the area, and had initiated and concluded the buying legalities without knowing of any selling agent's interest in the matter, no obligation to pay any commission whatsoever rested with us. Our Spanish lawyer, had he been called upon to do so, would surely have made that abundantly clear to the peeved Señor Hefty Percent. But he did eventually stop calling anyway, and although his aggressive attitude had been a bit disconcerting to us as new arrivals on the island, there was something strangely refreshing about an estate agent using a more 'direct' approach to a rip-off than those more subtle methods sometimes attributed to members of that much-maligned profession everywhere.

His threat to 'get his cut one way or another' was put to the back of our minds, only to emerge soon enough, when the house was broken into and all of our personal valuables stolen. None of the items were recovered, but we decided not to tell the police of our suspicion that the robbers may just have been tipped off about the arrival in the valley of a family of security-naïve *extranjeros* by a spurned real estate dealer. After all, who would have taken such a preposterous suggestion seriously! It was a fine illustration, though, of the truth in the old Roman maxim, caveat emptor, let the buyer beware – whether purchasing a valuable property, or just a humble sack of cattle feed.

Which brings us back to the uninvited purified-chickenshit salesman from Scotland. After he'd gone, I vowed to be less accommodating to Mr Recycling and his like the following summer. But time, as Ellie sagely commented, would be the test of that knee-jerk resolution, worthy though it may have been. And she did have a point, because for all that we enjoyed our regular, all-the-time-in-the-world chats with our Mallorcan neighbours, it was good to have the occasional opportunity to talk with people in English as well. Unless you are absolutely fluent in the language of your adopted country (and we were still in the 'trying hard' bracket as far as Spanish was concerned), it can be something of a strain just conversing casually with local folk over the gate, and even more testing when having to do business with them. For instance, when the difference between a modest profit and financial disaster depends on your unfailing recognition of the word for 'fifty' as opposed to the word for 'five hundred', both of which can sound confusingly similar in Spanish, a feeling of tension is never far beneath the surface for the learner linguist.

For all that, we had never been tempted to join any of the English-speaking residents' associations which exist in pockets of Spain favoured by émigré Britons, either living in retirement or running local businesses catering mainly for their own country-men. Such enclaves have developed over the years in Spanish coastal resorts best-liked, logically enough, by British tourists – or, equally, by Germans, Dutch and Scandinavians in their respective chosen spots. So, what you have are small communities of 'foreign' people who are living in Spain, but to all intents and purposes have never left 'home'. In popular locations like Palma Nova in Mallorca, for instance, so established are the communities of expat *británicos* that they have their own British doctors, dentists, hairdressers, a plethora of pubs and cafés, plus butchers, book and video stores, and maybe even a fish and chip shop all to hand. In such places there really isn't any need to learn to speak Spanish at all if you don't want to. It all adds up, I suppose, to a feeling of security that some regard as a prerequisite for living in a 'foreign' country. And for many expats, particularly those who may suddenly find them-selves living alone, such communities and their various clubs and associations can mean the difference between unbargained-for loneliness and the reassuring companionship of their own folk. Many are the dreams of living a wonderful life in the Spanish sunshine that have become nightmares when things haven't turned out just as wonderfully as the dreamers had hoped. It happens all too often within expat communities in favourite start-a-new-life places like Mallorca, when partnerships break up, illness strikes, spouses die, the over-optimistically calculated nest egg disappears in a puff of overspending, or those 'dream' businesses (usually bars, significantly enough) go bust.

We weren't immune to any of those dangers, of course, but our intention from the start had been to live in the real Mallorca, as opposed to a transplanted patch of Britain. At the same time, our aim was to blend in as best we could with the local people in our adopted home. It isn't that we had some daft notion of becoming *guiris*, the rather uncomplimentary Spanish term for foreign 'settlers' who eventually imagine themselves to be Spaniards. We'd always be foreigners, no matter how hard we tried to assimilate, and we harboured no delusions about that. It's simply that, facts being facts, there's absolutely no alternative to the precondition of integration if your business happens to be farming. And, so far, everything was going pretty much to plan – particularly if we ignored the possibility of our elder son Sandy not coming back from his working visit to Scotland,

and the lurking dread that we might not manage to make a living from our first attempt at commercial fruit-growing. The long-neglected and recently-doctored trees were still a long way from getting back to full production, after all, and now there was the unknown effect on orange prices of Spain joining the EU to worry about. In addition, never far from our minds was the sobering thought that we'd invested just about our holy all in this venture. Yes, there were times when it was good, if only in a therapeutic sort of way, to converse with people in our own tongue. And that's where young Charlie going to an English-language school came in handy.

When we left the Celler Ca'n Amer in Inca that Friday afternoon in September, instead of returning home the way we'd come, we took the fast new *autopista* motorway back towards Palma. Having lingered too long over Señora Cantallops' fabulous food, there was a risk that we'd be late picking up Charlie from school if we didn't get a move on. Not that Charlie would have been bothered that much. He'd taken to the laid-back environment of his new place of learning with an enthusiasm that was unrecognisable from the reluctant attitude he'd always shown towards school in Scotland. It isn't that his Mallorcan alma mater had a less robust policy towards studying than its British equivalents. On the contrary, being British-owned and catering predominantly for British kids, the school followed the official British curriculum, while also covering the criteria essential for those who would later go on to higher education in America or Germany. And its record of educational achievements and the percentage of its pupils ultimately gaining university entrance were nothing short of impressive.

But it wasn't such admirable scholastic attributes that attracted Charlie to his new school. His approach to studies was the same as it had always been; if he liked the subjects, he tended to do well at them, while showing a distinct lack of accomplishment in those that he found dull. No, it was the way of school *life* in Mallorca that appealed to Charlie. Firstly, there was the matter of the code of dress. Casual was the byword in that department – no boring blazers, grey slacks, white shirts and constricting neckties as is the norm in many British schools, but instead a go-as-you-please 'uniform' of tee shirts, jeans and trainers. All of which makes perfect sense in a Mediterranean climate, and should appeal, in theory at least, to parents in terms of cost when compared to an obligation to buy a formal uniform at the start of every school year. Not so, however. Peer pressure is a powerful force in the blossoming world of teenage kids, or those, like twelve-year-old Charlie, limbering up to join the self-interested ranks of that enigmatic fraternity of rookie adults.

I'd always thought that one pair of trainers looked pretty much like another, that denim jeans were denim jeans period, and that a simple tee shirt was about as basic and choice-free an item of clothing as you could get, except perhaps for selecting the slogan splashed across the front. At this time of year, with winter approaching, our main school-wardrobe concern for Charlie in Scotland would have been to check if last year's wellies still fitted him. But this was Mallorca, and he had become an accepted member of a circle of fashion-conscious youngsters who constituted much of the pupil population of a small international school. Here, the difference between Nike and Reebok – a seemingly minor detail to the uninitiated parent – was so crucial to the youthful cognoscenti as to be humiliating to the point of self-imposed purdah if they committed the shameful sin of getting it wrong.

'You only get what you pay for,' was Ellie's response to my gasps of disbelief on seeing the prices of the current trend in casual 'schoolwear' in one smart department store in Palma.

'But what's the difference between that tee shirt with the crocodile logo on it and the one over there with no logo at all – apart from the huge difference in price, that is?'

'The logo is the reason for the price, and the price is the reason for the logo.'

'Come again?'

'*Lacoste*, that's what the crocodile means, and the crocodile means quality.'

'Yeah, well that's just bloody typical of the woolly

thinking of a woman let loose in a clothes shop. Forget it, Ellie – I am not forking out silly money for the doubtful privilege of buying a kid's bog-standard tee shirt with a wee felt crocodile glued onto it, and that's final!'

'But you've got a couple of Lacoste shirts, Dad,' Charlie piped up. 'Great quality, you said they were when you got them. Last a lifetime, you said. Really neat.'

'Pipe down, Charlie. Your mother bought me those shirts, and if I'd known what she'd paid for them when she brought them home, I'd've sent her right back to the shop with them. Bloody outrageous waste of money.'

'But, Dad –'

'No arguments, Charlie. What I've got is one thing, and what you're going to get is another.'

'That's just not fair, Peter,' Ellie objected.

'It's perfectly fair. Like I said, my Lacoste shirts will last me a lifetime, but Charlie's tee shirts will be too small for him in a matter of months, provided he doesn't rip them to shreds in the meantime, of course. You know what boys of his age are like – up and down trees, always getting into scraps and everything.'

'Yeah, but *all* the guys are wearing them this semester, Dad – the ones with the little 'gator on them, I mean.'

'And that's another thing, Charlie – just because you've got a few American kids at your school, there's no need to speak like them. God, we've

99

hardly been here a year and you're already talking like Catherine Zeta Jones!'

'Come on, Peter, don't be so stuffy,' said Ellie. 'All the kids at international schools on the island pick up that way of speaking from their American chums. It just happens. Even your old pal Jock Burns uses it for effect when it suits. It's an infectious accent, and everybody everywhere has been picking up bits of it since the death of the silent movies. Get with it, for goodness' sake!'

'OK, OK, talking mid-Atlantic is one thing, but trying to keep up with the spending habits of some of those rich kids' parents is not an option for us.' My eyes lit on a rack of Reebok trainers. 'I mean, hell's teeth! How many tons of bloody oranges would we have to sell to pay for a pair of *those?*'

'Hey, not a problem, Dad!' Charlie smirked in that smart aleck way that kids do when they're entering the know-it-all era of adolescence. 'That brand's kinda *pasado*. Yeah, man, you gotta be into Puma sneakers now. Top-of-the-range Pumas is where it's at.'

'Whatever happened to the good old black sandshoes?' I groaned. 'Gutties, we called them in Scotland when I was at school. Gym shoes – plimsoles. They cost next to nothing and served the same purpose. I mean, what's the point in all those dayglo squiggles and flash bumpers and fenders and knobbles and pads and flaps and stuff they stick onto them these days? Useless falderals – any excuse to hike up the price!'

'It's known as style,' Ellie condescendingly informed me, the rolled-eyes glance she swapped with Charlie suggesting that they thought I'd just beamed down from Mars. 'Come on,' she muttered to him, 'let's have a look upstairs in the jeans department.' She took Charlie by the elbow and sped him away, adding in a voice pitched for me to hear, 'There was a sign in the window saying they've got the new Calvin Kleins in!'

I didn't know what the Calvin Kleins were, but I did know they sounded expensive.

'Jesus H. Christ, Ellie,' I yelled after her, 'what the hell chance have I got of teaching the boy to be careful with money if you encourage him to get kitted out in all this bullshit designer gear, for crying out loud?'

I hardly noticed the disapproving 'tut's and startled looks of the pack of immaculately decked-out Spanish lady shoppers in our immediate vicinity, nor was I that bothered about what they thought anyway. Ellie had her credit card cocked, so this was serious. I wouldn't have done in Britain what I did next, but it's funny how easily you lose whatever decorum you possess when surrounded by people you think can't understand you.

'Tell you what, Ellie,' I called out while pushing my way through a crush of shocked *señoras* in the lingerie department, 'let's compromise, right! Listen, Ellie! Hold it a minute, will you! Let's talk this thing –'

Over I went, my toe having collided with something – either the protruding foot of an innocent clothes rack, or the protruded foot of a mischievous *señora*. In a clatter of disintegrating tubes and rails, I was floundering about on the floor under an avalanche of Wonderbras, lace-trimmed negligées and assorted ladies' knickers.

'Ooya bastard!' I instinctively hollered. 'My bloody toe!'

'*SILENCIO!*'

I didn't understand much of the machine gun rattle of what was said next by the strapping floor manager who suddenly materialised above me, posing concave-backed like a matador about to deliver the *coup de grâce*. His speech was cotton-woolled with lisps and dropped sibilants, which suggested, as did his swarthy appearance, that he was a native of the cradle of bullfighting, the southern Spanish province of Andalusia. Confusing accent or not, however, the meaning of the word '*expulsión*' wasn't difficult to fathom, particularly when accompanied by the illuminative thrust of a rigid finger exit-wise. Apologising in Spanish was one thing I'd already become adept at, so I profusely did so, struggled to my feet and slunk past the store toreador with all the bravura of a hapless heifer in a bullring. I couldn't be sure if it was '*Olé!*' that he grunted as I sidled on my way, but there was no mistaking the shopping *señoras*' titters of amusement bubbling through the duvet of cosy background Musak. Always uplifting, they doubtlessly thought, to see a *loco extranjero* making an arse of himself in the bloomers department.

'Andratx street market next Wednesday morning,' I puffed when I eventually caught up with Ellie and Charlie. 'Let's face it, they've got all this designer-label stuff there too, but at a fraction of the price, right? So why don't we just wait and get the new school gear there? Makes sense to me.'

'All bootleg,' Charlie instantly pooh-poohed. 'Fake labels, sham shoes, third-rate threads.'

'So what? They look exactly the same as all the overpriced stuff in here.'

Charlie shook his head and shot me a pitying glance. 'Nah, no way, Dad. You can spot the difference a mile away.'

'He's absolutely right,' said Ellie, forging ahead. 'You only get what you pay for – which is where we came in.'

'But whatever happened to cutting your coat according to your cloth?' I asked in an almost pleading voice as Ellie pushed Charlie onto an escalator.

'Well, Dad,' Charlie shouted over his shoulder while I stood and watched his mother and him glide away from me, 'at least you *won't* have to buy me one of them. Strictly for Melvyns, coats are. Yeah, *so* uncool, man.'

Ellie shrugged her shoulders, patted Charlie on the head, and flashed me a 'that's my boy' smile.

After years of being dragged around such places

by my shopaholic wife, I knew when I was beaten. But luckily, one enviably humanitarian aspect of Spanish department stores is that they all have a built-in haven of solace for the downtrodden man-in-waiting. A bar. Which is where I headed just as soon as Ellie and a delighted Charlie soared heavenward into Calvin Kleinland. The eventual credit card slip would seem that little bit less painful to contemplate after a brow-cooling glass or two of ice-cold *San Miguel*, I reckoned.

Fortunately, as it turned out, Ellie had only been winding me up – well, to a certain extent anyway. She did like expensive clothes, and it was becoming clear that Charlie had inherited the trait. But Ellie was also the arch pragmatist when it came to shopping. She'd never had money to burn, so to get the things she wanted, she'd developed – to near virtuoso level, I may add – the rummaging and bargain-seeking skills of the kasbah marketplace that all women display when let loose in a clothes shop. When she eventually strode triumphantly into the bar, with Charlie shuffling along a couple of disgruntled paces behind, it was clear that she'd had a satisfying rummage. Somehow, she'd managed to strike an acceptable balance between the purchase of trendy togs and the employment of pecuniary prudence. I didn't bother to ask how. The bills for Charlie's 'uniform' still seemed wallet-shrinkingly extravagant to me, but when Ellie pointed out how much bigger they could have been if she hadn't done her kasbah thing, I just sighed a reluctant sigh of acceptance and ordered myself another beer.

Charlie's moans that the triple side stripes on the sneakers that had been bought for him weren't exactly what was currently cool, and his assertion that Calvin Klein jeans would have cut a funkier dash than the Levis his mother had 'lumbered' him with, went unheeded. Yet, for a kid who'd been brought up to do such messy farm jobs as bucket-feeding calves and, dressed accordingly, shovelling chopped turnips into cattle troughs in muddy winter fields, his developing sartorial pernicketiness had me slightly concerned. Here was one potentially expensive aspect of the influences that come to bear on a country boy exposed for the first time to *la vida loca*, the 'crazy life', the golden fleece of the fun-seekers who come and go on the ever-changing tide of youthful hedonism in holiday hotspots like Mallorca. And the island had more such distractions to lay in Charlie's impressionable path, as we were about to find out.

The school sits snugly on the brow of a steep, pine-spangled rise in a quiet suburb of Palma called Sant Agustí, or San Agustín as it was known until the Mallorcan government's re-conversion of many of the island's place names from the Castilian Spanish of the mainland establishment to the original *mallorquín*. The spelling of some town and street names, even road directions on *autopista* signposts, have been altered accordingly – a potentially confusing situation for any visitors already familiar with what was where and where was what when referred to in Castilian. For all that, it's a worthy change in the eyes of those who value the traditions of Mallorca and have fought long and hard for the survival of its language. Good luck to them, and even better luck to you if you happen to be struggling to find your way about with the aid of anything other than an absolutely up-to-date map – except in one or two of the more remote country areas, perhaps, where an out-of-date map may well be exactly what you need. Stick with it, though; it's Mallorca, and its little quirks are worth persevering with, even if you do get hopelessly lost occasionally. You can always take comfort from the knowledge that you're never likely to be far from a back-street or country-lane hostelry in which to ask directions, or simply to sit in and drown your sorrows while tearing up your map or looking up the phone number of the Samaritans.

Off the top of my head, I still can't tell you the name of the little street at the top of which the school is located, but it's easy enough to find, either by descending the switchback road from the Palma-to-Andratx highway as we did that day, or by driving the short distance up from the coast. The old road that skirts the sea was formerly the main link between the capital and the scattering of popular holiday resorts that adorn the south-west

Mallorcan shoreline. Randomly, though ever-more-closely spaced, these modern urbanisations resemble the 'gems' in a concrete necklace draped round the evergreen bosom of the Sierra de Na Burgesa mountains. While such 'progress' is perhaps inevitable, beauty, as ever, is in the eye of the beholder.

'Hey, Don Pedro! *Cómo le va, amigo?* Say-y-y-y, how ya doin', ol' buddy?'

It was Jock Burns, this time in schoolteacher guise, greeting me in histrionic mid-Atlantic from the top of the school steps. Originally built as a small hotel before being converted to its present use, the pristine white building has an unusually welcoming aspect for a school. Thinking back to the appearance of the school I first went to in Scotland, an austere Victorian establishment that was about as pleasing for a child to behold as the dog-catcher's van would be to a carefree stray, this place seemed like utopia in comparison. Sweet smelling junipers guard either side of the entrance, its elegant arches all but smothered under mauve cascades of wisteria. At one side of the wide sweep of steps that leads to the doorway, the shiny leaves and unmolested fruit of a lemon tree cast dappled shadows on a carpet of Livingstone daisies tumbling over a low drystone wall beneath. Adding a spectacular dash of colour to this pretty little garden, the red trumpet flowers of Hibiscus burst into a visual fanfare of cheer that contrasts vividly with the depressing, graffiti-daubed entrances of this school's counterparts in many a less favoured environment. Jock Burns himself had taught for a while at just such a place in a tough housing estate in Edinburgh before escaping to Mallorca to take up a teaching job that conformed with his previous one in name only.

Charlie was indeed fortunate to be a pupil at Sant Agustí, and his relatively short time at the school had already changed him noticeably from the unworldly wee Scottish laddie who had been so reluctant to enrol there the previous winter. His initial impression of life on a fruit farm in a fairly isolated Mallorcan valley hadn't been too favourable in any case, and the prospect of having to endure what he envisaged as the ordeal of being a new boy at a school so different in every way from the one he'd been used to had appealed to him even less. But, as I said before, it didn't take long for Charlie to alter his opinion, thanks to the relaxed procedures that permeated school life, the informal dress code, the feeling of not being confined that comes with the endless opportunities for outdoor scholastic activities in a Mediterranean climate, and, perhaps most significant of all, the outlook-broadening experience of mixing with young people of various nationalities and from many ethnic backgrounds.

It was heartening to see them pouring happily from school; all shapes and sizes, ranging from mere infants to gangly seventeen-year-olds, with every face a picture of sun-kissed health, and their behaviour, though as exuberant and noisy as that of school kids anywhere, revealing a refreshingly genial attitude as well. Few, if any, were the sullen expressions of disinclination so often associated with the first few days back at school after the long summer break.

'Nice to see such a contented bunch of youngsters,' I said to Jock when I met up with him at the bottom of the steps.

'Aye, they're no too bad at all, son,' he said in his 'normal' Scottish accent, having surreptitiously checked to see that no one else was listening. Clearly, his mid-Atlantic drawl was an essential part of the image that he chose to present to his students. Knowing Jock as I did, it was a foregone conclusion that he believed that adopting an 'international' mien would enhance his classroom cred at a school like this. And, judging by the cheery valedictions being shouted to him by home-going pupils, he was obviously a very popular member of staff.

'Mind you,' he went on, 'ye do get the occasional awkward wee twonk to contend wi'. Spoiled rich kids, mainly. Usually a handful o' them on the school roll here, by the way. A good hard kick up the arse is what they need. Aye, but ye cannae resort to that, unfortunately – no when their parents are coughing up good money for school fees.'

He had just touched on a subject close to my heart – or, more truthfully, a subject that was becoming increasingly close to giving me a heart attack. When we did our sums before coming to live in Mallorca, Charlie's school fees were high on the list of items of expenditure that we knew we'd have to budget for. And we did – first calculating the cost in pounds sterling, then, once we'd got used to dealing in the local currency, in Spanish pesetas. But as time went by and the commercial realities of what we had chosen to do for a living began to sink in, I'd instinctively started to work out the cost of Charlie's education in crates of oranges. It added up to depressive accounting. The success, or otherwise, of the orange harvest during the coming winter months would answer many crucial questions that were already beginning to creep into my mind.

Yet, ironically, our spending on Charlie's schooling was the one balance-sheet item on which, if we chose to, we could most easily make a substantial saving. All we needed to do was to send him to the local state school in Andratx. It had a good reputation after all, and, most importantly, was free. Moreover, both Charlie and Sandy – like Ellie and me before them – had known nothing but state-school education in Scotland, and it had served us well enough. We knew of other British families in Mallorca who had opted to send their children to local Spanish schools, and as a result the kids had integrated more quickly and much more thoroughly than their privately-educated counterparts. Consequently, there was the bonus of the children rapidly becoming fluent, by sheer necessity, not just in the formal Castilian Spanish of the classroom, but in the Mallorcan/Catalan of the playground as well. We'd already met one Scottish couple who had sent their five-year-old daughter to the little school in the village where they lived on the other side of the mountains from us, and after just a few months she could already speak considerably more Spanish than I'd managed to learn in years of poring over phrase books and grammars.

So why not just do likewise with Charlie and head off the possibility of school fees becoming a problem? Well, rightly or wrongly, our thinking on the matter was that he had already been subjected to the upheaval of being separated from everything and everybody familiar to him when we moved to Mallorca, had already had to cope with settling into one new school, and was now positively thriving on the experience. To put him through all that again, therefore, wasn't something we'd resort to lightly. He was a hardy kid both physically and emotionally all right, but at his sensitive stage of life, yet another uprooting could well have adverse results, and that wasn't a risk that we, as his parents, were entitled to take on his behalf. No, we'd keep sending him to school at Sant Agustí, and if economies to our family budget did have to be made eventually, we'd find other ways of making them . . . somehow.

'So, how *do* you deal with bad apples at a school like this?' I asked Jock. 'You know, the few disruptive pupils you were talking about.'

'Just leave it to the other kids most o' the time.

Any obnoxious wee chavvies are always in the minority here, and being made an outcast by yer mates usually has that type changing their ways smuckin' fartly. Nup, it's no often we need to take anything like what ye might call *disciplinary action*.'

'Sounds like a good place to be a teacher, then?'

'Aye, well, Ah've worked in worse, put it that way. Anyway, must rush, son. Got a man to see about a couple o' mobile phones he's selling.' Jock tapped the side of his nose. 'High-tech machines, low-tech price – know what Ah mean? Say no more, eh!'

I cleared my throat and had a furtive glance over my shoulder. 'Well in that case,' I said *sotto voce*, 'I might just be interested in buying one myself.'

Jock shook his head. 'Nah, nah, no danger. Ah wouldnae sell ye one, son.' He put his lips to my ear and hissed: 'They might need a wee bit o' what ye might call *adjustment* before they work in what ye might call the western hemisphere, see.' Now it was Jock's turn to take a sly peek over his shoulder before revealing: 'Ah'm getting them via ma mate Juan the bargain man along at the Palma docks. Straight off the back o' a North Korean freighter. No questions asked and no guarantees either.' He puffed out his chest and declared matter-of-factly: 'Ah'll sell them sold-as-seen, like. Oh aye, goes without saying, that!'

'Ah, the old caveat emptor, right? Let the buyer beware.'

Jock gave a roguish chortle. 'More like caveat

nauta – sailor beware! Yeah, Ah'm flogging them to a coupla Hooray Henry yachties who're setting sail for the Bahamas in about an hour's time. More money than sense. Aye, wi' a bit o' luck the daft buggers'll be cruisin' past the Canaries before they twig they've been patsied.'

With that he was gone, striding over the school-yard towards his car, breezily acknowledging parents and bidding farewell to pupils alike, and all in his loudest mid-Atlantic accent, of course.

Ellie wandered over from the shade of a spreading umbrella pine where she'd been having a chat with a few other waiting mothers she knew.

'How does he do it?' she asked, nodding towards the shiny new BMW Z3 roadster that Jock was shoe-horning his ample contours into. 'I mean, look at the clapped-out bangers most of the other teachers are driving. The value of the whole lot put together would hardly buy one wheel for Jock's car.'

'Well, credit where credit's due, he *is* a hard worker. Never stops. Straight from here to the docks for a bit of wheeling and dealing, then on for a swift earner down at the yacht marina. And after that he's got his nightly double gig entertaining hotel punters along the coast. That'll keep him busy until the wee small hours, but he'll still be up and about and back here at school bright and early in the morning.'

'I'm surprised he finds time to eat,' said Ellie, raising her eyebrows.

Right on cue, Jock's moon face beamed out at us from beneath the flared rim of a white Stetson as he swept past in his matching Beemer. 'So long, pardners!' he yelled between bites on a chicken leg that he'd produced from somewhere. 'YEE-EE – HA-A-A-AH!'

Ellie pulled a resigned shrug but said nothing. She didn't need to. Jock would never starve – no matter how busy he was.

The afternoon sun was still high above the Med, its jewelled waters lapping the shore only a Balearic slingshot away at the foot of the hill. Through the pines we could see the sails of two distant yachts, elegant and unhurried in their silent voyage. Farther out still, a thin chalk mark was being drawn across the rich blue of the sea by the wake of the daily Valencia ferry, heading for mainland Spain, lying unseen and seductive beyond the western horizon. We had parked our car by the high whitewashed wall that flanks the yard in front of the school. The heat in the reflected glare of the sun was intense, and my thoughts returned to Ellie's earlier harping on at me about making a start to the improvements that needed to be made around the house. If this sort of weather continued, I might still be able to play my *mañana* card for a while yet! The temperature was more conducive to sailing through a cooling sea breeze like the lucky folks on those far-off yachts, I mused, than to doing even relatively light work like watering fruit trees – a twice-daily chore that I'd have to face until the rains of autumn finally arrived. For the moment, though, I was pleased just to lean back against that whitewashed wall and soak up, eyes closed, the tranquillising warmth of the September sun.

'No sign of Charlie,' sighed Ellie after relishing a minute or two of like indulgence. 'I'd better go into the school and see what's keeping him. Probably playing computer games or something. Typical male – no sense of time!'

I must have dozed off for a bit, for when I opened my eyes again I could see that the last of the other parents' cars had left the yard, which was now completely empty, save for a huddle of the school's small contingent of boarding pupils, who were sitting under the big umbrella pine doing some giggle-punctuated homework. Ellie was coming back down the steps from the school entrance.

'No sign of him in there either,' she called to me. 'Head teacher said he left with one of his chums the moment the bell rang. Says he saw them heading off down the road.'

'Ah well,' I yawned, '– probably thought he'd meet us coming up. Not to worry, he's most likely sitting having a Coke on the terrace of the Bar Tu-y-Yo down on the corner of the coast road. I've known him to wait there before if I've been a bit late.'

'Like father, like son,' Ellie testily muttered while climbing into the car. 'Not even thirteen years old and he's already hanging around bars!'

'Time enough to worry when he starts ordering himself bottles of *San Miguel*,' I muttered back, allowing myself a little smirk of satisfaction at the way Charlie was preparing himself for adulthood in the free-and-easy atmosphere of Mallorca. And what was Ellie being so prudish about anyway? What harm was there in kids having an alfresco chat with their friends on the pavement terrace of a respectable café-bar? When all's said and done, they'd be much more likely to have a couple of tea-sipping old ladies than a gang of lager louts sitting at the next table outside a quiet establishment like the Tu-y-Yo in any case. It isn't a big deal for secondary school students in Spain to adopt such places as post-school rendezvous – though, admittedly, the kids frequenting them would generally be a few years older than Charlie. But the most important consideration is that it's a harmless cola rather than a sneaky beer that's the accepted order of the day at such see-and-be-seen watering holes. That's the way (publicly at least!) of Spanish young folk in that age group, and I was quietly pleased to know that Charlie was getting into the swing of things early. A commendably liberal precept on my part, I reckoned. Maybe so, you may warily think, but mightn't I ever come to regret having embraced it? A perfectly reasonable question, I would willingly concede, though little knowing that at least part of the answer would soon be revealed.

★　★　★

116

So silent was the approach of the gold Rolls-Royce up the school road behind us that I almost pulled out in front of it. A majestic toot on its horn obviated the inevitable shunt, however, and a big grin from the middle-aged lady driver assured us that an outburst of road rage clearly wasn't on her agenda.

'Well, hello there, me darlin's!' she warbled in a broad Irish brogue, waving to us through her open driver's window as if greeting long-lost friends. She pulled up on the other side of the yard. I had never seen a Rolls-Royce this big without the Queen sitting in the back, far less knowing the owner of one.

'Who the hell's *that?*' I gasped.

Ellie merely shook her head and somewhat sheepishly returned the Rolls lady's smile.

The most instantly-obvious features of her appearance were a devoutly-deep suntan, a pair of diamond-studded Catwoman sunglasses, gold hoop earrings big enough for a gymnast to swing on, and a towering 'blonde' hairdo that was somewhere between early Dusty Springfield and a high-rise biblical beehive. Striking though this image was, it was mild stuff compared to what our eyes were regaled with when she opened her car door and stepped out. I had once described Jock Burns' flamboyantly dressed wife Meg as a one-woman Rio Carnival, but this one was all of that and then some! The upper part of her lean frame was encased in a fluorescent pink boob tube spattered with big green polka dots, while the

117

lower half had been poured into skin-tight ocelot pedal-pushers. To add a final touch of individuality to this bizarre fashion statement, a chiffon scarf of Royal Stewart tartan was tied round her midriff. Looking like someone who had walked out of the wreckage of a collision between two circus caravans, she tottered towards us on a pair of mauve Manolo Blahnik stilettos that would have made acceptable stilts for a midget. That said, those shoes alone were probably worth more than our little second-hand Ford Fiesta.

'Sure it's grand to meet ya at last,' she beamed. 'You'll be Peter and Ellie, so ya will, and Oy hope ya didn't tink Oy'd kidnapped yer boy. Ah, Jaysus love ya, and a fine boy he is at that.'

It was only then that I noticed Charlie, sitting regally in the back of the Roller with a cat-that-got-the-cream grin on his face. Beside him was a boy I recognised as Dec, one of Charlie's school friends we'd met a few times before, but knew nothing about, other than that he seemed a well-mannered lad with a cheery disposition. Charlie had stayed over at his house on a couple of weekends (just as he'd done at the homes of other classmates), and had been driven home next day by Dec's older brother Mick in his rattly old beach buggy. No questions asked, no worries, and all part of the trusting, easy-going way in Mallorca.

'O'Brien,' said the Rolls lady, offering both of us in turn one of two gold-festooned hands, before launching herself with gusto into the

118

Spanish two-cheek-kiss routine. 'Colleen O'Brien, Oy am, but me friends just call me Col.' She erupted into cascades of raucous laughter. 'Col – Spanish for cabbage, don't ya know? Oh yeah, and a grand name for an Irish lass it is an' all, don't ya tink?' She elbowed me in the ribs, then murmured eye-twinkingly out of the corner of her mouth: 'Better still if me old man's name was Cannon, so.' She nudged me again. 'Colcannon, see – as Irish as feckin' stew!' She punched me on the shoulder, threw her head back, and an even louder peal of hoarse guffawing reverberated round the schoolyard.

Ellie and I weren't even given half a chance to speak before Mrs O'Brien's laughter dissolved into another deluge of words. They'd just moved into a new house, she informed us. Fed up with all the upheaval, she and her hubby were, so they'd decided to shove the 'owld' boat out this evening – just to blow the 'owld' cobwebs away, didn't we know. She'd left a phone message with the school secretary for her son Dec to get his little arse into gear when the bell rang and give her a hand to pick up some boat-shovin' supplies from the supermarket down round the corner there.

'And, Oy says to her, his wee friend Charlie's invited along for the craic an' all. Cream o' the milk bottle, yer boy Charlie,' she said to Ellie. 'We all tink the world o' him, so we do. He's a darlin' boy, and Oy hope ye'll let him stay the night t'night.'

We had no objection to that, I told her. In fact,

119

it was very kind of her to offer. 'The only thing,' I started to explain, 'is that we're planning to harvest our almonds tomorrow, and as it's a Saturday, we'd banked on Charlie giving us a –'

'Ah, away wit ya now and yer feckin' nuts! Holy mother o' Christ, yer almond trees'll still be there a hundred years after ye're dead and gone, so they will. Let yer boy enjoy his weekend. Enjoy yerself when ye're young, say Oy. And, tank chuckie, Oy'm still a young ting meself!'

She hit me with another straight left to the shoulder, then burst into that wild laugh of hers again. Here was a grade-A raver, if ever I'd seen one. Instantly likeable with it, though, and I admired her philosophy. A great attitude to life – if you could afford it, and judging by her car and the small fortune in jewellery glinting from every exposed area of her bronzed hide, Colleen O'Brien most certainly could.

'Come on!' she beckoned while getting back into the car. 'Come on and have a wee house-warmin' drinky-poo at me new pad, why don't ya? Sure it's good for what ails ya!'

Before we could say a word, never mind attempt to make any excuses, the Roller whispered off down the hill, with Charlie, still grinning, wafting us a queenly wave out of the rear window. Ellie and I looked at each other, exchanged what-the-hell shrugs, and duly followed on behind.

Perhaps the massive, gilt-embellished wrought iron gates that swung automatically open when the gold Rolls-Royce approached should have prepared us for the scene that would unfold before us as we drove through behind, but they didn't. Nothing could have. To describe what we entered as a driveway would have been like calling Mount Everest a molehill. This was a veritable esplanade, every square centimetre of it crazy-paved (for want of a better description) in white marble. Col parked the Rolls alongside a gleaming white Mercedes sedan of presidential proportions. Next to the Merc was a red Ferrari coupé that lacked nothing in ostentation except the presence of a half-naked film starlet draped over its bonnet. It struck me that the value of this trio of sheer auto-motive luxury would have amounted to more than that of several little *fincas* like Ca's Mayoral put together.

'They're all theirs,' Charlie enthusiastically assured us, opening our little Ford's door for his mother. 'The cars, I mean – yeah, all theirs, and there's more in the garage round the back.'

I hardly took in what he said. Even a fleet of such cars would have been worth mere peanuts compared to what my eyes had been drawn to behind them. The house rose from beyond the swimming pool like something out of a Hollywood dream sequence. Ellie and I just stood squinting at it with our mouths open.

Col O'Brien stiletto-wobbled over to us from the Rolls. 'Now then, the pair o' ya!' she scolded, linking her arms with ours. 'Ya know what happened to the owld lady who swallowed a fly, so come away inside now and Oy'll show ya around – let ya see the tinker's wagon yer wee boy's gonna be dossin' down in tonight.'

Now I knew why she was wearing those huge Catwoman shades. My unprotected eyes were smarting in the glare of sunlit white bombarding them from every direction. White – everything was white – the purest, dazzling white, broken only by fine details of gold. The front of the house appeared to be on three levels, yet the stepped and gently undulating contours of its wide façade gave it a pleasingly low-lying look. Clever. Sweeping, balustraded balconies ran the entire length of the upper floors, their arcaded fronts supported by columns of snowy marble. As new as the house was, little groves of miniature palms and the slender green fingers of 'skyrocket' cypress already graced either side of its spectacular entrance. Although real, the trees looked as though they had been purposely hand-crafted, each set carefully in a preordained place to effect a perfect balance of form with their surroundings. This was a palace straight out of a movie set, and if Fred Astaire and Ginger Rogers lookalikes had suddenly appeared swirling light-footed down the curving flight of marble steps, I wouldn't have been surprised. All that was missing were the lights, cameras, microphone booms and a guy with a clapperboard.

Colleen O'Brien must have read my thoughts. 'So then,' she said while ushering us through the grand doorway, 'ye're likely wondering where a common-as-spuds owld Irish tart like me got the money for all this, are ya? Must've won the lottery, ye'll be tinkin' to yerselves, Oy'll bet.'

We were both still speechless, so she was able to continue uninterrupted. No, it hadn't been luck that had been responsible for where she was today, she declared. It had taken hard work, a lot of it – yes, and a healthy dose of good old common-as-spuds Irish savvy an' all. Her husband's father had started the business, she went on.

'Owld Paddy O'Brien,' she chuckled, her emerald eyes twinkling again. 'Looked like a tramp, but could out-tink bloody Einstein. Onto the main chance like a ferret up the leg o' yer feckin' drawers,' she laughed, digging me in the ribs. 'After the war, ye see. Military surplus. Ye know, it's surprisin' the profit that's in owld army boots – *if* ye have the nerve to buy a mountain o' them in a job lot, that's to say. Then it was the scrap he went into. Not yer owld bike frames and rusty drainpipes and stuff, so. Ah, no, no, no, he was always tinkin' bigger than that, so he was. Battleships and submarines was his game – British, German, American or French, it mattered not a piglet's bollocks to owld Paddy.'

She then revealed that shrewd investments in property and the building of a retail empire with the help of his two sons had sealed the family's fortune. 'But sure,' she said with a philosophical shrug of her shoulders, 'there's a time to work and

123

there's a time to play. So, when owld Paddy – God rest his smelly feet – finally went to the big scrapyard in the sky, me and me hubby cashed in a few chips and came out here to live . . . and play.'

And were they playing in some style! The interior of the house was even more stunning than the outside. White and gold remained the dominant theme, offset by pink drapes and soft furnishings that simply oozed opulence. Slender columns rose dramatically through three floors to a glass dome enclosing a galleried atrium that created the centrepiece of the ballroom-sized reception hall. Piped music added to the impression of being in the lobby of a luxury hotel. Visions of Las Vegas came to mind. An indoor garden, complete with classical statues and a scaled-down replica of Rome's Trevi Fountain, led through a Moorish archway to a mirrored formal dining room, which in turn opened onto an entertaining area with a full-size snooker table. Taking pride of place was a lavishly-stocked oval bar that lacked nothing but Dean Martin slouched on one of its white leather stools. Instead there was Sean, Col's hubby, a gangly fellow with an unruly shock of black hair and a grin as open and as broad as Dublin Bay.

'All designed by Valentino, this, ye know,' he told us in a totally unpretentious way after pleasantries had been exchanged. He drew our attention to a white grand piano resting in the palm of a huge sculptured hand. 'Classy, or what? That's yer Eyetalian designers for ya.' He popped a champagne cork and filled four flutes. 'Oh yes, yer Eyetalian designers,' he declared expansively, '– we use 'em for everything. Quality and taste. Sure, it speaks for itself, ye know.' Sipping his champers with little finger appropriately raised, he gestured towards his wife. 'Just take them togs the missus is wearin' for example.' A discreet burp. 'Versace.' (He pronounced the last syllable as per 'ace' in 'ace of spades'.)

His next statement, directed at Ellie, was plainly inspired by the look of disbelief on her face as she once more ran her eyes over his wife's outlandishly assembled get-up.

'Fair enough,' he said blandly, 'it might look like shite to you, me darlin', but it's the best shite that money can buy!'

Sean and Col stared at us deadpan for a few moments, silently revelling in Ellie's tongue-tied attempts to come up with a suitably diplomatic response. Then they burst into a duet version of Col's rasping laughter. It was as infectious as it was gladly received.

'He's a terrible caution, isn't he now, so?' said Col, bidding us follow her again. 'Come away and Oy'll show ye the rest o' the shack.'

After a guided tour of the kitchens, breakfast room, morning room, study, servants' quarters, sauna and Jacuzzi, she led us up another Fred Astaire staircase, this one spiralling up beneath a crystal chandelier that Louis XIV wouldn't have turned his nose up at. I lost count of the number of bathrooms we were shown – one for each of the five luxury bedrooms and at least a couple more. The white and gold theme had been carried through the tiling of the walls and floors of those, with the added lavishment of giant ceramic scallops, each one permanently yawning open to reveal a bath with gold-plated fittings moulded into the shape of its lower shell. Signor Valentino had developed this mollusc mood to even more fanciful heights when designing the focal point of the master bedroom. Here a gaping oyster shell contained not a bath but a huge water bed. The image that it immediately conjured up in my mind's eye was not of Col O'Brien's angular frame rising from it, however, but rather the graceful curves of Botticelli's *Venus*. This was flamboyance so far over-the-top as to risk giving yourself a nosebleed just by looking at it.

'Christ!' my mouth said without any assistance from my brain.

Ellie choked, prompting Col to give her a hearty slap on the back.

'Ah, sure Oy can see ye're impressed,' she grinned. 'And Oy don't blame ya. Like me owld hubby says, ye can't whack yer Eyetalians for quality and taste, neither ye can.'

'The quality's unbelievable,' Ellie wheezed rheumy-eyed, tactfully leaving the matter of taste in abeyance.

'But if ya tink the bed's impressive as it stands,' Col gushed, 'just feast yer eyes on them here gizmos Oy had made for it.'

She plonked her bottom down on one side of the bed, causing a minor tidal wave to slop about under the gold-braided satin of the duvet cover. Then, her eyes wide with childlike anticipation, she pressed a button recessed into the lip of the oyster shell's base. With a gentle whirring sound, the tops of the two bedside tables slowly rose to reveal 'his' and 'hers' drinks cabinets containing bottles of champagne and various other alcoholic refreshments. A little bell pinged to indicate that operating altitude had been attained.

'And there's more!' Col enthused, glancing at us for encouragement – as if she needed any. She pressed another button, and the 'hers' cabinet started to revolve, disposing of any need for the lie-a-bed imbiber to stretch too far for the tipple of her choice.

'Christ!' I muttered again.

'Oy tought ye'd like it,' she said, nodding her head. Then she winked a knowing wink. 'But Oy know what ye're tinkin' – there's somethin' missin', right?'

She selected another button, and a clam-shaped tray, strategically positioned at pillow height, emerged from the side of the elevated minibar. A music-box rendition of 'Roll Out The Barrel' confirmed that this particular technical manoeuvre had been completed. Col reached into the tray with a pair of gilt tongs that had been concealed inside. She pulled out an ice cube.

'What did Oy tell ya?' she laughed. 'Feckin'

brilliant, eh? Refrigerated, the little wee bars are. Yeah, and all me own idea an' all!'

Signor Valentino had finally been upstaged. But still, the ultimate accolade was reserved for nature – or, more accurately, the location that nature had provided for the house. Stepping out from the master bedroom onto the cloistered balcony, the uninterrupted views over the Mediterranean were truly magnificent. Although I hadn't realised it when at ground level, from up here I could see that the house was sitting on its own little promontory, with private access to the sea. It was the type of location usually snapped up by developers for the construction of a five-star hotel, but all that had been built on this site was the O'Briens' new home. Old Paddy and his mountain of ex-army footwear had served his well-heeled family well. And, looking down at the swimming pool, it was now evident that it was in the shape of an 'owld' boot, a fittingly zany tribute to the old man's enterprise and foresight. To me, that pool provided a truer reflection of this unique family's character than all the overstated opulence lavished on the house by their much-revered 'Eyetalian' style guru.

Back down at the bar, Charlie was helping Dec and two older brothers load up a few coolie boxes with cans of soft drinks and bottles of beer and bubbly. On first impressions (usually the best), the O'Brien boys seemed like down-to-earth, ordinary lads living in an extraordinary house.

Nothing in their demeanour suggested the air of detached superiority that young fellows in their privileged position might be expected to display. They'd obviously been brought up under the influence of plenty good old common-as-spuds Irish level-headedness. Their father Sean was overseeing proceedings from his perch on the Dean Martin stool, a charged champagne flute still delicately clenched between forefinger and thumb.

'Ah, it's yerselfs again!' he shouted to Ellie and me. 'Come away wit ya and sit yerselfs down. There's time enough for another drop o' the champers for ya before we shove the owld boat out.'

I'd thought that all the talk about pushing the boat out had been purely figurative, an indication that the O'Briens were planning some sort of house-warming party that evening. But after helping to lug the 'boat-shovin' supermarket goodies from the Rolls-Royce down to a private jetty, it became obvious that the term had been used absolutely literally. Tied up alongside the little pier was a Riva motor launch – Eyetalian again, Sean pointed out. I don't know much about boats, but I recognised this one as a gleaming example of the luxurious wooden-hulled craft I'd seen ferrying the Queen to and from the Royal Yacht Britannia on newsreels covering visits to exotic corners of her dominion. Even the beautifully upholstered cream leather seats were identical to the boat's regal counterparts.

Sean was first on board, captain's hat quickly

donned and pushed to the back of his head. 'Jump aboard, me darlin',' he called to Ellie, extending a helping hand. 'We're just goin' round the coast a bit to meet up wit the boys' big sister and her hubby for a hooley on the beach. Ye'll have a ball, so ye will. And don't worry now – ye can stay the night, for there's bunks a-plenty in the boat for the lot o' us.'

The Riva being essentially a tender, albeit the most prestigious of its kind, I didn't see any likelihood of it having even one bunk. Not that it mattered to Ellie and me, because we couldn't accept the invitation anyway, no matter how reluctantly we'd have to decline it. Bonny the boxer had been left alone at Ca's Mayoral for most of the day and she needed to be fed. Besides, there was still the evening stint of essential tree-irrigating for me to do before dark, and to skip that to go to a beach party just wasn't an option. We made our apologies and waved our goodbyes.

It didn't take long for the mystery of on-boat sleeping accommodation to be solved. Sean steered the Riva directly towards a sleek, ocean-going yacht tied to a mooring buoy in deeper water just fifty metres or so off shore. It was like a two-masted, floating hotel. Charlie was first to clamber up on deck, followed by the O'Briens bearing 'boat-shovin'' goodies. Ellie and I stood and gaped slack-jawed again as the sound of raucous laughter and another champagne cork popping heralded the elegant ketch's departure across the bay. Even from this distance, we could see the grin of delight on Charlie's face as he mucked in with the other lads to follow Captain Sean's shouted instructions to his 'crew'.

'Reminds me of that old song,' I said.

'"Red Sails In the Sunset"?' Ellie murmured dreamily.

'No,' I groaned, returning Charlie's wave, '"How We Gonna Keep Him Down On The Farm, Now That He's Seen Paree?"'

CHAPTER 5

HERE WE GO GATHERING NUTS

The clatter of cane on wood had been echoing round the valley every day for the past week, a sure sign to novice nut-pickers like us that we'd better get on with our preparations for the almond harvest, small as ours would be in comparison with those of some of our neighbours. As Ca's Mayoral had a well that was capable of providing water for as many fruit trees as the land would accommodate, that's precisely how the *finca* had been developed. Thirsty citrus trees had taken precedence over almost everything else a long time ago. On the other hand, owners of *fincas* with no such source of water for irrigation are obliged to specialise in 'dry' farming, and in Mallorcan orchard terms that largely means the husbandry of either olives or almonds. The trees are indigenous to the Mediterranean area and, because of their deep, moisture-tapping roots, can exist happily all year on the water nature delivers from the sky during the months of winter. On the plains and on the terraces (or *bancales*) that scale many mountainsides like great, sweeping staircases, large expanses of the Mallorcan landscape have been devoted to almond production since time immemorial. The result is the wonderful 'snowy carpet' of pink-white blossoms that covers so much of the countryside during the month of February – an unforgettable sight that never fails to enchant any visitor to the island.

Yet, ironically, it's just such aspects of Mallorca's wealth of natural beauty that have come to threaten the very survival of the almond trees themselves. The millions of tourists who now descend on the island every year do not share the almond trees' meagre need of water. The result is that the underground sources that for so long satisfied the delicately-balanced ecosystems of Mallorca have become so depleted that shiploads of water now have to be imported just to satisfy human demand. But while such enterprising measures have looked after the interests of the tourism industry, they have done nothing to halt the menace that creeps unseen beneath the trees which traditionally contributed so much to the island's economy. With over sixty percent of Spain's total production, Mallorca once laid claim to being the world's largest exporter of almonds, and even now, with competition from places like California, where more modern harvesting techniques are used, the quality of its produce cannot be bettered anywhere. But as the island's freshwater resources have been exploited ever more greedily, salt water from the sea has seeped in to replace it in the deep aquifers that once prompted an unusually lyrical geologist to describe the island as being akin to a great turtle shell covering a honeycomb of underground lakes and lagoons. There is certainly evidence of the damage already done round some of the coastal fringes of Mallorca, where dead or dying almond trees stand as silent witnesses to the poison that their own tap roots have drawn up in the way that nature intended for their very survival. Even more disturbing is the theory that, once such a pattern of salination has started on an island, its progress inland will be irreversible, unless the process is undone by rapidly getting rid of its cause. And what chance is there of Mallorca closing its doors to those millions of tourists who have brought the island riches beyond the wildest dreams of the almond farmers of old?

Old Pep's was just such a 'dry' farm, though fortunately still far enough inland to remain unthreatened by subterranean contamination from the sea. Pep also utilised the land between his hundreds of almond trees to grow another crop that needs only seasonal rain to thrive. That crop is oats, the grains to feed his little flock of sheep and other livestock, the straw to provide their bedding when housed, with the resultant manure fed back to the land in exchange for its yielding another crop in another year. It's a simple 'you scratch nature's back and she'll scratch yours' method of farming that's as old as farming itself. 'Organic' is the buzz word for it nowadays, but there are few of the modern converts to the system who could claim to employ an absolutely chemical-free regime like the one still followed by Pep in the way of countless generations of his kinsfolk before him. In Pep's situation, 'self-sufficiency' wasn't just a glib handle of the type bandied about by suburban 'good-lifers' with enough money in the bank to subsidise their back-to-our-roots whims. For Pep, self-sufficiency was an absolute necessity and as much part of his life as the way he skilfully harnessed nature to make it possible.

'*Hombre,*' he once told me, 'the only thing this *finca* does not supply for my needs is electricity, and I existed well enough without that before the power company came along and ran the cable in. Poles everywhere! *Bastardos!*'

He wasn't *quite* telling the whole truth, however. He did throw his leg over his rickety old two-stroke moped for occasional shopping trips to the village store, and he also had an ancient paraffin-powered tractor that he trundled out just once a year to drive his little threshing mill. There was no evidence of an oil well on his place, though, far less a refinery. Yet, to be fair, the few litres of fuel he bought in a year to feed those two machines would have amounted to little more than we spent on petrol to do the seventeen-miles-each-way school run during a single week. Yes, Pep was about as self-sufficient as it's reasonably possible to be in this day and age. Even the bills for what electricity he did *reluctantly* make use of would

135

have amounted to very little. I had never been inside his ramshackle little house, but if Pep's workaday clothes and the dilapidated state of his farmstead were anything to go by, it's safe enough to assume that he would have indulged in precious few domestic mod cons of the electrical variety. That said, he did have a forty-watt light bulb in a wall lamp outside his front door that he turned on at dusk. But even that was switched off as soon as he had completed his end-of-day farmyard tasks and retired indoors for the night.

It isn't that Pep was mean – far from it. Necessity was the mother of thriftiness in his case, and that, combined with his well-cultivated grumpy air, could give the impression of his being something of a Mallorcan Mr Scrooge . . . until he got to know you, that's to say. Despite the frugality that was the hallmark of his own existence, he would never see you stuck for anything, if it was within his means to help out. I'd never forget, for instance, how he'd provided us with enough almondwood logs to keep us warm during our first calamitous Christmas at Ca's Mayoral, when the fickleness of the winter weather and the very fibre of the old house itself seemed to have conspired to make us miserable, if not to drive us away altogether. Pep didn't have much of anything, certainly not materially, but what he did have he'd gladly share with you in time of need. What's more, he neither sought recompense nor entertained the offer of it.

Now, almost ten months on from that traumatic Christmas, I had grown to respect Pep more and more as a person, as well as having taken a real shine to him as a character. He was a man who had the traditional ways of Mallorcan farming in his blood. He also knew the valley's temperament and the telltale signs of any forthcoming quirks of its weather better than anyone else – with the possible exception of old Maria. I valued his advice greatly. I had also learned to passively accept the benign, though ostensibly barbed, ridicule that so often came with it.

It was late in the afternoon when I made my way over the lane to his place, having decided to delay flooding the irrigation channels round our citrus trees until some more heat had gone out of the sun. One thing I had quickly learned in Mallorca was that water is too valuable a commodity to risk wasting through evaporation. I had waited until the bamboo rattle created by Pep's little troop of almond-gatherers from the village fell silent, signalling that they had temporarily downed tools to take a thirst-quenching break from their labours. Their job was to knock the ripe almonds from the branches with their long canes, causing the nuts to fall onto large nets spread on the ground round the base of each tree. The almonds would then be gathered up and put in sacks, ready for Pep to load onto his mule cart.

I could see him at the far end of his farm steading, if indeed steading isn't too grand a word for such a higgledy-piggledy conglomeration of shacks and pens. And 'shack' had been how Colleen O'Brien had described, albeit with tongue-in-cheek, her Hollywood-style mansion that I had been wandering through just an hour earlier! In the space of such a short time, I had stepped into two diametrically opposed worlds, separated by only a few miles and the capriciousness of fate on this most enigmatic of islands. But were the O'Briens any more content in their Mallorca than Pep was in his? I doubted it.

'Weh-*ep!*' he called out to me, employing the old Mallorcan expression of greeting that's as much used on the island as the equally meaningless 'Hiya!' is elsewhere.

He was standing in the pose he invariably chose when relaxing – shoulder propped against the wooden-spoked wheel of his mule cart, baggy-trousered legs crossed, his black beret drawn down over his forehead to shade his eyes. He pulled a hand-rolled cigarette from the top pocket of his scuffed leather bomber jacket, struck a match on the steel rim of the cart wheel, and lit the *cigarrillo* amid the usual mini fireworks display of sparks, crackles and pops.

'*Cómo va su vida?*' he spluttered, smoke belching from his nostrils. 'How goes your life?'

I'd only just begun to reply when Perro, Pep's dopey dog, came loping round the corner of the nearest shed. *Perro* also happens to be the Spanish word for 'dog', a name Pep had always bestowed upon his successive canine companions. '*Coño!*' he'd exclaimed on noting my quizzical expression when he first told me of this curious custom, 'it is the logical thing to do, no? Would you address a man by calling him anything other than *hombre*, for instance?'

Game, set and match to Pep, as ever.

Perro was big, black and, as Pep never tired of pointing out, a fine specimen of Mallorca's native breed, the *Ca de Bestiar* – literally 'Cattle Dog' in *mallorquín*, though actually a multi-purpose animal, equally skilled at hunting, animal herding and (like Perro, according to Pep) acting as a fearless guard dog with an instinct to attack anyone or anything that threatens his master or his domain. Perro certainly was a prime physical example of the strain, judging by other *Cas de Bestiar* I'd seen at agricultural fairs on the island. It's just unfortunate, although Pep would never admit it, that at birth Perro had swapped his breed's inherent intelligence and alleged aggression for a generous streak of disarming gormlessness. Apart from his colour and rangy, Labrador-like build, he could well have been a throwback to the doggy ancestor that inspired Walt Disney to create Goofy. The first time I'd ventured into Pep's farmyard, Perro had indeed attacked me – with his tongue. He had also peed all over me after pushing me to the ground in a frenzy of unbridled friendliness. In fairness, though, he'd been little more than an overgrown pup then, and the intervening months had seen his impulsive nature tempered by slowly creeping maturity. *Very* slowly creeping maturity!

The Castilian Spanish name for the *Ca de Bestiar* is *Perro de Pastor Mallorquín*, meaning 'Mallorcan Shepherd Dog', and although his sheepdog's hat was the one he wore most often for Pep, Perro still hadn't grasped the basics of the job. Pep supplemented his sheep's home-grown fodder by taking the little herd to graze on other *fincas* in the valley, logically enough to *fincas* whose owners had no livestock of their own to nibble down the weeds growing between their trees. This involved shepherd and sheepdog combining their skills to drive the animals along various country lanes until the predetermined destination had been reached – never any more than a few kilometres distant from Pep's own farm. Perro's responsibility, like that of a Border collie in the hills of Scotland for instance, would have been to perform the duty of outrider, ducking, diving and running around hither and thither to make sure that no sheep or lamb strayed from the body of the flock en route. He would also have been able to follow his master's instructions as to which route the sheep should take when approaching a fork in the road. To do that, it follows that Perro would have to run ahead of the herd to block off the wrong route in order that the sheep would be obliged take the right one. But it never worked out that way, and Pep's bellowed curses and threats to his thick-headed mutt would invariably result in total farce – sheep scattering in all directions, with Perro desperately trying to chase each and every one of them into an even more confused state than they were already in. And that took some doing. The senior ewes – wiser than Perro would ever be, no matter how brainless their reputation – had made those journeys so often that they instinctively knew where they were going anyway. If those older matrons of the group had been left to their own devices, they'd have led the others along with no fuss whatsoever. In fact, the sight and bell-tinkling sound of orderly little flocks of long-legged sheep ambling along, while pausing here and there to munch a roadside tuft, is one of the delights of rural Mallorca. Perro had turned the destruction of that delight into an art form.

But at least his method of welcoming had calmed down a bit since our first encounter. Instead of knocking me over, he now threw himself to the ground, rolling onto his back in a show of submission combined with an open invitation to have his belly tickled. One thing that hadn't changed, however, was his inability to hold his water when excited. Watching the pulses of pee arcing upward from Perro's nether regions, it struck me that this would be about as close as Pep would ever get to emulating the O'Brien household's replica of the Trevi Fountain.

'Just as well I'm here, *amigo*,' Pep advised me while looking down admiringly at his best friend and doting aide. 'Otherwise he would have had your foot off!'

141

The truth of the matter, however, was that Perro, big and gangly though he was, would have been happier sitting on my knee than gnawing on my ankle. I gave his chest a friendly rub with my toe, then deftly pulled my foot away in advance of the resultant squirt of urine. Judging by the smile on his face, Perro seemed happy enough with that. Pep feigned indifference, though I knew from experience that his mind was working overtime. He would already have worked out the reason for my visit, of that I was sure. He would keep it to himself for as long as it suited him, however. The *interludio dramático* was Pep's stock in trade. But, for all his quirky ways, I felt comfortable in his company. There was something familiar about his idiosyncrasies, something that reminded me in many ways of my own grandfather, himself an islander and a mud-on-his-boots farmer who didn't suffer fools gladly, wasn't without his own eccentricities, but had a mind that was as sharp as a razor. It seemed, too, that the two thousand miles that separated my grandfather's native Orkney Islands from Pep's Mallorca made no difference to the essential nature of both men. Neither seemed to care too much about his appearance, yet both had an undeniable presence. They had charisma, perhaps without realising it, though I suspect that they *were* quietly aware of their own particular magnetism. It mattered little that my grandfather expressed his individuality by wearing rolled-down, straw-filled wellies that were purposely bought two sizes too big, while Pep's trademarks were his jauntily-cocked black beret and his rakish neckerchief. It was an inner quality that set them apart from the crowd, not so much their appearance, strangely arresting though it could be. And animals seemed to recognise that too, as both old fellows had an uncanny way of communicating with their livestock by employing just a word or two, or even by eyeballing them in a certain way. It was a kind of telepathy, I suppose, but it worked – well, most of the time, and with the obvious exception of Perro.

I watched Pep as he struck another match and re-lit his *cigarrillo*, which had extinguished itself in a minor grenade burst of sparks that must have stung his face like a hundred hot darts. He scarcely blinked an eye.

'*Cuarenta putas!*' he grunted. 'Forty whores! Too much saltpetre in that wad!'

He was referring, of course, to the fact that he both grew and cured his own tobacco, a noxious concoction that smelled like a spontaneously combusted muck heap when lit, and must have tasted even worse. But Pep swore that his tobacco plants were genuine Havana and that his secret curing method was unique. Most importantly, he liked the resultant mix better than any store-bought equivalent – of which, he was at pains to add, there was none in any case. I believed him on the last point at least. But, foul-smelling or not, Pep's home-grown tobacco was just one example of the breadth of his self-sufficiency expertise. Had he not signed the pledge years ago, there's little doubt that Pep would still have made his own wine too, with perhaps a little copper still secreted in one of his sheds in which to cook up something 'medicinally stronger' for the winter months. But Pep's legendary drinking days were over, and he now concentrated on his one surviving sin – smoking.

'Sex is an overrated pastime,' he said, right out of the blue.

'*Sí?*' I replied, taken aback.

'*Sí*,' he said. 'Just take your neighbour, that old bat Maria, for example.'

'Sex? Maria! But she's ninety if she's a day, so surely she still doesn't –'

'Have you not seen her new teeth?' he cut in, inclining his head backwards, the better to observe my reaction from under the dark overhang of his beret.

'Well, y-yes,' I stammered, not wishing to be drawn into any behind-her-back bad-mouthing of the old woman. 'I – well, I mean, we – we did sort of notice some sort of, you know . . .'

Pep raised a silencing finger. 'Do not be embarrassed, *tío!*' (Calling someone *tío*, meaning 'uncle', is a Spanish term of familiarity, even if the person being addressed is, as in this instance, young enough to be your nephew.) 'You see,' he calmly proceeded, adopting the learned air of a medical specialist about to deliver a diagnosis, 'old Maria has lost her marbles.' Reading my look of puzzlement, he

144

nodded his head and dropped the corners of his mouth. 'Ah *sí*,' he solemnly confirmed, 'in the words of the young people of today, she has gone completely off her fucking trolley. *Totalmente loca* – and all because of sex.'

I started to snigger. I couldn't help it.

Pep wasn't amused. 'You doubt the strange power I have over women?' he snapped.

That did it. I burst out laughing so loudly that even Perro, who'd been snoozing at my feet, pricked up his ears and wagged his tail. Pep's body language didn't match his dog's, however, and I knew I'd have to pull myself together quickly if I was to avoid a tongue-lashing.

'Sorry, Pep,' I said, flicking a tear from the corner of my eye, 'I didn't mean – I mean, I wasn't laughing at *you*. It was just that –' Another snigger escaped my nostrils, this time inflating two matching snot bubbles in the process. I could tell by the inquisitive sideways inclination of his head that Perro was more impressed by this amazing feat than his master was.

'Go on, get it out of your system,' Pep muttered. 'Laugh your head off.' He shrugged his shoulders in an uncharacteristically nonchalant way. '*Va bé, hombre*. See if I care.'

I suspected that what Pep really wanted now was for me to eat humble pie by pleading with him to reveal more about old Maria's alleged sex-driven insanity. Yes, beneath this show of insouciance, it was fairly obvious that Pep was actually bursting to spill the beans. I decided to play him at his own game for a while.

The click-clack of the almond harvesters' canes rattled out once more from the field behind the farmstead. Pep raised an eyebrow, but otherwise remained impassive. He coughed an involuntary puff from the cigarette wedged in the corner of his mouth, and so still was the warm evening air that the consequent wisp of smoke hardly wavered as it rose and spread into a little flat cloud above his head. It looked like a halo. 'Saint Pep of the *Cigarrillo* Rollers' was the name that came immediately to mind. He'd have made an unlikely candidate for canonisation, though – particularly now that he had admitted his attraction to the opposite sex, or rather *their* attraction to him. Anyway, the notion of any woman, particularly a cagey old chicken like Maria, going crazy for a rough-and-ready old fox like Pep didn't really strike true. Then again, there *was* that rumour about them having had some sort of 'attachment' in the dim and distant past – the three-cornered romance, according to local chinwags, that had been the cause of the long-standing animosity that still existed between Maria and Francisca Ferrer. Maybe there was something in it after all. My curiosity was getting the better of me.

I was just about to broach the subject of Maria's new teeth again when Perro created an unintentional diversion. He yawned, pulled himself up into the sitting position, stretched, yawned again and went skittering across the yard on his backside, hind legs splayed, rear paws in the air. His ears were clapped back like a whippet's in the wind, and the corners of his mouth were drawn into a kind of manic grimace. I'd seen our old collie bitch do this on occasions back in Scotland, but she'd always picked a grassy spot to do it on. Perro was performing the act on the sharp, gravelly surface of the yard, which suggested to me that he either had a very acute case of worms or a corrugated iron arse. Knowing Perro, it was probably a combination of both, the latter being proof of the old adage: 'No brain, no pain.'

'A sign of contentment in a dog,' said Pep, his eyes following Perro's swift, front-paws-propelled circuit of the yard. 'A sign of complete trust in his surroundings.'

'Not a sign of worms?' I ventured.

None of his dogs had ever suffered from worms, Pep confidently proclaimed, then reminded me of the 'natural' preventive measure he swore by and had told me about once before. 'Stuffed a garlic clove up his hole only yesterday,' he stated matter-of-factly. 'Garlic – better than any of your *medicinas sintéticas* for the worms.' A smirk spread over his leathery face, indicating that a pertinent afterthought had entered his mind. He pulled the cigarette from his mouth and pointed the lit end at the flies of his trousers. 'Eating the raw garlic puts fire into a man's blowlamp as well,' he concluded with a knowing wink. 'I swear by it. Ah *sí, claro*.'

If this was Pep's way of clumsily guiding the conversation back to the subject of old Maria's reversion to long-forsaken ways of the flesh, it almost worked. I was just about to raise the subject again when his mule, spooked by the scuffling sound of Perro's sledgeless sleighride whizzing past his hooves, suddenly stirred from the standing slumber he'd been enjoying between the shafts of his cart. The backwards jerk of the cartwheel knocked Pep off his balance. He staggered sideways, letting out a yell of pain while grabbing his right shin with both hands.

I leapt forward, anxious to stop him falling over and perhaps hurting himself even more. But Pep had regained his balance *and* his composure long before I'd got within grabbing distance. Succumbing to physical assistance from anyone wasn't something that Pep would do willingly. Which reminded me of the rumoured reason why we hadn't seen anything of him for several weeks during the hottest period of summer. We'd assumed that he was just lying low in his shack during the daylight hours, hiding away in the shadiest, coolest spot indoors until sundown, when he'd take his sheep on their customary foraging journeys round the valley. There would have been nothing odd about that. Everyone, including ourselves, complied with that essential siesta-taking approach to life in the oppressively humid summer temperatures that even born-and-bred natives of the valley like Francisca Ferrer described as *horreeblay* and *terreeblay*. In fact, it was Francisca herself who told Ellie that Pep had been laid up with a broken leg, sustained, she'd added laughingly, by being butted in the behind by his billy goat and thrown headlong over the edge of the high mountain terrace on which he had been grazing the crotchety beast and his little harem of nannies. Naturally, it isn't an occurrence that Pep would ever have admitted to. Such a mishap, as comical to envisage as it must have been painful to experience, would have done his image of being a master controller of animals no good at all.

'Shrapnel,' he said, rubbing his shin. 'Civil War.'

I said nothing. I doubted that Pep had ever been a soldier, but that poker face of his revealed not the slightest sign that he may have been telling anything but the whole truth.

The wound still hurt occasionally, he went on, the pain striking at any time and for no apparent reason. 'About as predictable as a fart in a whirl-wind, *amigo*, and a lot more difficult to control.'

'Isn't brought on by the weather, then,' I suggested, leading him on. 'Not like a sign of impending rain or anything like that?'

Pep swallowed the bait, hook, line and sinker. 'No, no, nothing to do with rain,' he blurted out. 'To tell the truth, sometimes it can be worse in the heat of summer. Ah *sí*,' he said, eagerly taking up more of the line I'd fed him, 'and that is why I was housebound during much of the month of

August this year. Agony!' He squinted at me through the haze of smoke wafting from his cigarette, the words 'Don't you want to know more?' written all over his face.

'So where do old Maria's new teeth come into all of this?' I obligingly inquired.

He was quick to reply. For all her womanly quirks and foibles, Maria was a good neighbour, he conceded, though not without a hint of reluctance. Pep now adopted an air of confidentiality. 'I tell you this,' he confessed, 'no sooner had she heard the news about my acci – . . . uhm-ah, *perdón*, I mean about the onset of my war-wound *problemas*, than she was at my door offering to help. *Sí, sí* – you know, feeding my partridge, milking the goats, collecting the eggs and little things like that – simple things that women are good at.' Pep nodded his head discerningly, spat the butt of his cigarette onto the ground, tapped the side of his nose and confided: 'It was only a matter of time before she yielded to temptation, *amigo mío*.'

Without any urging from me, he went on to tell how, on one particularly hot day, he had been resting on his bed, unable to move because of the pain in his leg, when Maria entered his room uninvited. She'd said that she only wanted to tidy the place up a bit, but, in Pep's irrefutable opinion, that had only been an excuse, a crafty womanly ploy, to get herself into his bedroom.

'I have seen nanny goats and ewes sniff the air in the way she did as soon as she came through the door,' he informed me, his expression deadly serious. 'They have the same look on their faces as she did – *muy sensual, muy erótica* – a sure sign that they are on heat. The nostrils twitch, the top lip curls – a signal of sexual desire in the female that is well known to the experienced stockman.'

I had to cover my mouth with my hand to hide the smile that was doing its best to graduate into a full blown guffaw. Fortunately, Pep was now too engrossed in his storytelling to notice.

'And it was then that I first saw her new teeth,' he continued, 'shining bright in the dimness of my room like a couple of glow-worms warming up for a good hump!'

I faked a cough, raising my hand to my mouth again.

Pep paid no heed. His warming to the theme had now reached boiling point. Because of the stifling heat, he keenly divulged, he had been lying clad only in his underwear, his woolly *combinaciones*, the lightweight summer ones that he wore permanently from the beginning of May 'til the start of the October storms.

'"Get them off!" she yelled at me. I tell you, *tío*, she was, as the young people say today, gagging for it.'

If, as he claimed, he had been wearing the same one-piece drawers and undershirt for the five hottest months of the year, it was little wonder that Maria was gagging, particularly when having walked into an airless room that probably smelled like a polecat's nest at the best of times. Pep's partiality to eating raw garlic wouldn't have helped either. Sex would have been the last thing on Maria's mind. An overwhelming urge to throw his smelly duds into the washtub would have been her sole motivation for telling Pep to 'Get them off!'. That was my reading of it anyway, but certainly not Pep's.

'She was like a woman possessed,' he exclaimed, 'like a wildcat, clawing and yanking at the ankles of my long-legged *pantalones*, and all the while screaming, "Off with them! Off with them!" I tell you, I was off that bed and hopping out into the yard quicker than a man with two good legs could have done. Puh!' he scoffed, his brows gathering into a frown beneath the eaves of his beret, 'did she think that simply stuffing new teeth into her *boca* would ensnare a man like me? New teeth? *Coño*, it would take a lot more than a few new teeth to make me yield to the wicked ways of that rampant old nymphomaniac!'

So intense was the compulsion to laugh, and the necessity not to, that I wished I'd taken the precaution of going to the toilet before paying Pep this visit. I crossed my legs, suddenly sympathising with Perro in the spontaneous-pee department, and only just managing to stem the threatened flood of incontinence. I couldn't speak, and I wouldn't have known what to say anyway. Pep came unwittingly to my rescue by suddenly announcing that he was a busy man and couldn't

152

afford to stand around talking to me any longer. I took it that he felt he'd accomplished the dual mission of affirming his masculinity while making what he perceived to be a plausible cover-up for the indignity of having been knocked off a mountain by a goat.

'*Adéu*,' he grunted as he took hold of his mule's bridle and started leading him out of the yard to pick up another cartload of almonds. '*Hasta luego, eh!*'

'*Hasta luego*, Pep,' I said, turning to walk away and having a good chuckle to myself at the same time. You never knew what to expect in a conversation with this old rascal, but somehow you always seemed to come away from it feeling a whole lot better than you had before. The one imponderable, though, was whether, on such occasions as this, he took what he was saying as seriously as he made out, or whether he was simply pulling your leg mercilessly. To me, it didn't matter either way. Listening to Pep's banter was invariably the highlight of the day.

I'd almost reached the gate when his voice rasped out again:

'*Oiga!*' he bellowed at me. 'Forgotten what you came for, have you?'

Indeed I had, which says a lot for the quality of the entertainment.

Pep didn't wait for a reply. 'Over there by the woodpile,' he shouted. 'A few stout bamboo *cañas* and an almond-catching net. I knew you would need to borrow them. *Sí*, it was a certainty that, that mean *hijo de puta* Ferrer would not have left you any when you took over the place.'

'*Gracias*, Pep,' I called back, my right thumb raised in acknowledgement of his thoughtfulness. '*Muchísimas gracias!*'

'*De nada, hombre.* You are welcome. But, hey . . . there is a big hole in the net. Get your wife to mend it, eh. *Sí, claro*, women are good at simple things like that.'

'*Sí, claro*,' I shouted, thumb raised in ostensible agreement this time, while I silently thanked the gods of two-facedness that neither Ellie nor old Maria were within earshot.

'And another thing, *amigo*,' Pep added before disappearing round the far corner of his yard, '– old Maria's new teeth – there is something *very* strange about them. *Ah sí*, I tell you, *tío*, they are just not . . . *normal!*'

Now, where had I heard that before?

Ellie was rushing out of the house to meet me when I staggered back into the Ca's Mayoral yard lugging the bulky almond net and an ungainly clutch of nut-knocking canes.

'You'll have to give the orange trees a *very* quick watering this evening,' she panted. Her face was wreathed in smiles, her cheeks flushed with un-disguised delight.

'Let me guess – you've won the lottery and we're dashing off to the Bahamas, right?'

'No, better than that. It's Sandy! He was on the phone just now and he's coming back – tonight!'

I couldn't stop myself grinning either. 'For good?' I asked, hoping that Ellie's answer would be in the affirmative.

'He didn't say – didn't have time. He was calling from a payphone in International Departures at Edinburgh – ran out of change – just said he'd managed to get a stand-by seat on the next plane to Palma.' Ellie was beside herself with excitement. 'So come on!' she urged, grabbing the bamboo poles from me. 'Get those trees watered fast, and let's head for the airport!'

CHAPTER 6

COMING HOME, OR GOING HOME?

Typically, perhaps, for a growing youth of eighteen, Sandy's first words to us when he walked through the arrivals gate weren't, 'Great to see you again', or even, 'It's nice to be back', but, 'Jeez, I'm starving! Crappy wee meals on these flights – one sawdust sausage, six squashed peas and a polystyrene spud – not even enough to fill the guts of a mouse. Yeah, and all cold at that. Telling you, I was so hungry I even ate three of the brickworks rolls they came round with!'

The bar-restaurant Punta Son Gual sits almost directly under the flight path of Palma Airport's main runway, and only a short drive (once you know the back roads!) from the terminal building itself. Ellie and I calculated it was both close enough to reach before Sandy died of malnutrition and generous enough in the size of its portions to satisfy his ravenous appetite. It's the type of unpretentious establishment you'd quite easily pass by without giving a second glance to. One of two modest-looking bar-restaurants situated on either

156

side of a minor T-junction on the busy Palma-to-Manacor road, the Punta Son Gual's only external asset would appear to be the surrounding Pla de Sant Jordi, the windmill-dotted central plain of Mallorca. We had originally been tipped off about the wonderful reputation of the little restaurant's food by no less an epicurean authority than Jock Burns himself. He in turn had learned of it from a Mallorcan friend, unthinkingly divulging what had been a jealously-guarded secret known only to local folk who recognised good value when they ate it.

The Punta Son Gual, or 'The Lamb Joint' as revealingly dubbed by its devoted patrons, is one of those rare finds, a no-nonsense eatery whose owner sticks unwaveringly to doing what he does best, strives to do it better than anyone else, and charges no more than a fair price for it. Miquel Serra had built the reputation of his place by making a speciality out of a simple, traditional dish so familiar to Mallorcans that it was almost taken for granted, and would have been regarded by many as an unlikely candidate for attaining legendary status in the annals of the island's cuisine. That dish is *cordero asado*, roast lamb. And the secret of Miquel's success? Again 'simplicity', and his inspired decision to forego the use of modern cooking equipment in favour of roasting the meat in a stone-lined, wood-fired bread oven of the type that, in bygone times, was built into the kitchen wall of every farmhouse in Spain.

157

Miquel's decision was to prove the making of both his fame and, ultimately, his fortune too. The food at Punta Son Gual became so renowned that he and his chef-partner Matias were eventually obliged to open a much larger and grander restaur-ant, called, appropriately enough, Ca'n Matias Miquel, on the same road, but back towards the outskirts of the city. And a very fine establishment it is, the overflowing car park at mealtimes proof of its popularity. But there's still something special about the little place that was Miquel's spring-board to all that success. Even now, and despite the competition from its grandiose younger sibling, unless you're very quick off the mark, there's about as much chance of getting a table at The Lamb Joint at Sunday lunchtime, when much of the population of Palma decants into the countryside to eat, as there is of Jock Burns becoming anorexic. And as the typical Mallorcan weekend gets off to a flying gastronomic start on a Friday evening, we were also extremely fortun-ate to find a free table when we arrived with the starving Sandy at eleven o'clock that night – right at the peak of the dining rush hour for Spanish folk.

Vegetarians beware! The toothsome aroma of roasting meat cuts through even the thick blue fug of cigar smoke that permeates the cramped little bar you have to shoulder your way through to reach the restaurant proper. And once inside, you immediately realise that it isn't the ambience of the place that attracts people in their droves. For a 'joint' is what it is – in the most complimentary sense of the word, of course. It's just that, as far as luxury appointments go, everything has been spared. What you have is a plain, narrow room filled with plain tables and chairs, the tables themselves covered in plain paper, the walls adorned with no more than the bare necessity of unprepossessing pictures. The only visual feature of any note, in fact, is a clear view through the windows to a procession of big passenger jets descending at what seems like windmill height towards the nearby runway. But even the scream of their engines is drowned out by the babble of animated conversation that is so much a hallmark of communal eating in Spain.

The subject of whether or not Sandy had come back to Mallorca permanently hadn't arisen during the short drive from the airport, and, keen as we were to know what he had decided, Ellie and I thought it best to leave the matter unmentioned until Sandy himself decided the time was right to bring it up. And the prompt arrival of the food ensured that this was likely to be delayed a while yet. Eating out in Mallorca just wouldn't be eating out in Mallorca without the customary opening 'picks' of olives, crusty bread and garlicky *all-i-oli* mayonnaise. They were soon followed by a shared platter of *gambas a la plancha* – large, unpeeled prawns turned to smoky pink perfection on a hotplate while drizzled with olive oil and lemon juice, then served with a sprinkling of salt and herbs and a generous garland of lemon wedges. I say that it was a 'shared' platter, and that indeed was what it was intended to be, except that Sandy's starved state ensured that the description was purely academic. Peckish as we were, Ellie and I hardly got look in. But when you're the parents of teenage boys you're used to making such dietary sacrifices. And anyway, it was good to see Sandy tucking into his first meal back on the island, tearing the heads from the prawns and sucking out the roasty-toasty juices inside (as is the Spanish way), before deftly stripping the papery skins from the bodies and popping the luscious crescents of flesh into his mouth.

'It's as if he's never been away,' Ellie whispered to me, while lovingly watching our elder offspring refuelling.

'It's only been two bloody weeks,' I muttered back. 'He's hardly likely to forget the intricacies of stuffing his face in a fortnight!'

There were now only two whole prawns left on the communal platter.

'I, uhm, take it you've already eaten,' Sandy remarked on noticing the comparatively tiny smattering of prawn debris on the side plates lying forlornly in front of Ellie and me. 'Come on,' he benevolently invited, '– help yourselves anyway. Not much eating in these wee fellas, you know.'

It took only the merest negative hand gesture on Ellie's part and a compliant shake of the head from me for Sandy to respond with a suit-your-selves shrug, before swiftly committing the final brace of *gambas* to the mercy of his digestive juices. I was tempted to suggest to him that he should try the cure for worms that old Pep habitually administered to his dog, but, in the interests of prandial propriety, decided against it.

Still feeling slightly guilty about having gorged ourselves at the Celler Ca'n Amer in Inca earlier that day, Ellie and I, unlike Sandy, had resisted the temptation of ordering ourselves a main course of Miquel's celebrated leg of lamb. We'd opted instead for baby lamb chops, *costelles d'anyell*, which we felt would be kinder to the waistline *and* the conscience, though none the less delicious for all that. What sets Mallorcan lamb apart from its northern European counterparts is that local climatic conditions and the consequent dearth of natural fodder in typical 'dry' sheep country have dictated that the animals are slaughtered at a very young age. This, combined with the naturally slim build of Mallorcan sheep, ensures that the flesh of the lamb is both tender and devoid of the thick coating of fat for so long regarded as a desirable characteristic in certain British breeds, for example. The result, when skilfully cooked, is lamb that is melt-in-the-mouth succulent and totally lacking in what can be (in older, less lean animals) the strong, muttony taste so reminiscent of the smell you get when hand-washing an old woolly jumper. In short, the best Mallorcan lamb is in a class of its own, and it doesn't come any better than at the Punta Son Gual.

Although Sandy's dismissive glance at our baby lamb chops revealed that he reckoned the little medallions-on-the-rib would, like the contents of his earlier airline meal, be insufficient to satisfy the hunger pangs of a mouse, their diminutive size was no reflection on the fullness of their flavour. They had been cooked, in typical Spanish fashion, *a la brasa*, the intense heat of the charcoal grill quickly browning and sealing the surface of the meat while leaving the inside gloriously pink and juicy. And the rich tang of the olivewood smoke from the fire had added that final touch of Mallorcan magic to the taste.

You have to have a man-size appetite to be able eat a whole leg of meat on your own, even the slim limb of a young Mallorcan lamb. So, Sandy's effortless polishing-off of the well-turned shank that spilled over the rim of his plate suggested that he was no longer in the ranks of the boys; not in the eating stakes at any rate. Thanks to the inimitable cooking properties of the old stone bread oven, the joint had been roasted to the crispy texture of parchment-like crackling on the outside, while retaining its savoury moisture all the way through to the bone. Conforming to Miquel's principle of simplicity, it had been served, as had the baby chops, with an accompaniment of golden roast potatoes and a bowl of refreshing *trempó*, a classic Mallorcan salad comprising sweet onions, mild green peppers, tomatoes, pears, pickled capers and a dressing of olive oil and purslane-flavoured vinegar. It's hard to contemplate any addition to this straightforward but dedicated presentation of first-rate ingredients that would be likely to improve it. To attempt to polish such unpretentious excellence would surely only result in dulling its shine.

Smacking his lips as he savoured the last delicious morsel of lamb, Sandy declared, 'You know, I never said so before, but when we came out here to live, one of the things I missed most about Scotland was the food.'

Ellie and I looked at him askance, and then enquiringly at each other. Had he been harbouring, perchance, a secret craving for the unsung glories of mince and tatties, we silently pondered?

'Telling you,' he said, 'the first thing I did when I went back was to go to the chippy and order up a white puddin' supper. Mmmm, magic!'

While not wishing to underrate its gastronomic charms (there's nothing I like more than a white puddin' supper myself), the Scottish white, or 'mealy' pudding as it's also known, is a sausage-type creation that consists mainly of oatmeal, with only the slightest hint of seasoning and flavouring added. As bland as that may sound, when deep fried and served in paper with a helping of chips smothered in brown 'nippy' sauce from the chip shop counter, the white puddin', like its close cousin, the sadistically-named battered haggis, is indeed a treat to be relished. Comparison with more sophisticated international dishes would perhaps be a bit unfair, though. I suggested this to Sandy.

'Oh aye, I couldn't agree more,' he readily conceded. 'Honestly, coming back here to Mallorca tonight and having those big juicy prawns and that fabulous leg of lamb and everything has got me thinking.'

'Uh-huh?'

'Yeah, really! No kidding, I reckon the Mallorcan food's just about as good as the Scottish stuff after all!'

Clearly, the likes of Miquel and Matias still had a way to go before their cuisine would appeal one hundred percent to Sandy's tartan taste buds, but I'm sure that they'd have been relieved to know that they were making some progress. And it could have been worse. Just imagine, he might have set their 'simple' food up in comparison with that other uniquely Scottish culinary delight, the deep-fried Mars Bar.

'So, Sandy, does that mean you're glad to be back?' Ellie asked, unable to contain her need to know any longer.

'You bet, and not just for the grub.' Sandy rubbed his hands and grinned. 'Yup, that hot air hitting you when you step out of the plane. And the warm smells, you know – I mean, I don't know what they are – something like pine trees and wild herbs and whatever, but not like the smells you get anywhere else, if you know what I mean.

You can even sniff it through the pong of the jet fuel at the airport. Yeah, magic.'

I knew the question that Ellie was dying to ask next, so I gave her leg a curbing nudge under the table. I needn't have bothered. Her brain had already dispatched the words to her mouth on a one-way, express-delivery ticket.

'So you've come back to Mallorca for good, have you?' she gushed. Her eyes were lit up like those of a little girl who's about to open her first present on Christmas morning. I knew that she'd be shattered if Sandy said no – and, to his credit, Sandy recognised the fact, too.

'Well, I've been giving it an awful lot of thought over the past couple of weeks,' he said, with a glance towards his mother that gave nothing away, 'and I've come up with a couple of ideas, but . . .' Sandy paused and shifted uneasily in his seat, his fingers reaching out to fiddle with the stem of his water glass.

'But – but what?' Ellie prompted.

Sandy smiled at her, then gave the back of her hand a pat, in what for him was an unusually tactile show of empathy. 'It'll maybe take a day or two back here before I can make my mind up, Mum,' he said softly. 'That OK?'

Ellie tried gamely to disguise her feeling of disappointment with a nod of her head and a little smile of assent.

'Right,' said Sandy, resolutely rubbing his hands together while looking round for the waiter, 'let's see what they've got in the way of sweets on the menu tonight. Jeez, I'm still starving!'

Then I *did* advise him to consider self-administering Pep's 'folk' cure for worms.

'Nah, can't stand the taste of raw garlic,' was his droll reply. 'But that reminds me – where's Dog's Balls?'

Ellie's expression switched from disappointed to confused.

'Probably a pet name for his brother,' I advised her, putting two and two together.

'But what've dog's thingies got to do with it?' she came back, her look of confusion switching to puzzlement. '"Balls" doesn't even rhyme with Charlie.'

'Well, it probably isn't supposed to be rhyming slang,' I told her. 'More likely just a lads' thing. You know – embarrassing nicknames – harmless insults and all that stuff.'

'Yeah, Mum,' Sandy grinned, 'his chums at school call him D.B. for short, but don't let it worry you. It doesn't actually mean he's got nads like a greyhound. Mind you, they say it was that sixteen-year-old American bird they call the Texas Cowgirl who first gave him the handle, so . . .'

'*Cow*girl?' Ellie queried. 'A cowgirl at an English school in Mallorca?'

'That's right,' said Sandy, a mischievous smirk spreading over his face as he added, 'and with the emphasis on the word cow.'

Ellie was aghast. She turned to me, her brows

166

knotting into a frown of angst. 'But Charlie's still only twelve, Peter. A wee boy, and Sandy says a sixteen-year-old girl knows the size of his – his – his *nads*? Tell me it isn't true.'

'It isn't true, Ellie,' I assured her, while discreetly crossing my fingers. 'Sandy's just pulling your leg.'

'But anyway, where is he?' Sandy repeated. 'Too busy watching telly to come to the airport and welcome his big brother back, is he? Typical!'

Sandy's reaction to being told Charlie's actual whereabouts was entirely predictable, though ironic in that, of our two boys, he had been the one who'd shown by far the most enthusiasm for the family moving to Mallorca in the first place.

'At a beach party!' he gulped. 'Gone to a beach party on a multi-millionaire's yacht?' A series of huffs, puffs and muttered swearwords followed. 'I mean, isn't that just typical of Charlie?' he eventually continued. 'He was only in Mallorca for two minutes before he wanted to get back to his Granny in Scotland, and now he's so slotted into the scene here he's even hobnobbing with the millionaire set. Telling you, if Charlie fell into the septic tank he'd crawl out smelling of air freshener!'

It would have been easy enough to read into Sandy's words a sense of resentment at the ease with which his younger brother had taken to his new life, while he himself was now struggling with the dilemma of whether to stay in Mallorca or return to Scotland. But there was more to it than that, and Ellie and I understood his predicament only too well. It was essentially a matter of the boys' respective ages. While Charlie's having to go to a new school had certainly flung him abruptly in at the deep end as far as life-change was concerned, it had also been his passport to making lots of new English-speaking friends, the vast majority of whom shared the common denominator of being the sons and daughters of expatriate parents, and of many nationalities at that. Sandy, on the other hand, had found himself in a comparatively isolated position socially, working alongside his parents on a little farm in a fairly remote valley in which the majority of other residents were native Mallorcans who didn't speak his language and who were, by and large, about a couple of generations older than he was. And, incongruous though it may seem, his problem wasn't alleviated by the fact that, in the summer at least, a few coastal resorts within easy reach by car were brimful of thousands of young English-speaking people of his own age group. Those youngsters were holidaymakers, visiting the island for a week or two of sun and fun, and more than likely with very little in common with a lad who was helping his parents run a small fruit farm in a location that most of them would regard as being in the back of beyond. That said, Ellie and I had to count ourselves fortunate that Sandy hadn't been attracted to getting involved in that particular scene. He wouldn't have been the first expat youngster to fall into the ruinous trap of living every day on the island as if he were on permanent holiday. For us, making ends meet for a family of four was going to be hard enough without subsidising that type of profligate lifestyle, and we could now only hope that young Charlie would turn out to be as prudent in that regard as his older brother – dog's balls notwithstanding.

Finding Mallorcan contemporaries who shared his own agricultural interests had proved difficult for Sandy and, in all likelihood, would continue to do so, no matter how hard he tried. It was simply a fact that there were precious few young Mallorcan chaps in our area still interested in working the land. And in fairness to him, Sandy *had* tried to integrate, as witness his driving halfway across the island twice a week during the winter months to train and play with one of the local-league Mallorcan football teams. But that apart, we knew that the one thing, perhaps more than any other, that had drawn him back to Scotland for his recent visit had been that he missed working with big, modern farm machinery in a familiar environment that was much more extensive and progressive agriculturally than the one we were committed to now. On top of that, he was a perceptive young fellow and he must already have worked out for himself that it was liable to take as much good luck as hard work to turn a small, run-down farm like Ca's Mayoral into a business capable of providing a decent livelihood for us all. To complicate matters, though, he valued the closeness of our family life and, all things being equal, would doubtless have chosen to remain part of it. Yes, Sandy had difficult decisions to make, and it was only fair to give him all the time he needed to work things out. But for tonight, the most important consideration was to help him feel good about being back with us in Mallorca, no matter how temporary his return might still turn out to be.

Although not quite adding up to the proverbial killing of the fatted calf, I did the next best thing by hailing the waiter and asking for the sweets menu.

Manually knocking almonds off trees with a long pole in the fierce Mediterranean heat could hardly be farther removed from the relative luxury of sitting inside a climate-controlled glass cocoon atop a huge agricultural machine with just about every mechanical and electronic working aid imaginable at your fingertips. Back in Scotland just a couple of days previously, Sandy, single-handedly, had been transporting several tons of barley at a time while shuttling non-stop between combine harvester and storage silo without doing anything more physically demanding than tweaking his tractor's power steering to stay on course and pulling a little hydraulic lever at the side of his seat to empty the trailer. By the end of our little one-day almond harvest, he'd probably feel as if he'd lost as much weight in sweat as the fruits of his labours had gained in the quantity of nuts gathered. Handfuls, rather than tons, are all you have to show for your efforts after fencing with the branches of an almond tree for arm-aching minutes that can seem like hours until your muscles get used to the work. And, paradoxically, even the soothing sound of cane rattling against wood when heard from a distance can soon descend into jarring annoyance when you're actually having to produce the effect yourself. Bits of twig and little hailstorms of bark dust falling into your eyes and creeping under the collar of your shirt do nothing to improve the mood of the reluctant almond harvester either.

'I read somewhere that they use tractor-mounted implements to get the nuts off almond trees in the States and Australia,' Sandy said after his first twenty minutes of pole-brandishing work. 'The machine grabs the tree trunk and shakes the whole caboodle – that's how they do it. None of this antiquated, knock-'em-off-with-a-stick stuff for them.' He wiped his brow and gave his neck muscles a rub. 'Phew! Prehistoric, this way of doing things.'

What Sandy said about the 'New World' method of harvesting almonds was absolutely correct, but contrary to what he may have thought, Mallorcan farmers hadn't been slow in attempting to emulate the modern technique themselves. Two factors had gone against them, however. Firstly, in countries like America and Australia, special strains of almond tree had been developed with the prime purpose of being able to withstand the rough treatment that mechanical harvesting would impose upon them. The traditional Mallorcan varieties simply didn't like having their trunks grabbed and violently joggled by a machine. During field trials on the island, it was found that the trees' roots were being damaged to such an extent that there was every chance that what was intended to make life easier for the farmer was liable to completely kill off the source of his livelihood. Secondly, so many Mallorcan almond orchards are located on narrow mountain terraces that, even if the trees *could* have withstood the rigours of mechanical harvesting, the difficult terrain would have rendered the entire exercise impractical in any case. Perhaps the introduction of those machine-friendly varieties of almond trees would replace the old ones on the wide Mallorcan plain one day, but on little mountain *fincas* like those surrounding Ca's Mayoral, the autumn clatter of bamboo on branch is certain to be heard for as long as almonds are harvested there.

'Think yourself lucky we only have a few nut trees to bother about,' I said to Sandy, giving him what was intended to be a heartening slap on the back. 'At least you know we'll have the job done in one day.' I nodded in the direction of the lane.

'Imagine if we had as many almonds to harvest as old Pep over there.'

His grunt of reply spoke volumes. But I knew how he felt. There are certain aspects of farming everywhere that you have to be born to. The teams of motorbike-mounted stockmen who herd huge flocks of sheep in the sun-baked outback of Australia would take it ill if made to swap places with a lone shepherd trying to cope with lambing his ewes on a blizzard-swept mountainside in the Scottish Highlands, for example. Equally, if old Pep were to try piloting a mighty diesel tractor round a pancake-flat barley field bigger than his entire valley, he'd feel just as out of place as Sandy did wielding a bamboo version of a Jedi light sabre in a little Mallorcan almond grove. Time, however, was running out for Pep's seemingly timeless way of life. The very fact that there were no young Mallorcan men of Sandy's generation left working on their families' *fincas* in the valley testified to that. And, looking at Sandy gamely attempting to adjust to what he had rightly referred to as an antiquated method of doing things, the likelihood of his staying on with us at Ca's Mayoral seemed all the more remote. Perhaps our dream of starting a new life for our family as an enduring unit had been ill-conceived after all, no matter how idyllic the location, no matter how agreeable the climate, no matter how enviable the lifestyle had seemed from afar.

The sight of Ellie making her way over the field

173

from the house provided welcome relief from what was threatening to become quite a doleful working atmosphere. She was carrying a tray loaded with a large jug and three tumblers. Bonny was leaping up and down excitedly at her side, a big grin on her face, her stumpy tail seeming to wag her entire body all the way to her shoulders and back, the way that boxers' tails do. She was looking up at Ellie with that unique doggy mix of contentment, trust and happiness shining from her face. Seeing Ellie and Bonny like this was a cheering sight, and they couldn't have appeared on the scene at a more opportune moment. My flagging spirits were instantly revived. Ellie, as had become her wont during the hot summer months, was dressed in her 'working' clothes of floppy shirt hanging loose over a bikini swimsuit. Her skin glowed with a healthy tan that was a tribute to the benevolent Mediterranean climate we'd enjoyed during our first summer in the valley, her smile reflecting the same feeling of bonhomie displayed by Bonny, albeit in a noticeably less exuberant way. We'd certainly had our share of difficulties since our arrival at Ca's Mayoral the previous winter, and no doubt there would be many more trials to cope with in future. But the picture of happiness created by Ellie and Bonny as they made their way between the rows of fruit trees on this sunny September morning reminded me of how lucky we were to have been given the opportunity to experience a way of life that most can only dream of. Moments like this never failed to tip the scales of deliberation away from self-doubt. We'd get by, I was sure.

'Made you some lemonade,' Ellie shouted. 'Thought you'd like something to cool you down a bit.' She reached up and plucked a lemon from the tree she was passing. 'I'll slice this one up and pop it into the glasses. Can't get much fresher than that.'

How right she was. And what an obliging creation a lemon tree is, thoughtfully providing you with ripe fruit while simultaneously nurturing emergent lemons to take their place. A sort of endless production loop. I had already taken for granted how easy it was to simply pour myself a gin of an evening and pop outside to grab a complementary lemon from a tree. It was almost as easy as going to the fridge for some ice cubes, and at virtually any time of the year at that. Yes, a wonderful thing, the lemon tree, and pleasing to behold, too.

Jordi had told me that if you have a favourite one and want to clone it, all you have to do is pull off a small branch and plant it upside down, leaves in the ground, the stem sticking out. Before long, the leaf nodes will produce roots, and soon you'll have a brand new tree that will produce lemons every bit as good as its parent. I hadn't believed Jordi at first, thinking that he'd merely been taking the mickey out of a gullible *extranjero*, but on checking his assertion with a few old farmers I bumped into at the agricultural supply store in Andratx, I was assured that what Jordi had told me was no leg-pull. The same trick could be done with fig trees, one of the old fellows told me.

'*Sí, sí, señor*,' he said, nodding his head sagely, '*es cierto*.' It was absolutely true, he reaffirmed, for he had done it many times himself. '*En serio!* No kidding, *amigo!*'

Well, that's what he said, and he'd seemed sincere enough. But something still told me that I was being set up, and as curious as I was to put the tip to the test, the thought of old Pep or Maria popping their heads over the wall just as I happened to be planting an upside-down lemon twig prevented me from trying. I'd never have lived it down if it turned out that I'd been the one guileless patsy in living memory to take seriously what may have been, for all I knew, the oldest Mallorcan practical joke in the book. A bit like the first-day-on-the-job apprentice engineer who was told by his journeyman mentor to go to the stores and ask for a bucket of S-H-one-T. I was still gripped by a compelling fascination about the whole issue, though, and it wasn't long before an opportunity to satisfy my curiosity presented itself.

Margarita de Freitas Balmés, an elegant and gracious Spanish woman, the wife of a well-to-do Palma businessman and the doting mother of Carlos, one of Charlie's classmates, occasionally asked us to take fresh fruit for her to buy when we were picking Charlie up from school, which she lived close to. I had never thought that our lemons were anything to write home about, always much smaller than those on old Maria's well-maintained trees, for example, but Margarita swore after first sampling a few that they were the juiciest she'd come across, irrespective of their modest size. Here was the chance I'd been waiting for. Would she like a tree or two of her own, identical to the one from which these particular lemons had been picked? I didn't have to ask her twice, but I did have pangs of foreboding when she accepted with almost childlike trust my explanation of the miraculous method by which I would provide the trees. However, having let my impetuosity overcome my better judgement, I was left with no alternative other than to put my lemons where my mouth is – so to speak.

I planted twelve carefully selected little branches in Margarita's back garden, telling her by way of insurance against my own lack of conviction that we'd be lucky if one in four took root. Those were the percentages to play for in this game, I assured her with a feigned note of confidence. Unknown to Margarita, in the ensuing weeks I would peep over her garden wall when passing, praying to Mother Nature that some sign of life would be popping optimistically from those exposed sticks of lemon wood. Weeks soon graduated into months, but nothing popped – not even one solitary bud. Margarita and her family eventually moved from that house in Sant Agustí to another on the opposite side of Palma, and although we had met her in the school car park several times in the interim, she never once mentioned the failed lemon tree miracle. She was simply too much of a well-mannered Spanish lady to rub my nose in it, I concluded. And, being too much of a faint-hearted Scottish gentleman myself, I chose never to ask.

I tried to put all thoughts of Jordi's so-called tree-cloning dodge out of my mind, but as ever, nosiness eventually prevailed. A couple of months after Margarita left the house, I allowed myself one final peek over the garden wall, and to my astonishment there were four extremely healthy-looking little lemon saplings growing in the same patch that I'd planted the branches in. Admittedly, there were also four young orange trees growing beside them, so it's not impossible that the new owners of the house had actually bought conventional baby trees from the garden centre and had planted them to replace my long-dead, upside-down twigs. It would have been easy enough to knock on their door and ask, but I preferred to leave it as an open verdict, with the possibility, no matter how slight, that my lemony percentage game had come good in the end. And maybe, just maybe, one of those dark, moonless nights when the risk of prying neighbours' eyes seeing me was at its lowest, I would yet put the theory to the test in a secluded corner of a Ca's Mayoral field.

As chance would have it, the tree from which Ellie had just plucked a lemon was the very one whose twigs I had planted for Margarita. Ellie had a quiet chuckle to herself when I reminded her of the saga. Even Sandy was prompted to put on a happier face at the thought of what he was convinced had been his father's unbelievable naivety. But I didn't care; I had been laughed at for plenty of other things while making the inevitable mistakes that come with trying to adapt to a new life in a new country. It's par for the course, and if you can't see the funny side of your own innocent misdemeanours, then you're better not to leave the refuge of familiarity behind in the first place.

'Could be worth checking the upside-down lemon tree caper with one of the lecturers when you go to agricultural college,' I said to Sandy, grasping the chance to broach the subject of what his immediate plans were. 'You never know, there might be something in Jordi's ploy after all.'

But Sandy didn't rise to the bait. 'Yeah,' he coyly smiled, hunkering down beneath the almond tree we were in the course of stripping, 'as you say, you never know.'

Ellie and I joined him, sitting down on the big nut-gathering net we had borrowed from Pep, and sipping our homemade lemonade under the porous shade of the tree's spidery branches. As antiquated as the cane-rattling method of harvesting almonds may be, there's something strangely satisfying about doing a job that you know has been done in exactly the same way since time immemorial. It's like stepping back into another age without the need for a time machine. Certainly, sitting there in the orchard, enveloped in the serenity of the surrounding mountains, there was nothing to suggest to our senses that we were living in the latter stages of the twentieth century. It was that time of late morning when tractors in the fields of the valley farms had fallen silent one by one as their owners prepared to make their way back to the village for a midday meal followed by a well-earned siesta. All that could be heard was sleepy bird-song echoing from the wooded slopes of the mountains, a dog barking lazily on a *finca* hidden behind the pines on some high *bancal*, and the yodling crow of a bantam cockerel strutting his stuff over a little farmyard farther up the valley floor. Not even the distinctive, and often irritating, Spanish sound of a two-stroke moped carrying its owner from field to village intruded on the total tranquillity that had descended on the landscape. If a troop of Roman legionnaires had passed by along the lane at that very moment, they would not have seemed out of place. Time, for a few brief moments, was standing still, and we were experiencing exactly the same sounds, sights and smells as people in our present position had been familiar with throughout the ages. It was a strange feeling – almost eerie in a pleasant sort of way, and totally calming as well. I had that illusive sensation of being at one with nature, a feeling of belonging in and being an integral part of our surroundings. Sandy must have felt it too.

'I didn't fancy all this when I came here first,' he said, casting his eyes round the orderly rows of trees in the orchard and glancing up at the summits of the craggy sierras reaching for the sky away to the east. 'Didn't fancy being closed in by the mountains, being hemmed in by trees. Felt a bit, you know, claustrophobic. But now . . .' He took a deep breath, leaned back against the tree trunk and closed his eyes. 'Well, I've got to admit, it's pretty special.' He opened one eye, squinted over at us and let out a little chuckle. 'You maybe won't believe this, but I actually missed this place when I was back ho –, I mean, back in Scotland.'

His catching himself before completing the word 'home' was immediately picked up by Ellie. 'More than you miss Scotland when you're here?' she asked.

Sandy gave her a knowing little smile, but said nothing. The three of us sat in silence for a minute or two, each of us with our own thoughts. I knew what Ellie's were, but there was still no way of guessing whether or not Sandy would tell her what she wanted to hear – that he had decided to stay on in Mallorca with us.

'Still a lot of work to do with these,' I said after a while, picking up an almond and prising off its

181

rough outer hull. 'Even after we've knocked them off the trees and gathered them up, we still have to pull all their jackets off by hand like this, nut by single nut.'

'A bit hard on the fingers,' Sandy remarked, having a go at de-husking an almond himself. 'Jeez – must be a machine for doing this, no?'

'No doubt,' I said, 'but hardly worth it for us to spend good money buying one, not for the few sacks of almonds we'll finish up with.'

'Even so, it'll take ages doing it by hand.' Sandy placed his newly-hulled almond on a rock, picked up a large stone, cracked open the shell and flicked the plump kernel into his mouth. 'Hope it pays at the end of the day.'

I answered with a shrug, knowing within myself that all the work of harvesting the almonds, de-husking them, spreading them out to dry in the sun, then gathering them up in sacks would prove not to be worth the bother financially. It'd probably be a waste of time and petrol to take such a small quantity all the way to the almond mill run by the farmers' co-operative near Consell over in the middle of the island. By the same token, Mallorca's renowned international trade in almonds was hardly likely to founder for want of our insignificant input. So, instead of taking them to be ground down for culinary purposes, or to end up in some of the thousands of packets of delicious sugared almonds that are sold on the island every year, we'd probably just store ours

182

in the *almacén* for our own consumption, with any surplus being used, like most of our kakis, for bartering purposes. We had already learned how handy the dry husks and shells are for kindling the fire during the winter, and it's surprising how many almonds you can consume when they are as fresh-from-the-tree good as Sandy had just discovered them to be. Mallorcan almonds do deserve their reputation for excellence, and after taking the trouble to harvest them, we'd feel no twinges of guilt at gorging ourselves on them when the fancy took us during the coming months. Wc wouldn't go short of fire-lighting material.

Sandy cracked open another one. 'Never realised how good these things could be,' he said, smacking his lips. 'Always thought the shop-bought ones were as dry as dust when I tried them before. But these – well, they don't just taste great, but they're almost juicy, if that's the right word to describe a nut.'

'Yes, well, we're never likely to be as rich as Charlie's friends, the millionaire O'Briens,' Ellie pointedly observed, 'but living and working on a little *finca* like this does have its rewards you know, Sandy – simple though they may be.'

'I'll eat to that,' Sandy replied, scoffing another almond. If he had taken Ellie's somewhat unsubtly-made point, he certainly wasn't about to elaborate on it.

'Weh-*ep!*' came the cry from the gate leading

through the high stone wall to the lane. Old Pep was standing there waving at us. 'Oy, Sandee!' he cried. 'Hey, how are they hanging, *muchacho?*' A phlegmy chuckle rasped through the stillness of the morning. '*Benvinguts!*' he yelled cheerily. 'Welcome home, eh!' At that he beckoned Sandy over. 'I have a favour to ask of you, *tío.*'

Sandy's face lit up. From the day, shortly after we arrived on the island, that Pep had praised his prowess at ploughing with our little Barbieri tractor, Sandy had been a big fan of our crusty old neighbour. A wholesome sort of grandfather/grandson relationship had built up between them. Despite the generation and technology gaps that separated them, they seemed to enjoy a mutual respect that isn't uncommon between folks who share a love of the land. Pep didn't try to disguise the fact that he was glad to see some young blood returning to the valley, even if it had flowed from a far-off country with farming methods and customs quite different in so many ways from his own. Grinning delightedly, Sandy stood up and walked over to greet his old chum. We couldn't hear what they were talking about, but we could see Pep making plenty of animated hand gestures and pointing his finger at various locations around the valley. Sandy was clearly paying close attention to what he was being told, his head nodding intermittently, a well-pleased smile tugging occasionally at the corner of his mouth.

'*Va bé!*' Pep eventually cried out, giving Sandy a hearty slap on the shoulder. '*De acuerdo!* So, we are agreed, *sí?*'

We could see Sandy nodding his head once more, this time very positively. Pep gave his shoulder another thump, then ambled with that John Wayne swagger of his back towards his little farmstead over the lane. Sandy was still grinning from ear to ear when he came back to join us again on the almond-gathering net.

'Well then,' he sighed, 'that's it decided, I suppose.'

'That's what decided?' Ellie's expression was a mix of excited anticipation and instinctive foreboding.

'Whether I'm going to stay here or go back to Scotland.'

'And?'

He had been on the horns of a real dilemma, Sandy explained, showing obvious relief that he was about to get the whole thing off his chest at last. For all that he had enjoyed being back in Scotland for those two weeks, working with the best of modern agricultural equipment in surroundings and with people that he knew so well, he'd been unable to dispel the nagging thought that there was still so much for us to do to restore Ca's Mayoral to the little model farm that it has once been, a goal that he knew Ellie and I had set our hearts on achieving. We were going to need all the help we could get, and he was only too pleased to give us all he could. But he also realised that it would be stretching our financial resources to the limit to cover family living expenses while making all the improvements to the place that would have to be done before optimum income could be realised. His going to agricultural college in Scotland now would at least mean one mouth less for us to feed, and he'd manage to keep the wolf from his own door by doing weekend and holiday work on one of the big farms back there. He'd already fixed all that up.

'So you're going back?' said Ellie, more as a statement of fact than a question.

'Well, I had more or less decided that I would . . . until a moment ago, that is.'

'So you're staying?' Ellie warbled, her emotions now going up and down (to borrow one of Pep's more colourful expressions) quicker than a Palma whore's drawers when the fleet's in port.

Sandy raised his shoulders. 'Seems Pep's got it all figured,' he said with a look of resignation-tinged relief. 'Says he wants me to give him a hand with his ploughing and cultivation work this winter. Got a bad leg, he says – some old war wound or other playing up.'

'And he'll *pay* you?' asked Ellie, never slow to check the financial prerequisites of any business offer.

'Yeah, and better than that, he reckons I can pick up the same kind of work for quite a few old

186

farmers round about here. Old guys that aren't as fit to work their mules as they used to be. Old folk whose sons have upped and offed years ago. Says I should be able to work out some sort of share farming deal with them – a cut of the produce, that sort of thing.'

'Wait a minute – you're telling me you're going to work with a *mule?*' I said, unable to hold back a snigger. 'Well, old Maria *will* be delighted.'

'You must be bloody joking,' Sandy scoffed. 'Nah, all I need is your OK to borrow our wee Barbieri machine for the smaller fields. Pep says I can have the use of his old Fordson tractor for heavier work. Admittedly, it's a giant leap backwards compared to the tackle I've been using lately, but at least it'll give me an earner until the spring. By that time we'll have a lot of the essential work done on this place, too, then we'll see what's what as far as the future goes.'

'And college?' Ellie probed, suddenly more concerned about Sandy's further education than keeping him within easy reach of her apron strings. 'What about agricultural college now? You surely don't want to give up the chance of going, do you?'

'All sorted, Mum.' Sandy gave his mother a reassuring wink. 'I spoke to the principal when I was back. Explained the situation. He was dead understanding about it. Said I could either go this year, which would mean going back to Scotland next week, or take a year out to help you guys, then

187

start the course twelve months from now, if I still have a mind to. No problem as far as he's concerned. Plenty blokes take a year out to go to places like Australia these days, so what's the difference?'

Much to Bonny's delight and Sandy's embarrassment, Ellie rushed over and gave him a hug. 'Welcome home,' she beamed. 'I owe old Pep a huge cuddle too.'

'Rather him than me,' Sandy squirmed, struggling to free himself from his mother's arms.

'And rather you than me, Ellie,' I said. 'I'd think twice about giving Pep a cuddle if I were you – especially if he happens to smell of garlic.'

'What do you mean?'

'It's a long story. But, hey, never mind about that for now. Sandy's news calls for a celebration, so where's it going to be? Your shout, Sandy.'

There was no need to waste time thinking about that, Ellie advised. Colleen O'Brien had been on the phone to her a little earlier, and it was all taken care of already. A big house-warming party had been arranged for her place that evening, and as we would be going along to pick up Charlie anyway, we'd all been cordially invited to participate in the 'hooley'. It was going to be a night to remember, *if* we could remember anything at the end of it, according to our inveterate raver of a hostess.

Suddenly, thanks to two people at opposite ends of the island's social ladder, life at Ca's Mayoral had taken a turn for the better once again. Even what was left of our first Mallorcan almond harvest was completed to the enlivening sound of Sandy keeping time to his cane-swinging work by whistling a jaunty tune – albeit a Scottish one!

CHAPTER 7

WHEN YOU WISH UPON A STAR

I was twice reminded of the *Star Wars* movie that day. The first instance had been when, in my mind's eye, I'd likened Sandy's wielding of an almond-harvesting stick to a Jadi warrior fencing with his light sabre. The second was when we arrived at the O'Briens' house-warming party, and this time the comparison was even more striking. It was like walking into that outer-space bar which, in the film, is crowded with all sorts of freaky creatures – some comically attractive, others suspiciously chary, many cheerfully bizarre, a few threateningly sullen, and all adding up to a curious mish-mash of alien life forms. The O'Briens' version was equally fascinating, particularly so when considering that it wasn't a fancy-dress party. Nor were any of the guests extraterrestrials. These were clearly beings of the earthly variety, and all but a very few of them expatriate settlers, apparently delighted to be members of what they saw as the high-life clique of Mallorca.

'Full o' superficial, pretentious wankers, this scene, son,' Jock Burns advised, appearing at my elbow toting a cocktail glass adorned with what

190

appeared to be a mini tropical rainforest sprouting a paper parasol and a brightly coloured Perspex drinking straw in the shape of a curly pig's tail, complete with dangling testicles. 'Plastic people. Bunch o' wannabe *dolce vita* merchants, pseudo jet-setters and in-their-dreams millionaires, a lot o' them without a pot to piss in. Ye see the same set at all these parties where there's free booze flowin'. Aye, just a load o' two-faced spongers.'

At that, a sun-wrinkled elderly woman with peroxide blonde hair and toting a miniature poodle under her arm sidled past us. Her make-up looked as if it had been applied to her deeply tanned face with a plasterer's trowel, and her flesh-coloured fishnet catsuit was so revealing that even someone a fraction of her age would have thought twice about wearing it in public for fear of being arrested for indecent exposure. She was flashing enough gaudy jewellery to deck a municipal Christmas tree.

'Well, hey there, Babs honey!' Jock called to her, effortlessly switching his accent from Scottish to mid-Atlantic. As she turned to face him, he opened his arms and looked her up and down. 'Wow, babe, are you a sight for sore eyes, or what! Yeah, ya just get younger every time I see ya. How *do* ya do it, darlin'? Bee-oo-ti-ful!'

He threw his arms around her and gave her the customary air kiss on either cheek, the poodle snarling and baring his teeth at him all the while. Jock then introduced the woman to us as one of

Hollywood's all-time great actresses, a description that Babs accepted with a casual shrug before continuing on her shoulder-rubbing way without as much as saying a single word to any of us.

Ellie was patently unimpressed. 'I've never heard of her,' she told Jock. 'What films was she in?'

'Nah, that's all bullshit, hen,' Jock replied, reverting to his natural Scots. 'She's dined out on that Hollywood actress baloney here for the past forty years. Aye, the nearest she ever got to starrin' in a movie was a walk-on part in a TV commercial for diarrhoea tablets.' He gestured towards where she was now standing, ostensibly engaged in conversation with another garishly-dressed woman, while glancing around for signs of someone higher up the food chain that she might more profitably latch onto. 'I mean, just look at her – she's had so many face lifts she has to wear that spangly choker thing round her throat to hide her belly button, and she *still* has more wrinkles on her clock than an elephant's arse.' Jock then smiled sweetly and blew her a kiss as their eyes inadvertently met. 'Freeloadin' old bag,' he muttered ventriloquist-fashion through his teeth.

We had entered the grounds by way of the swimming pool terrace, which was swarming with people sporting matching tans, the women largely in the mutton-dressed-as-lamb category, many of the men with shirts open nearly to the waist, the better to reveal their medallion-adorned chest hair. Hollywood Babs' practice of carrying on a conversation with someone while looking around to see who else could be zeroed in on seemed to be the order of the day. To complete this picture of self-absorbed swank, there was enough bodily gold on show to fill the ore store in a Klondike assay office. By contrast, Ellie, who had a gift for always looking right for the occasion no matter what she wore, managed to stand out from the crowd by simply appearing as if she wasn't trying to outshine anyone. Classically classy would be how I'd put it. For myself, putting on a pair of never-worn white trousers that Ellie had bought for me when about to go on a Spanish holiday years ago, and completing the ensemble with a white shirt and a pair of white shoes of the same vintage, was the best I'd been able to do. And although I felt a bit self-conscious in this un-familiar get-up, I reckoned I'd done all right for someone who was neither interested in nor knew anything of the fickle fads of fashion.

Colleen O'Brien's cackling laughter rang out from the direction of the house, its wide French doors flung open to reveal even more see-and-be-seen revellers milling about inside. A team of formally-dressed waiters was drifting through the throng, some exchanging full champagne glasses for empty ones, others carrying large silver platters of savoury titbits.

'Cop yer whack for the champers and grub, son,' Jock urged as he beckoned a couple of the waiters. 'You too, Ellie. Come on, Sandy – for Christ's sake get stuck in before this crowd o' gannets scoff the lot.' Three caviare-topped canapés had disappeared down Jock's gullet almost before he had finished warning us about the alleged competition in the guzzling stakes. 'Right, must mosey,' he said between gulps of bubbly. 'Gotta do a bit o' shmoozin', know what Ah mean?' He dug me in the ribs with his elbow. 'That's the only way to survive on this island, by the way. Networkin' at freebie capers like this is the name o' the game. So mingle, boy, mingle. Make yerself a few contacts. Flog a few bags o' yer oranges or whatever.' He turned and headed into the crowd, then paused and shouted back over his shoulder, 'And get a right gutful o' the nosh and bevvy down ye!'

We spent the next few minutes doing nothing more sociable than standing gawping at the scene and trying to take it all in. In my time as a pro jazz musician, and subsequently while combining record production with farming, I'd been to more media receptions and album launch parties than I cared to remember, many of them flaunting a fair smattering of big showbiz names, with all the glitz and glamour that such people assiduously radiate. But I had never been to a bash quite like this. Perhaps it was the setting; a modern mansion of film star proportions, in which no detail of ostentation had been neglected; the huge, eccentrically-shaped swimming pool, with its underwater illumination and backdrop of palm trees; the lavish façade of the house bathed in the warm glow of concealed

194

floodlights; the velvety black Mediterranean sky, its stars seeming strangely dim in comparison with the fairground glitter surrounding us. And then, of course, there was the warm, caressing ambience of the Mallorcan night, its natural charms diffused (if not completely overcome) by a surfeit of unsubtle perfumes and aftershave lotions, the nearby lapping of the sea and the nocturnal chirping of crickets drowned out by the hubbub of chit-chat and the broken-glass jangle of Richard Clayderman piano music being relayed throughout the property on the house PA system.

'Let's find Charlie and get back to Ca's Mayoral pronto,' said Sandy. 'I'd rather sit in the *almacén* husking almonds all night than get involved in this,' he grimaced. 'It's just unreal – false – not my scene.'

False was what it appeared to be all right. But it was what Colleen O'Brien saw as the true Mallorca, the side of island life that she regarded as attractive, even to the point of having laid on this sumptuous shindig just to celebrate being part of it. More than that, she was making a statement that said she'd become queen of it. We could see her now, descending the wide sweep of steps from the house, obviously revelling in showering her subjects with generosity – as well as basking in the atmosphere of what she doubtless regarded as the envy-inducing trappings of her affluence. Yet, from what little we already knew of her, she could be equally down-to-earth and, to use her own description, 'common-as-spuds' unpretentious as well. A real enigma was Col O'Brien, but a likeable character for all that. She was a woman who wore her faults on her sleeve, called a spade a spade, and was more than likely as good a person as she was over-the-top flamboyant. In any case, courtesy dictated that, having been invited, we had to stay at her party for a polite amount of time at least. I explained this to Sandy, who took the point, though a tad grudgingly.

Just then, Col caught sight of us and came scything through the throng, acknowledging all salutations en route with asides which, judging by the explosions of shocked hilarity they evoked, must have been well and truly on the indelicate side of genteel. Queen Colleen was in her element, dressed, to outdo the most eccentrically garbed of her female guests, in a flowing gold lamé kaftan, embellished with what appeared to be a psyche-delic version of a snakes and ladders game, with the characters depicted in zany arrangements of coloured sequins. Her usual beehive hairdo was encased in a Carmen Miranda selection of exotic fruits that the average street market stall-holder could have retired on the proceeds from.

'Holy Mother o' Jaysus! Where the feck have ya been hidin' this one?' she gasped, taking an appraising eyeful of Sandy. 'Sure, this is never the ugly, pain-in-the-backside big brother yer wee boy Charlie has been tellin' me about, is it? Well,' she gushed, after we'd made the necessary introductions,

'Oy've got a nice young lady in me house who'd *really* like to meet *you*, ye darlin', handsome hunk o' a boy that ye are.' Linking arms with Sandy and preparing to whisk him away, she stage-whispered to Ellie, 'In fact, missus, if Oy was but a coupla years younger, Oy'd be lockin' this one up for meself, so Oy would!'

With Sandy going through the motions of objecting – though not too energetically, we noted – he disappeared houseward with Col, leaving Ellie and me to stand gaping slack-jawed once more, though this time for a very different reason.

'Since when did Sandy become a handsome hunk?' I asked, flabbergasted by what I'd just seen and heard.

'Well, he *is* – he's a very good-looking young man. You've just never noticed him sort of, well . . . growing up, that's all.'

'But he doesn't come over as the Casanova type – not even flirty or anything like that. Quite the opposite. And suddenly there's Col O'Brien, a grown woman, drooling over him. I mean, he's never even had a girlfriend.'

'Not that we know about, but that proves nothing.' Ellie let out a discerning little chuckle. 'Keeps his cards close to his chest, does our Sandy. Hmm, and you know what they say about the quiet ones.' She winked suggestively, then gave me a nudge. 'Anyway, no point in us standing about here like a couple of spares while the boys are

197

having fun. Come on, let's do like the man said. Let's mingle, son!'

First impressions can be deceptive. I'm a habitual believer in trusting them, but on this occasion, I eventually had to admit that I'd been a bit premature in assuming that all of the O'Briens' assembled guests were shallow, sycophantic extroverts. I'd surmised they'd all be outdoing each other in boasting about showy material possessions, loud status symbols that in reality might well amount to more symbol than status. But while a fair percentage of them probably would have fitted snugly into such a pigeonhole (a pigeonhole notoriously well-populated by expats of that ilk in certain of the more popular Spanish *costas*), there was also a scattering of people of a more unassuming nature. These folk, once identified, added a welcome modicum of normality to what seemed an overwhelmingly vainglorious gathering. Jock Burns' effervescent wife Meg helped make the distinctions for us.

'Hello-o-o-o there, flowers!' she piped at the top of her voice, momentarily silencing chattering groups of house-warmers as she breezed between them, her eyes sparkling like newly-charged champagne glasses, her enduringly pretty face wreathed in the infectious smile that made her instantly liked by virtually everyone she met. But it was Meg's overall personality that was the real key to her popularity with people of all nationalities and social backgrounds on the island. She was like a walking giggle, a well-upholstered parcel of fun, loosely but trendily wrapped as usual in billowing clothes that combined an eye-catching splash of jazziness with a deliberate element of comfort. Like Jock, Meg was an unashamed devotee of food and drink, and when out on the razzle-dazzle she made sure she was dressed in preparation for a fair intake of both. And she was a veritable fount of information about what seemed to us like almost everybody in Mallorca. Meg's unisex salon on the western outskirts of Palma was more than a hairdresser's shop, it was a meeting place for friends and strangers alike, a cauldron of convivial gossip, hot scandal and hush-hush info passed 'in confidence' one to the other, hour after hour, day after day, year after year. And, like most hair-dressers worthy of their professional reputation, Meg had been blessed with a good pair of ears. Also, to her credit, she had lost none of her Scottish accent since leaving her native home in Edinburgh's port of Leith almost twenty years earlier. Not for her the affected speech and infected mannerisms of the more easily-influenced émigré. As far as Meg was concerned, you could either accept her as she was, or go stuff yourself.

'See that sleazy-lookin' wee creep over there?' she muttered, shepherding us towards the house while directing our eyes towards a group of people standing by the near side of the swimming pool. 'Says he's an ex-jockey. Says he's Irish, but he's as

English as tripe and onions. Yeah, and tripe's the operative word. Sixty if he's a day, but tries to kid everybody he's half that age. Conceited wee bastard. Honest, if he was chocolate, he'd eat himself!' Meg proceeded to tell us that he'd arrived in Mallorca with, as she put it, 'nothing but a big ego' a few years previously. 'Got his hooks into an old dear with bags o' dough,' she continued. 'One o' ma customers. Big Lil, alias Lamplight Lili. Inherited a fortune from her old man's condom-dispenser company when he kicked the bucket. Some say he was king o' the pimps back where they came from as well – network o' brothels and all that. Anyway, I've heard that the so-called ex-jockey there – Tim McCoy, he says his name is – is actually an ex-safe-blower from Liverpool. Grassed on his gangster mates to save his own hide before he shot the crow out here. His arse is in a sling if they ever find him when they get out o' the slammer, by the way.'

'Meanwhile, he lives a life of luxury with the old sex-empire heiress, does he?' asked Ellie, keen to avail herself of as much juicy detail as possible.

'Naw, naw, petal! Nah, he saw her off a few months back. Officially, she fell off the balcony o' their penthouse apartment overlookin' Palma Bay. Twelve storeys up.' Meg shook her head and put on a pull-the-other-one face. 'Yeah, yeah, yeah – and I'm Audrey Hepburn reincarnated, right?'

'You mean you think he *pushed* her?' I asked, raising a shocked eyebrow.

Meg adopted an air of wearied resignation. 'Put

it this way, Pedro,' she sighed, 'the old bird was no oil paintin', right? Drank like a baskin' shark, had a temper like a chimp that's had its banana nicked, but was also said to have a few million dollars stashed in a Swiss bank account. And the old softie was stupid enough to promise to leave the lot to her toyboy Tim over there. It was one night when she was out of her skull after downin' the best part o' a bottle o' *Larios* gin at a party at her place. I was there. I heard her!'

'Still doesn't prove the guy pushed her off the balcony.'

The look of utter disbelief that Meg shot me left little doubt that she believed my head zipped up the back. 'Aye, and what's Santa Claus bringin' ye this year, china?' she gibed, before concluding the Tim McCoy saga by informing us that the last laugh had been on him. Old Lili, more subtle than soft, as it ultimately turned out, had actually willed all her worldly possessions to two impishly-apt charities – one running a home for down-and-out prostitutes, the other a refuge for retired racehorses. So, Tim was now on the lookout for another lonely old female mark with more money than marbles. 'Plenty o' them on this island, by the way,' Meg assured us. She then launched herself into a running commentary on the background, character and financial standing of selected guests who caught her eye as we progressed slowly up the steps and on into the teeming reception hall of the house.

It seemed that the O'Briens' invitation list had

201

been drawn up in order to bring together a micro-cosm of the entire English-speaking expatriate community of Spain, but with the emphasis firmly on the side of the colourful and cryptic. And Meg had a story to tell about them all. In this sort of company, she advised us, you had to 'keep yer lug to the rug and yer nose to the prose', which was her way of telling us to keep our ears and eyes open. She then commenced, for our ears only, a series of character assassinations befitting selected victims who caught her eye.

There was the suave, pink-suited man with a broad cockney accent, and with chameleonic eyes that constantly scanned the gathered company like searchlights. Another predator, according to Meg – a self-styled international financial advisor with a slick line in promising huge profits to those prepared to entrust him with investing their cash for them. Meg knew of several gullible souls he'd already sweet-talked into parting with more nest egg contents than they could afford to lose. And the talk in her shop that he was also a serial bigamist did nothing to dispel Meg's distrust of this geezer either.

'He's livin' with two women right now,' she divulged. 'His actual wife and their ex-nanny, who's become his *spiritual* missus, according to what he's supposed to have told one o' ma clients. Weird set-up. Mark my words, he'll be off this island for pastures and mugs new as smartly and mysteriously as he arrived, just as soon as he's raked in enough readies from a few more suckers.'

Then there were the two gay plumbers, camping it up outrageously for a gaggle of giggling ladies under the shimmering light of one of the Valentino chandeliers.

'*The Sheiks of Leaks*, that's what they call themselves,' said Meg. 'And it's leaks as in drips, by the way – *not* because they happen to come from Wales, which they do. Yeah, and the drips angle can only apply to their appearance, because I can tell you for a fact that neither of them knows his arse from his elbow-bend when it comes to fixin' burst pipes. Oh aye,' she stressed straight-faced, 'even Noah would've been pushed to survive some o' the floods that pair o' daffodils have created.'

There were plenty of chancers like them around, she assured us – bogus British brickies, joiners and the rest, dredging the expat community for work, *and* getting it, simply because they touted their alleged skills to unsuspecting people who couldn't speak Spanish well enough to communicate confidently with legitimate local tradesmen.

'OK, there's a few genuine non-Mallorcan builders and such on the go,' Meg conceded, 'but ye have to know who ye're dealin' with, or ye're liable to get screwed big-time.' She chuckled at the thought, then added, 'Take it from me, flowers, there's more cowboys on this island than deep in the heart of Texas. Yep, some real desperados.'

She pointed out a few examples as we wove our

way through the crowded hall and on towards the bar area. Lurking in a corner away to our left, for instance, was a Norwegian yacht captain, a sextant-for-hire freelancer who sidelined in house painting when not at sea. He was said to be lying low at the moment, keeping an inconspicuous profile after being under surveillance by Interpol for alleged drug running between the Middle East and Holland.

'Carries a gun, that bugger,' Meg said out of the corner of her mouth as she gave him a cheery wave.

'You're pulling my leg,' I laughed.

'No way!' Meg retorted. 'I mean, check the rise in his Levis. Don't tell me ye think it's just a sign he's pleased to see me!'

There was no polite answer to that, so I dropped the subject.

Meg then pointed out a huddle of people being entertained over to our right by a gregarious-looking and loudly-attired couple who openly boasted, according to our in-the-know guide, that they'd done a runner from the British Customs and Excise.

'Had a second-hand van and truck business in the north o' England. Went bankrupt on purpose, left a list o' debts as long as yer arm, did a big VAT rip-off and scarpered out here with the proceeds.' Meg pulled her characteristic none-of-my-business facial shrug, then added matter-of-factly, 'Nice folk, though. Fabulous dress sense. Always look great. They come into ma shop to have their roots done, actually.'

The leggy, middle-aged blonde perched on a tall stool at the bar, ostensibly oblivious to the blatant ogling of all the men in her immediate vicinity, was, Meg divulged, a Danish career divorcee called Brigid.

'At the salon, we call her Brigid the Frigid for a laugh,' said Meg. 'Frigid? Forget it! She's laid more men on this island than Mother Goose laid eggs in fairyland.' Brigid was also nicknamed the Black Widow, Meg informed us. 'OK,' she keenly continued, 'maybe she doesn't actually *eat* the guys like the spider after she's shagged them – just marries them, bleeds them nearly dry, then cops for a divorce and settles for a nice slice o' alimony outta whatever they've got left.' Meg nudged Ellie and confided: 'Came here as a rep for a Danish package tour company. Absolutely skint, she was. Snared a wealthy local businessman within a coupla weeks – ye know how the Spanish guys go ape for blondes – and she's never looked back. Just ditched rich hubby number four last month, so she's on the prowl again.' She gave Ellie a warning look. 'Stand by yer man, petal!'

There'd be no need to bother taking that precaution, Ellie dryly observed. 'Not unless she fancies a divorce settlement calculated in a few dozen oranges every month, that is!'

'Yeah, ye're right,' Meg agreed, looking askance at my clothes as she spoke, 'and anyway, she only goes for guys with a bit o' style.' She flashed me a hairdresserly smile which, in anyone less genial than her, could have been taken as a touch condescending, then bluntly appended, 'Do yourself a favour, flower. Get rid o' the white gear – especially the shoes. OK, they may still cut a dash at yer farmers' barn dances back in Scotland, but they went out over here with Bill Haley and the Comets.'

Suitably deflated and feeling more conspicuous than ever now, I watched Meg sashay off, enough technicolour linen flapping in her slipstream to kit Joseph out with a new dreamcoat. Her irrepressible love of socialising had finally taken precedence over the temporary buzz she'd got from giving us a bit of insider info on the assembled cross-section of the 'beautiful people' of Mallorca. From now on, we were on our own.

'Let's find the boys and get the hell out of it,' I mumbled to Ellie. 'Sandy was right. Not my scene either. I'm a fish out of water in here. I feel like a – like a –'

'A milk bottle in a stained glass window?' Ellie giggled. She took an oblique glance at my all-white rig-out. 'And don't be so sensitive. Meg didn't mean to hurt your feelings. She was just sort of, well . . . she was just kind of –'

'Taking the piss? Yeah, yeah, I know, Ellie. Say no more – I've got the message.' I muttered a few expletives, then huffed, 'Bill Haley and the Comets shoes, eh! Next time, I'll go the whole damned

1950s hog and wear a tartan jacket *and* a bloody kiss curl!'

I thought Ellie was going to wet herself. There was nothing she enjoyed more than seeing me go off the handle about some futile little thing that had stung me into a purple-faced tantrum. She knew that, after a few seconds of foaming at the mouth, I'd usually see the funny side of things and join in the hilarity myself. This time was no exception. And she'd been right in what she'd attempted to say about Meg's comment on my lack of sartorial nous. As a dedicated follower of fashion herself, Meg had only been trying, in her own no-messing way, to mark my card about how *not* to look like a fish out of water at 'chic' gatherings like this. I still had no idea of how better to dress for such occasions, however, and I had no intention of bothering to find out either. Taking a leaf out of Meg's book, I decided there and then that the 'beautiful people' could either take me as I was, or go stuff themselves. In any case, another glass or two of champagne was all it took to restore my self-confidence sufficiently to finally get on and mingle with some of them, be they desperado, 'beautiful', predatory or otherwise.

Those we spoke to all had their own stories to tell about themselves, of course, and although a few CVs really did have to be taken with a liberal pinch of salt, a surprising number of people turned out to be just as 'ordinary' (if that's the right word) as ourselves, even if they all looked the part of what

Jock had described as '*dolce vita* merchants' better than I was ever likely to do. But what did that matter anyway? It's said you can't judge a book by its cover, and the old adage couldn't have been more graphically illustrated than by a retired bank manager and his wife, who could have passed as lookalikes for ageing pop stars. He was dressed à la Tom Jones in full Las Vegas mode, while his wife had tarted herself up, at least in my opinion, in the likeness of one of the members of Abba – albeit the one with the beard who plays the piano, as Ellie somewhat cattily remarked later. They turned out to be straightforward people, though – in reality not as flash as their appearance suggested, and certainly not as dull as the popular image of bankers would have led us to expect. They were, in fact, just as mesmerised by the outrageous opulence of this O'Brien party as we were, though at the same time patently thrilled to be included in it. The annual barbecue for the bank staff this most certainly was not!

And there were more couples just like this – superannuated professionals and early-retired business people, all having come to live in Mallorca with ideas of opening that little English tearoom with home-baked cakes they'd always promised themselves, or perhaps with notions of buying a small charter boat in which to take groups of holidaymakers on trips round the bay. They all had their own version of the life-in-the-sun dream, but none that we spoke to had thus far made it come true.

'I've become too lethargic, old boy,' was how one former civil servant from Surrey accounted for it. 'Bitten by the jolly old Spanish *mañana* bug as soon as I got here. Next thing I knew we were on the G-and-Ts-on-your-terrace-today-and-my-terrace-tomorrow treadmill. Damned difficult to get off once you're on board, I can tell you.'

It was, I surmised, on that same treacherous social roundabout that many of these people had met the O'Briens. And the longer they succumbed to the unyielding temptations of the ever-expanding cocktail hour, the more remote would be the chances of ever realising their particular dreams. The purposeless lifestyle they'd slipped into could too easily descend into a war of attrition between bottle and liver, and the record showed that the smart money would invariably be on victory for the bottle. It could be said that this was one of the pitfalls of having the luxury of a substantial pension to live off, but not everyone we met was in that arguably fortunate position, nor were they all in that particular age bracket either.

Not untypical of the younger generation of party animals present was a twenty-eight-year-old Glasgow lad called Shuggie Stewart, who had arrived on the island for a holiday with several of his mates some ten years earlier. He and a couple of others had decided to stay on in Mallorca when the rest of the gang returned home, their idea being nothing more ambitious, as he readily confessed, than to do a bit of beach-bumming, bird-pulling, suntan-perfecting and see what developed from there. When their money ran out after the first week or so of modest hedonism, they had picked up jobs working as ticket touts for a popular disco in the teen-friendly resort of Magalluf. Inevitably, the novelty of living *la vida loca* soon wore off, and his two pals bought plane tickets back to Scotland. But not Shuggie. He recognised the potential of carving a future for himself by building on experiences already gained on the midnight pavements of neon-lit Magalluf. He talked himself into the job of doorman at the same disco, soon graduating to barman, and then, after a few years, to becoming manager of the establishment. By keeping his eyes and ears open, as well as keeping his nose clean and being careful with his money, 'Sharp' Shuggie, as he'd now become known, was eventually able to take the plunge and open his own place in what was then a fairly unfashionable location further along the coast on the east side of Palma. Through determination and hard work (plus, I suspect, a fair bit of ducking and diving), he'd now built that into one of the most popular nightspots in the area. The rewards for his risk-taking had been as welcome as they were considerable when they did eventually materialise, and he was now planning to diversify by investing some capital in what he described as a 'revolutionary' retail project that he'd dreamed up.

'Not exactly selling fridges to Eskimos,' he confided, 'but not a million miles away from it either.' And that was all he'd say on the subject, except to state that it was surprising what tourists high on the euphoria of a holiday would buy, given a bit of slick spiel, a scenic bus trip and a free drink.

A variation on the Mallorcan maxim that many foreigners leave their brains at the airport when they arrive on the island? Perhaps. We'd watch Shuggie's progress with interest, but if indeed first impressions were anything to go by, I was fairly sure that he'd be sharp enough to get wherever he decided to go in life. And he was by no means unique among the younger expat element enjoying the O'Brien hospitality that evening. A drop-out from medical school told us how he had teamed up with a young local car mechanic to start a scuba diving centre; a secretary from the Home Counties of England said that she and her partner had given up the drudgery of life in London's commuter ant hill in favour of opening a house-sitting agency to look after holiday properties for absentee owners; and a disillusioned young maths teacher was delighted to announce that he had swapped his logarithm tables for the shovel that went with a minor share he'd bought in a pony-trekking stable. They had all taken their first highly individual steps towards establishing a new life for themselves on the island, and we wished every one of them well. Just how many would succeed in what they'd set out to do was the eternal moot point, but they all exuded the confidence that's born of the enthusiasm of youth and were forging ahead accordingly. Curiously, however, like most of their retired counterparts to whom we'd spoken earlier, they all seemed less bothered about their own future prospects than about how Ellie, the boys and I would fare on our little *finca* out among the Tramuntana Mountains.

'Are you *sure* you can make a living growing oranges in Spain?' was what they'd all asked in their own particular ways. 'I mean, oranges are so cheap in the shops here that I've always wondered how the poor farmers can survive on what little they must get for them.'

Naturally, as fair a point as that may have been, it didn't do much to assuage the doubts I was already harbouring about the potential viability of Ca's Mayoral. But it's surprising how easily such worries become temporarily relegated to the back of your mind when the bubbly is flowing as freely as the O'Briens' was.

Sean O'Brien himself was ensconced behind his bijou bar. He already looked at least two sheets to the wind, but was still liberally and cheerfully dispensing drinks to all and sundry, not least to himself. There was a noticeably exaggerated air of mateyness about the coterie of male imbibers clustered around the bar opposite their host, and it was plain to see that Sean was lapping up being on the receiving end of all their back-slapping bonhomie. He was king of his own castle in Spain, and would doubtless never be without such an entourage of doting liegemen as this – not for as long as he continued to ply them with such unstinting amounts of booze, that's to say. Bought 'friendship' has a nasty habit of turning out to be unworthy of the name, though, and it was impossible not to speculate about how few of Sean's current crop of chums would even stop to give him the time of day should his luckpenny ever fail to land the right way up when he spun it.

We left him to enjoy the pleasures of faithful companionship while it lasted and moved on to the games area, where we noticed Sandy playing snooker with two of young Dec O'Brien's older brothers. It was immediately apparent that no girls were in their company, and Ellie was quick to give vent to her maternal curiosity. Where, she wanted to know from Sandy, was the young lady that Colleen had said would be so keen to meet him?

There was a hint of diplomacy about the way the O'Brien boys pretended not to have heard Ellie's question. They deliberately moved to the far end of the table on the pretext of discussing the best way of playing the next shot. Sandy, on the other hand, couldn't hide his embarrassment as he discreetly shooed his mother out of their earshot and hissed that it was actually her own daughter that Mrs O'Brien had wanted him to 'hook up wit'.

'What's wrong with that?' Ellie came back. With a little jerk of her head, she drew his attention to

213

the lavishness of the immediate surroundings. 'Let's face it,' she whispered encouragingly, 'you could do a lot worse.'

'But she's ten years older than me!'

Ellie shrugged a you-may-have-a-point-there kind of shrug, then unthinkingly added insult to nosiness by asking Sandy, 'Is the O'Brien girl a bit *plain*, then?'

'Are you sure you didn't mean to ask if she's got a white stick?' Sandy retorted, well miffed. He took a deep breath, silently counted to three, then calmly informed his mother that the reason he'd declined Mrs O'Brien's invitation to 'hook up wit' her daughter was because the daughter just happened to be married, and to a very famous Spanish sports personality at that. One of her brothers had discreetly tipped him off about this before the daughter had had a chance to get too, well . . . 'chummy'. Sandy then revealed the identity of the husband – a top football player in Spain's *Primera Liga*, an international star who, although slight in stature, was known to be one of the hardest nuts in the game. The O'Briens' daughter had elected to live with her parents in Mallorca, while he plied his trade in Madrid during the football season, returning to be with his wife for a day or two whenever team commitments allowed. The last thing Sandy needed from him when he came back next was a hammering for mucking about with his 'lonely' wife, and he told Ellie so in no uncertain terms.

'So, ehm . . . where's Charlie?' she hesitantly asked, her face a picture of startled foreboding. Her younger son's 'Dog's Balls' tag and the image of sexual wantonness that it conjured up had clearly got to her. Yes, and there was that huge oyster-shell water bed upstairs to add fuel to her imaginings. We could read Ellie's thoughts like an open book – the sort of erotic women's book with a half-naked pirate on the cover that she was known to become engrossed in occasionally.

Sandy shook his head in despair. 'Look, don't worry, Mum,' he droned, 'even Charlie's not so daft as to get mixed up in that kind of scene, even if the bird did happen to be desperate enough to get humped by a twelve-year-old.'

Ellie's expression revealed that she was far from convinced, however. 'He's almost thirteen,' she muttered, as if reminding herself of the fact. 'Old enough *and* big enough to be preyed on by that type of brazen hussy.'

'So what?' said Sandy. 'You were keen enough for me to be preyed on by her a minute ago!'

Ellie's brows were already lowered into a pre-occupied frown. 'That's before I knew she was a baby-snatching Jezebel,' she mumbled, putting two and two together and making twenty-two. Then, slipping her train of thought into instant reverse gear, as was her wont, she shot Sandy a reproving look and snapped, 'Incidentally, young man, hump's a four letter word, and I'm surprised

215

to hear you using that sort of language in front of your mother!'

Sandy rolled his eyes skyward.

'But where *is* Charlie anyway?' I asked, telling myself that he wouldn't be up to anything untoward, but unable to quell the impulse to check all the same.

Sandy nodded towards the far corner of the crowded room, to one of the house's side entrances, through which Charlie and Dec were emerging at that very moment.

I watched Ellie's jaw drop. 'They're wearing tuxedos!' she warbled. 'And bow ties!'

Only Ellie knew what suspicions of youthful depravity those exclamations denoted. For my own part, I was too astounded by the suave, mature look of Charlie to think of anything other than how suddenly a kid can turn into an adult – if only in appearance. As had been the case with Sandy, I just hadn't noticed that he'd been steadily growing up. And here he was now, the jeans-and-tee-shirt schoolboy of only yesterday, looking every bit the self-assured young man. All he needed to complete the sophisticated image, at least from a distance, was a glamorous young supermodel on his arm.

Sandy started to laugh. 'What a complete numpty!' he mocked as his brother approached. 'Look at you – you're like something that escaped from the penguin enclosure at the zoo!'

Charlie shrugged off that gibe without rising to

216

Sandy's bait. 'Hi, Mum and Dad,' he grinned, 'sorry if I've kept you waiting. Dec and I just borrowed his brother-in-law's Mercedes and drove along the *autopista* to Tito's in Palma for a few boogies.'

Ellie's sigh of relief was all but drowned out by Sandy's guffaw. They both knew as well as I did that Charlie had to be joking. Being only eighteen months Charlie's senior, Dec was still more than a couple of years shy of being old enough to hold even a learner's driving licence. On top of that, Tito's Palace was regarded as one of the swankiest nightclubs in Europe, occupying a privileged position overlooking the Paseo Marítimo boulevard that skirts the spectacular Bay of Palma. It was hardly likely that two young boys would be allowed past the door, no matter how grown-up they looked in their formal evening wear.

'So, where did you get the dinner jackets?' I asked, my feelings a mix of Ellie's sense of deliverance and Sandy's unconstrained amusement.

'Oh, they belong to my big sister's husband as well,' Dec stated quite openly. 'He's got loads of suits in his wardrobe. Big-Time Spanish football player, you know. Yeah, and he's only a little guy, so they fit us fine. Just the job for us going cruising in his Merc.'

Ellie gave him a reproachful little smile, the sort of lightly-chiding smile that mothers reserve for kids caught telling fibs that are no more than a harmless product of an over-fertile imagination.

'Well, you've had your bit of fun dressing up for Mrs O'Brien's party,' she told Charlie, 'but I think you'd better go and change back into your own things now.' She looked at her watch. 'It's way past your bedtime. Time to go home.'

'That's right, kiddo,' said Sandy, 'and make sure you put the poncy gear back carefully where you got it. From what I hear, the owner is liable to give you a right doing if he finds out you've been messing with his property!'

Charlie offered no objection, but merely exchanged what I thought were slightly conspiratorial little smiles of resignation with Dec, before they both sloped off obediently upstairs. Ellie, meantime, went in search of Colleen to thank her for her hospitality, while I pushed my way through to the bar to pay my parting respects to Sean. He was so blitzed by this time that I doubted he recognised me, and by the look of vacant wonderment in his eyes, I suspected that he believed I was identical triplets anyway. Taking careful aim, he shook hands with the triplet in the middle, grinned, and slurred what I took to be the words of a traditional Gaelic farewell, but which, for all I could make out, might just as well have been a Swahili incantation for exorcising evil spirits from a herd of stampeding wildebeest. And how appropriate that would have been. From outside came the sound of breaking glass, followed by the screams and bellows of delight that accompanied the splash of someone falling (or being pushed) into the swimming pool. As the Mediterranean night air cooled to a balmy tepid, the temperature of the house-warming party was rapidly reaching boiling point. Ellie was right – it was time to go home.

Stepping out onto the terrace, we heard Jock Burns' amplified mid-Atlantic tones booming out. 'Wull, hi there, laydees 'n' jennelmen,' he drawled, 'it's time for the dancin' to commence right here at the *Palais de Dance* O'Brien, so grab a gal, you guys, and let's see ya jive yer socks off!'

Typical Jock, I thought, chuckling to myself. He never missed a trick. Not only had he and Meg partaken unstintingly of the freebie goodies on offer at the party, but he'd evidently negotiated for himself what I was sure would be a handsome earner for providing the live music as well. Perhaps I'd have to take lessons from him on 'how to survive on this island, by the way, son' after all. We'd certainly mingled with a lot of new people, as he'd told us to, but contrary to what he'd urged, I hadn't sold a single orange to anyone – not that I'd tried to, it has to be said. And maybe that was the vital difference between Jock's proven ability to succeed in Mallorca and our first tentative attempts to do likewise. He pressed the relevant buttons on his cutting-edge electronic keyboard and, magically, the instrumental sounds of a full rock band thundered out of his speaker stacks.

'And this first number is dedicated to an ol' pal a' mine,' he announced over a thumping intro, while exaggeratedly returning my wave of goodbye.

'Yeah, a real blast from the past, this one, folks, so let's cut a rug for ol' Pedro there with the legendary . . . *"ROCK AROUND THE CLOCK"!*'

Jock launching into Bill Haley and the Comets' greatest hit was, I knew, much more a mischievous reference to my white shoes than any kind of dedication to me. Everyone there quickly latched onto the fact as well. I was now obliged to take, with as much good humour as I could muster, the resultant ribbing directed at me by all those gyrating fashion plates who had to be passed on our way over the pool terrace and on into the sanctuary of the car park. Ellie and the boys maintained a diplomatic silence. I, for my own part, was so busy muttering curses to myself that I didn't even notice the unsightly scrape along the side of the snazzy Mercedes sports coupé parked near to out little Ford Fiesta. Nor, apparently, did anyone else in the car, with the possible exception of Charlie, that is . . .

It was a relief to return to the unsullied, rustic pleasures of Ca's Mayoral in the wee small hours of that September morning. Lying in bed with the shutters and windows flung open to let in the soothing sounds and aromas of the Mallorcan night invoked feelings so different from those we'd experienced at the O'Briens' party that it was hard to believe we were on the same planet, never mind the same small island.

'You know,' Ellie announced after a while, 'I was

propositioned no less than three times in the few minutes I was looking for Col O'Brien before we left her house.'

'Only three times,' I grunted, eyes closed, sleep beckoning. 'You're losing your touch!'

'No, seriously – there's always bound to be a few lechers at these things – boring creeps who reckon their ladykilling chances improve with every drink they take. But that place tonight seemed to be crawling with them.'

'It's the warm climate. Brings out the horniness.'

'Not in everyone, I notice!'

I decided to ignore Ellie's barbed remark. It had been a long day, and I was suffering from the over-powering feeling of droopiness that comes in the wake of over-indulging in champagne. 'Goodnight, Ellie,' I mumbled. 'See you *mañana*.'

Ellie, however, was wide awake. Fortunately, though, she wasn't *really* in the mood for anything more energetic than conversation. 'Two of them claimed to be builders,' she said. 'Dripping with gold chains. You know, the type of sleazebag Brit cowboys Meg was on about. Hmm,' she continued pensively, 'both promised big discounts if I'd agree to meet them in private to discuss my, ehm, *requirements*. Duff patter, virtually identical, except one suggested we meet up at the English fish and chip shop in Palma Nova tomorrow night, while the other was all for going upstairs there and then.'

Under most circumstances, I'd have been keen

to find out who these characters were, so that I could give them a firm word of advice if we ever met again. But this pair, whoever they were, struck me as being too pathetic to even bother about. 'Shows you can still turn 'em on,' I said as a sort of backhanded compliment, which, because of my drowsy state, must have sounded unintentionally crass.

Ellie seemed not to have noticed, though. 'And the third one was a weirdo with a pigtail who said he runs a transvestite pub in Palma.' She started to giggle. 'Asked if I'd be interested in a job behind the bar – dressed up as Marlene Dietrich, would you believe!'

'Must be the high cheekbones.'

'Mmm, it wasn't anything as high as my cheekbones he was leering at, though.'

'Yeah, well anyway, if you decide to do it, just speak to Charlie if you need to borrow a tuxedo.'

Ellie let that spiky little crack go without comment, then informed me, 'No, I think it was more the stockings-and-suspenders image he was interested in.'

'OK, OK,' I said wearily, 'you did well to escape the clutches of all those randy blokes, Ellie. Now for Pete's sake go to sleep.'

A few moments of blissful silence followed, before Ellie, unusually bright for this time of night, elbowed me in the back. 'Just look at those stars,' she enthused. 'Come on, Peter – wake up! Look! When did you ever see stars like that?'

I knew when I was beaten. I rolled over, opened my eyes, blinked and squinted through the open window. Sure enough, the stars in the moonless sky were dazzlingly brilliant. The same easily-recognisable constellations that we'd gazed up at in Scotland were all there – the Plough, Orion, the Little Bear and countless others whose names I'd long forgotten – but never had I seen them quite like this, not even in the clearest of frosty northern nights. And it wasn't just that the fifteen hundred miles that lay between Mallorca and Scotland appeared to have tilted the starry group-ings in a way that made me instinctively incline my head to see them lying at angles in which I'd been used to seeing them. They appeared bigger, brighter and closer, too – so close, in fact, that it really seemed as though you could reach out and touch them.

'Just like fairy lights on a black satin curtain,' murmured Ellie, sounding refreshingly sleepy at last. Then she perked up again and pointed through the window. 'And look!' she gasped. 'There's a shooting star. And another! And another! I could almost catch them!' Suddenly, perhaps due to the apparent proximity of the actual signs of the zodiac, she seemed overcome by some strange romantic notion, snuggling down beside me on the pillow, her voice soft and dreamy. Taking my hand in hers, she whispered, 'That's three wishes we can have.'

'One'll do for me,' I yawned.

'Don't tell me what it is, though – or it won't come true.'

'It's too late for that,' I muttered, succumbing once more to the soporific after-effects of the evening's surfeit of champagne. 'So I don't mind telling you.'

'I don't understand,' Ellie replied, cuddling in closer. 'What *did* you wish, then?'

I turned away, pulled the sheet over my head and barked, 'I wish I'd never let you talk me into buying that pair of bloody white shoes!'

CHAPTER 8

THE SEASON OF WINTER SPRING

Translating an old Mallorcan farming almanac I'd been given by Tomàs Ferrer had taken me many studious evenings with much delving into my Spanish dictionary to complete, but it had been a useful exercise, not just in learning some new words, but also in finding out how the island farmers of old had timed their monthly work to coincide with the phases of the moon. And they appeared to have trusted, perhaps justifiably, as much in the influence that the movement and relative positions of the sun, moon and planets have on nature as present-day believers do in relation to their love, career and financial prospects. For the month of October, whose zodiacal sign is Scorpio, the almanac states that:

'This sign depicts the scorpion, with a corresponding effect on the weather of biting and stinging. So, when the sun enters this sign in October, it starts to nip, the cold chafes, and there are tempests, thunder and lightning.'

Everything is relative, however, and as far as feeling the cold goes, it all depends on what you're used to. Certainly, the benign weather of this, our first October in Mallorca, reminded us more of reasonably good summer days in Scotland than of the sort of autumn temperatures we regarded as liable to nip or chafe, never mind bite or sting. Be that as it may, though, the almanac's forecast of '*tempests, thunder and lightning*' for this month was absolutely accurate, and would soon prove to be the mark of the change of seasons. We had already experienced the spectacular storms of late February and early March, unrestrained exclamations of nature which Mallorcans recognise as the infallible signal that winter is giving way to spring. And the fact that the weather of October was remarkably similar to that of spring tallied with the assertion of the more senior of our neighbours that, in the old Mallorcan language, there was in fact no word for 'autumn', the third season of the year being referred to as simply 'winter spring'. For all that it may sound quaintly poetic, the term 'winter spring' is actually a fair description of the state of the natural conditions that prevail in the more favoured parts of the Mediterranean area at this time of year. For the most part, the typical autumnal tasks of harvesting grapes, almonds and olives have been completed, but as the almanac states, this second spring of the year is a time to plant and sow things as well – cherry trees and flower bulbs, for example, as well as cereals, broad beans, lupins and other seeds that will germinate and grow during the mild Mallorcan winter. But, lest the olden-days farmer be lulled into believing that this mellow season of nature's graces has no inconvenience in store for him, a few words of caution are offered by the scribes of the almanac, too:

'During this month of October, plants and late fruits, like pomegranates and quinces, are liable to be damaged by ants and wasps.'

The remedy?

'Destroy the wasps' nests.'

If that sounds deceptively simple, the prescribed way to avoid ant damage is equally so, although potentially less dangerous for the perpetrator.

'Remove the ants,' the almanac states, *'by "washing" the trees (and even animals that you want to protect from flies) with the juice of pumpkin leaves.'*

It isn't said how many pumpkin leaves you'd have to squeeze to extract sufficient juice to be able to 'wash' a fair sized orchard or herd of goats, but I fancy that even contemporary no-chemicals-on-my-farm stalwarts like old Pep would balk at the prospect. I'd certainly never seen even one pumpkin plant on his *finca*. No doubt he'd have his very own and equally effective old-time cure for ant infestations, however – even if it was just scaring the tiny invaders off with swearwords and a few lungfuls of noxious reek from his home-grown-tobacco *cigarrillos*.

For us, the problem of ants in the fruit trees hadn't yet arisen, and if it ever did, I'd be content to let Pepe Suau, the local tree maestro, advise me what best to do. It had been little Pepe, after all, who had rescued our orchards from those ravages of neglect that, in our total ignorance of this type of farming, we'd failed to recognise when buying the *finca*. And although he was by no means an advocate of the indiscriminate use of potentially lethal pesticides, he did temper an inherent concern for the welfare of the environment with the pragmatic outlook of a small farmer whose livelihood depends on protecting the health of his livestock, crops and trees in a commercially-efficient way as well. He and his forefathers had been ecologically-aware farmers since long before 'green' became a buzz word, and maybe even before the almanac was written. But he was also a realist, who knew as well as anyone how to balance tradition with progress. Pepe would keep us right. Just as old Maria had tried to keep us right when dealing with an ants problem of a purely domestic nature . . .

'Chimney soot!' That had been her tip for how to stop a legion of ants from persistently marching into our house through the front door. 'Chimney soot! Sprinkle a line of it across the threshold – that will keep the little *bandidos* out. They cannot stand soot on their feet, you know. Ah *sí*, it is the truth – as true as what I once told you about spreading a ring of wood ash round your cabbages to keep the slugs at bay. Chemicals?' She faked a spit over her shoulder. 'Pah! Modern poisons, all of them – just like the stinking smoke from your infernal tractors. Chemicals? *Jesús, María y José!* I would never pollute even my conscience with the use of them!'

But for her squeaky voice, this could just as well have been Pep talking. Both of our venerable Mallorcan neighbours were passionate upholders (verbally, at least) of the country ways of their beloved 'old days'. And long might such eco-friendly traditions survive – that was my attitude. But we knew that even Pep, though using the trouble with his 'war-wounded' leg as an excuse, had already yielded to the use of a tractor in reluctant preference to his trusty mule in certain situations. And on Maria's *finca*, I had seen for myself the telltale blue of the substance that had been dusted onto her tomato plants to ward off fungal attack. It was a copper-sulphate powder which, though long used by market gardeners everywhere and perfectly safe if used carefully, was a toxic chemical, nonetheless. However, although I already knew about the potential consequences of the irresponsible use of such copper-based substances in agriculture, I'd had no real qualms about applying the powder to our own tomato plants, especially after Jordi had told me, with an insistence bordering on the dictatorial, that to fail to do so would be to gift the precious plants to certain tomato-deadly spores that thrive in the warm, humid air of Mallorca. Judicious use of copper-laced fungicide, he'd said, and timely applications of good old derris powder insecticide, would be all that was required to keep our tomato plants in tip-top condition. And he would entertain no questioning of the safety to nature of their sensible use, either. I found that out the hard way.

'Bloody 'ell!' he'd exclaimed, while surveying our neat rows of tomatoes under the dappled shade of an old fig tree one soft, early-summer evening. 'I tell you, man, the baster powders be doing less harms to the good sex than the baster stuffs you being use to water them tomaties being do to your neighbours.' He held his nose, gagging. 'Ugh, bugger Jordi for the stinks! Phew, is bloody ridickliss!'

I knew what Jordi was referring to as far as the stench was concerned. For reasons that could be regarded as being as 'organic' as they were businesslike, we used the nutrient-rich liquid content of the house's septic tank to irrigate and simultaneously feed our tomato plants. It was a practice that made perfect sense in a land where water is valued by its relative scarcity, and where store-bought fertilizer is as expensive as it is anywhere.

Purposely planting the tomatoes well away from our own house, but as close as possible to the Ferrers' weekened retreat, may well have appeared to the uninformed as inconsiderate, if not down-right antisocial. And indeed there had been an element of spite behind our decision to locate our little tomato plantation right behind the wall of our occasional neighbours' *casita*. It was our way of giving them some of their own back, so to speak, for having been less than honest with us about the 'efficiency' of the house's sewage system when selling us the place. Jordi knew that, and I knew what he meant about the discomfort that the pong must have caused the Ferrers when 'in residence'.

What I didn't know, though, was what on earth he'd meant when he'd said in the same breath that chemical powders applied to my tomato plants would do less harm to 'good sex' than the smells from the septic tank's outflow would do to the Ferrers. Could it be that, unknown to me, breathing in copper-sulphate and derris powder could have an adverse effect, no matter how slight, on the male libido? Could this, and not the overdose of champagne, have caused my disinterest in Ellie's tentative bedtime advances the night of the O'Briens' party? This required immediate investigation.

'Good sex?' I asked Jordi, scratching my head. 'Sorry, but how can sprinkling stuff on tomato plants be in any way harmful to sex, good or otherwise?'

He shook his head and looked at me in that

distinctive way of his – a slightly pitying look that suggested he could read the letters 'C-R-E-T-I-N' clearly stamped on my forehead. 'Bees!' he said, then raised his eyebrows in anticipation of the letters on my forehead changing to 'E-U-R-E-K-A!'

They didn't. In fact, I was more confused than ever now, and it must have showed.

'Bees!' Jordi barked, as if raising his voice would increase the chances of what he was telling me penetrating my thick skull. 'You must being careful the powders no being harming to the baster bees.'

I was none the wiser. 'Bees?' I repeated. 'Sex? *Bees?*'

Jordi clenched his teeth, his bony little frame tensing in sheer exasperation. 'Yes, *bees!*' he spluttered. 'Bees and spiders in the tomaties, aunties up the fruit trees, Margarets in the turnips – all bloody damn sex, OK! All baster sex, but only the bees is good sex for the forking farmer! Bloody 'ell, man, your English is being get more damn worser since you coming live here!'

Knowing the evolution of Jordi's improvised English vocabulary a little better with every meeting, it didn't take me long to work out that 'aunties' meant 'ants' and 'Margarets' was his ad lib word for maggots. It only took a second or two more to finally tumble to the meaning of his determined use of the 'sex' word. I hung my head in feigned shame, trying, as ever, not to smile. 'Sorry, Jordi,' I muttered, 'I should've known when you said "bees" that you were talking about insects.'

'Crice sakes! This being exackly what bloody Jordi being say. *SEX!*'

Coming a poor second to Jordi on the finer points of linguistics was something I'd grown to accept, and when all's said and done it was a lot easier for me to put up with that, and the little idiosyncrasies of his English, than to converse on equal terms with him in *his* native tongue. From that day on, the words 'sex', 'aunties' and 'Margarets' took on new meanings for me, at least when talking to Jordi. But what he had been trying to get across, in his own inimitable style, was the same advice Pepe Suau had once given me in *his* distinctive way – simply that, in order not to harm the bees, whose pollinating work is vital, care has to be taken when applying insecticides to plants and trees when they're flowering. As old Maria had once told me, bees are the little cupids of the field, without whose little arrows the act of love between potentially fruit-bearing blossoms would not take place. For all that, Pepe Suau's cautious chemical-spraying services were now being called upon when it came to controlling pests and diseases in *her* fruit trees, too. She would doubt-less claim, however, that this was being done without her permission, claiming it to be the muti-nous, underhand work of her de facto *finca* factor, her long-suffering son-in-law Jaume, no spring chicken himself, though a juvenile, tractor-loving whippersnapper and an enemy of tradition in Maria's eyes. Times were changing, nevertheless, and no matter how often good old folk like Maria and Pep sang the praises of the past, even they were now discreetly listening to, if not actively singing, the music of modernity as well.

My own little contribution to maintaining the 'green' ways of the past (as well as satisfying my Scotsman's natural desire to save a few pesetas!) was to suggest to Ellie that we try Maria's soot-across-the-threshold method of dissuading ants from paying us unwanted house visits. Ellie's reaction was both swift and to-the-point:

'Soot, in case you hadn't noticed, is not green. It's black! And just in case you really are suffering from a sudden attack of colour-blindness, the expensive rug on the floor inside the front door is off-white. Call it cream, parchment, alabaster, eggshell or ivory, if you prefer, but *not* black – which is precisely what it will be if you, the boys and Bonny start walking all over it with sooty feet.' She handed me an aerosol can. 'This is ant repellent. I bought it from the hardware store this morning.' And before I could make my point about the economic benefits of soot, she added, 'This little tin of chemical spray may have cost a bit more than a free handful of muck from up the chimney, but it still cost a hell of a lot less than that rug!'

So, with apologies to global warming, I did as instructed and fired off an invisible salvo of anti-ant droplets across the floor of the doorway. It worked, of course. The leader of the next parade

234

of ants simply took a cursory sniff of the chemical niff, waved his antennae impatiently, then wheeled right and marched his troops off – no doubt to find another house to visit, a house with a less questionable welcome mat on its doorstep. It appeared that, even if my fleeting use of an aerosol spray had contributed further irreparable damage to the ozone layer, the ants clearly couldn't have cared less. Old-fashioned soot or modern insect repellent, it was all the same to them. The grotesque, two-legged giants who wasted valuable working and marching time in dispensing such annoying stuff were only temporary visitors to their world anyway. Every thinking ant knew that his species had been around for a few million years longer than that meddlesome lot, and would doubtless still be around millions of years after they'd sooted and aerosoled themselves into extinction as well. And perhaps it would take a foolhardy human indeed to argue too forcibly with that. If the prophets of doom have got it right, soot smudges on our rugs will soon be the least of mankind's worries.

Still, I couldn't blame Ellie for emphatically rejecting yet another of old Maria's folk remedies. I had put several others to the test already, and no matter how much I'd have loved them to work as well as (or even better than) their modern 'scientific' counterparts, their general effectiveness had been marginal at best. But to be fair, perhaps I just hadn't been administering Maria's nostrums properly. For instance, maybe I hadn't been placing walnut leaves close enough to the cockroaches' bolthole under the freezer to send the horrible bugs scurrying out of the *almacén* forever. Or it could well be that I hadn't been secreting the optimum amount of salt-sprinkled lemon wedges about the kitchen to ward off perpetually-intruding houseflies. Whether or not, and while not qualified to write such things off as being merely old wives' tales, I did finally have to admit that, in those immortal words of Kermit the Frog, 'it's not easy being green'.

Not that I could claim to be a committed convert to the cause in any case. A supporter of it? Yes, in broad principle at least. But a card-carrying, banner-waving disciple of it? Well, no – to claim to be that would be stretching things a bit too far. On the farming front at least, I was firmly in the ranks of the middle-of-the-road brigade, as championed by the equitable Pepe Suau. On a personal-health basis, however, I *had* become a bit more actively interested in the sort of 'alternative' cures whose panacean qualities old Maria had preached to me since I'd fallen prey to her sermons on such favoured 'old days' subjects.

Her 'natural' method of discouraging the blood-sucking attentions of mosquitos had been a good case in point. I don't suppose mosquitos bite me more than they bite anyone else (although I'm not entirely convinced about that!), and their actual *bites* certainly don't bother me unduly. The effect of the anti-coagulant spit a mosquito squirts into me with its hide-penetrating proboscis in order to facilitate the theft of as much blood as possible with as little bother as possible to the thief does bother me, though. A lot!

Before going any farther, though, perhaps I'd better point out that there are virtually no creepy-crawlies in Mallorca that pose a serious threat to humans. You could spend a lifetime trudging over mountain and plain without ever encountering a venomous snake or poisonous spider, for instance. Even Mallorcan mosquitos are no more dangerous to human health than are their annoying northern cousins, the infamous Scottish 'midgies' that swarm around and nip to distraction hapless visitors to the Western Highlands in summertime. For some reason, however, Scottish midgies had never troubled me that much. Maybe they just left me alone because they'd grown indifferent to native 'food', and preferred the more exotic blood that flows through the veins of foreign tourists. If that same principle applies in reverse, that could be why Mallorcan mosquitos, ubiquitous as ants and cockroaches as they are in the Mediterranean climate, had become the bane of my life since back at the onset of the warm weather in spring – the *first* spring of the year, that is.

It took but seconds from feeling the almost imperceptible tickle of spindly feet on my skin, and the ensuing pinprick of that tiny siphoning tube, before the temperature started to rise in the immediate vicinity of the mozzy's raid on my unguarded blood bank. Then came the itch – a bitch of an itch that insists on being scratched, and becomes all the more itchy for it. Torture. Within an hour or so, while the itching got more unbearable and the scratching more frantic, the little red pimple on my knuckle that marked the spot of the attack had started to swell. Panic-stricken antibodies were pumping rivers of histamine into ground zero. Eventually, my still-itching hand looked like a rubber glove filled with water. And that is no exaggeration. I truly believe that my metabolism's reaction to mosquito bites warrants an entry in the Guinness Book of Records.

On one unforgettable occasion, I was attacked by what must have been an entire squadron of the miniature Stuka dive-bombers while I was sound asleep in bed. I awoke in the morning to discover that they had been gorging themselves in the area around my left eye, with the uncomfortable telltale signs of an even better-attended vampire feast having taken place on one exposed shoulder. When I got up to go and survey the damage in the mirror, I was halted by Ellie letting out a blood-curdling scream. I wheeled round to see her sitting bolt upright in bed, the terror in her eyes clearly visible, even in the shuttered half-light of the bedroom. She screamed again – louder this time.

'What the hell's got into *you?*' I snapped. 'Jesus H. Christ, Ellie, you nearly scared the pants off me!'

'Oh, it's only you,' she exhaled, patently relieved.

'Who the hell did you think it was?' I was too itchy and irritated to be bothered by one of her 'Oo-oo, I've had a terrible nightmare' dramas.

Ellie started to snigger. 'Well, I got a big enough fright waking up to see this strange figure shuffling about in the gloom with a lump on his shoulder.' Another fit of tittering. 'But when you turned round and I saw your face, I honestly did think I'd been paid a visit by Quasimodo.'

That really was an exaggeration, of course, but not a particularly big one, as I was about to discover. Switching on the light above the bathroom mirror, I saw not myself staring back at me, but the Hunchback of Notre Dame – the definitive version, as portrayed in the old 1930s movie. The left side of my face was pure Charles Laughton, and the only aspect of deformity in which old Quasi appeared to have one up on me was in the hump department, though there only debatably.

Something had to be done to deliver me from such recurring miseries. I'd already tried all the usual proprietary unguents and smelly spirits which the manufacturers claimed would protect me from mosquito strike. They didn't. So, it follows that I'd been obliged to buy and apply whatever itch-relieving and inflammation-reducing ointments were recommended by the Andratx *farmacia* as well. I was buying so much of all this stuff that I was about to ask the owner of the shop for a trade discount. In desperation, and risking ridicule, I plucked up sufficient courage to pour out my tale of woe to old Pep while having a typically protracted chat about this, that and nothing in particular over his farm gate one morning.

'*Basuras!*' he grunted. 'Rubbish! All of those chemical remedies for insect bites are about as much use as a single chopstick to a hungry Chinaman!' Vinegar, as strong and pungent as I could find, was, in Pep's irrefutable opinion, the only solution to my problem. I should apply the vinegar to all exposed skin, and no mosquito would venture within a metre of me. And, he proclaimed, with no bites to trouble me, no after-effects creams would need to be bought either. *Coño* – I would save a fortune!

Just in case he'd been pulling my leg again, I decided to check out Pep's recommendation with old Maria before actually trying it. Her reaction was a shrug and a facial expression that told me she assumed everyone knew about this particular property of vinegar.

'*Naturalmente,*' she said, '*el vinagre* will make all mosquitos retreat from the wearer of it. And it will also take the pain out of a wasp sting, as well as putting the shine back on dulled glass, soothing sunburn, removing sweat stains from the armpits of your working shirts, and a hundred other handy uses. *Los mosquitos?*' She swatted the air. '*Ay-y-y, no problema!* Splash on *mucho vinagre* and they will avoid you like my son-in-law avoids work!'

That was good enough for me.

'You smell like a fish supper,' was Ellie's reaction the first time I gave it a go. 'Honestly, the whiff you're giving off reminds me of something that's just been carried out of a chip shop in a piece of newspaper.' She glared at me and turned up her nose. 'I am *not* going out with you smelling like *that!*'

As we had been about to leave on an expedition to check out a hunters' eatery we'd heard about, a little-known but highly-recommended little shack of a place hidden away in the forest on the other side of the mountains, I realised this was serious. I'd never known Ellie turn down a chance of going out to eat. I had to face it, the days of tinkering with my problem were over. It was now time for the appliance of science.

Some swift research revealed that it's only the female mosquito that bites you – and only a pregnant one at that. The reason is that she wants your blood to nourish her fertilized eggs, and, being pregnant, the last thing she's interested in is any further advances from amorous male mosquitos. As far as the female is concerned, these guys have served their purpose, so if they're still feeling a bit horny, they can go hump a hornet – or themselves. Clearly, the multi-million-year survival of the mosquito was not based on notions of ungrudging passion masquerading as love, certainly not as far as the females are concerned. And, being as hard-bitten as that, you could just imagine the disdain with which they regard modern man's futile attempts to foil their continued procreation . . .

'What did all those recently-arrived human beings think they were going to achieve by smearing themselves with their smelly chemical lotions and so-called foolproof mosquito repellents?' That, I fancied, would be the most frequently-asked question when mosquito matriarchs meet at egg-laying time on some fetid, stagnant pool. 'Let's face it,' they'd continue, 'nothing smells worse than a dinosaur's crotch, and millions of our foremothers thought nothing of sticking their built-in drinking straws into those to ensure a wholesome future for their unborn babies.'

Thinking about it that way, I was inclined to concede that my battle against the biting mosquito was probably doomed to failure, even without Ellie's recent words of discouragement. A single Jurassic fart would have been sufficient to wipe out, in one fell poop, countless thousands of bloodsucking mosquitos from the vicinity of a brontosaurus's arse, so if the little prehistoric blighters had been happy to risk that for a feed, there'd be no chance of their present-day descendants being dissuaded from having a go at me just because I'd splashed some vinegar on my face – no matter what Pep and Maria said. Things were looking bleak.

But, as so often happens, cometh the problem, cometh the man with a solution. A couple of days after I'd mugged up on the gestational needs of the pregnant mosquito, I happened upon a mail order ad in the *Majorca Daily Bulletin*, which, quoting a potted version of the results of my recent studies, stated that a small device had been developed that emitted a high-pitched whistle which emulated exactly the frequency of the whine of a sex-mad male mosquito. Battery-operated, the mozzy-bamboozler was small enough to clip into your shirt pocket like a pen. And what's more, its audio signal, although coming over loud and clear to the female mosquito, was all but inaudible to the human ear. Unlike odour-based products, there would be no antisocial side effects for the user. Salvation! I sent away for one straight away.

Can you imagine how my spirits soared when I discovered that it really did work? Suddenly, with the gadget in my pocket, I was no longer the target of blood-thirsty lady mozzies. At last, I could go to the most mosquito-abundant places and sit enjoying an alfresco meal or drink without having to endure the constant dread of being bitten. Even the manufacturer's claim that the device would present no aural annoyance to the user or nearby human companions proved to be absolutely genuine. You really did have to stick the mini-loudspeaker into your ear before you could catch even a hint of the shrill whistle that it emitted. Admittedly, passing dogs did tend to flash me a troubled look before making quick their departure, ears pinned back, tails firmly between their legs. But, the way I saw it, this was a small price to pay for peace of mind and freedom from the itching agony of the suppurating lumps on my flesh that I'd been enduring so frequently up 'til then. And that, unfortunately, was to prove the very rock on which my ship of whistling salvation was all too soon to perish.

Bonny, being a dog, didn't appreciate my selfish and unfeeling attitude towards the sensitive hearing of her species, and she made her point in the bluntest of ways. After weeks of mosquito-free living, I'd become a bit blasé about what I now saw as my ex-problem, and had started carrying the little buzzer only after sundown, when mosquitos are at their vampire-like most profuse. I'd got into the habit of leaving the mozzy-bamboozler lying switched off on the kitchen table when out during the day, thus saving its battery life for the more perilous hours of darkness. On such occasions, especially when we were going to be away from the farm for an hour or two, Bonny, in her capacity as house-minder, normally stayed behind in the kitchen, with a free run through the open door to an enclosed terrace, from where she could keep an eye on things outside. Bonny took her work seriously. Though still not quite a year old, she had rarely fallen into that mischievous category expressed in the old saying that 'the devil makes work for idle paws'. The worst she had ever done, on the odd occasion when the boredom of lone watch-dogging did get the better of her, had been to pull a few baubles off the fly screen hanging in the kitchen doorway, or to 'weed out' a geranium or two from flower pots on the terrace. Even then, the guilty look on Bonny's expressive boxer face gave the game away as soon as we returned home. She knew she had done wrong, and the merest 'tut, tut' and a wag of a reproaching finger from Ellie or me was all that was needed to make her sink into a wallow of shame.

The look of sheer elation and pride that lit her face on the day she ate my mozzy-bamboozler spoke volumes, therefore, about how much she had hated the thing from day one. And I should have recognised the signs. Whenever I'd switched the buzzer on when Bonny was about, she would cock her head to one side, looking at me with her big brown eyes full of puzzled pleading. 'Will you *please* turn that infernal contraption off?' was what her expression seemed to be saying. And just in case I hadn't got the message, she'd then whimper a little, before flicking each of her ears in turn with a front paw. I did feel guilty about the obvious discomfort I was causing her, but again, I felt it was a small price to pay for what was being achieved. My view was that, whatever minor annoyance I was causing Bonny, the means justified the end of my own much more unbearable torture. Mistake. If I hadn't realised it before, I was soon to learn never to underestimate the resolve of a disgruntled dog. Unthinkingly, I had polluted Bonny's world in a way that was much more instantly-obvious and irritating to her than my occasional use of aerosols and chemicals were to the human race – or, for that matter, to Bonny and her four-legged pals. Everything is subjective, even in a dog's world.

Two paw marks on the kitchen table, a little gnawed battery and a tiny tangle of chewed electronic circuitry was all that remained of my treasured anti-mosquito device when we got home from a shopping trip to Palma that day. No doubt, Bonny's undisguised show of pleasure in what she had done was based on the belief that she had done us as big a favour as she had done herself. She was blissfully unaware, after all, that her 'masters' are literally deaf to the high frequency sounds that she and her canine chums can hear so vividly.

While sympathising with her problem and appreciating how she felt about her well-intentioned destruction of my mozzy-confounder, I ordered a replacement immediately. Fate turned out to be on Bonny's side, however. By the time I tried to contact them again, the gizmo's suppliers had moved on from their originally-advertised box-number address, the way certain mail order companies so often do. They had simply disappeared, perhaps pursued by packs of whistle-crazed dogs. And although I did eventually manage to find similar devices operating on the same principle as the original, none of them worked, at least not for me. Bonny's pleasure was matched only by my despondency. I was back to square one.

Then Fate, in her most even-handed of moods, threw *me* a lifeline. Some months earlier, old Maria had told me that the 'old days' way of keeping mosquitos at bay if you were dining outdoors was to throw a lump of dried donkey dung onto your cooking fire or barbecue. The resultant fumes would do the trick, she promised. I'd never put the method to the test, simply because I didn't fancy exposing myself to the indignity of being seen scouring the lanes and byways of the valley in search of donkey droppings, particularly if Maria had only been kidding, which I suspected she had been, in her typically impish way.

'But it is true, *amigo*,' enthused Gabriel, the genial owner of the Ferretería Capri, the Aladdin's Cave of a hardware store on the western outskirts of Peguera. '*Sí, sí, sí*, the smouldering Calcutta Coil will keep *los mosquitos* at bay just as efficiently as the burning of the donkey shit. *Sí claro!*' He couldn't have been more unequivocal in his confirmation.

Purely by chance, I'd found the Calcutta Coil he was referring to while rummaging in a bin of miscellaneous 'on sale' items outside his store while Ellie was shopping in the nearby Supermercado Casa Pepe. It was the large drawing of a dead mosquito on the box which caught my eye.

'It is the last one we have,' said Gabriel. 'Old

stock, you understand. But!' He held up an emphasising forefinger, then quickly appended, 'I can order more should you require them. *Absolutamente no problema, amigo mío.*'

I was back in his shop making an urgent order for further supplies the very next morning. The Calcutta, wafer thin and looking not unlike a khaki-coloured paper saucer when removed from its packing, comes with a little tin stand to fix it on after you've carefully separated the fragile rings of the coil. According to the instructions, all you have to do then is light the end of the outer ring, make sure it's smouldering nicely, then place the coil on the floor beneath your chair or table while you're enjoying your open-air meal or drink. No mosquito would venture near – guaranteed!

To my eternal delight, the manufacturers hadn't made their claim lightly. The Calcutta Coil worked a treat. I tested it by sitting for three hours in a copse of pine trees in the garden the same night I made the crucial purchase from Gabriel. Areas immediately beneath pine trees are widely recognised as being happy hunting grounds for marauding mozzies, and although I could see plenty of them making fly-past recces in the light of my storm lantern, not one of them came near me, cocooned as I was in my invisible cloud of protective Calcutta fumes. And the smell? Well, Bonny was the only member of the family sufficiently considerate (or stupid enough, according to Ellie and the boys) to keep me company during my lonely vigil, and even her super-sensitive dog's nostrils were not offended by the gentle Calcutta redolence. Admittedly, the smouldering coil didn't exactly give off the fragrant odour of a joss stick, and even if, as its name implied, the substance of the coil was based more on elephant excrement than old Maria's recommended donkey dung, you'd never have guessed. You sensed nothing more noxious than the faintest whiff of burning organic matter drifting by as if from a distant forest clearing on the warm night air.

My mosquito problem was finally over, and I had solved it by employing a modern derivative of a traditional solution. It's said that the simplest ideas are often the best, and I took my hat off to whatever crafty brain had devised this beautifully uncomplicated way of harnessing the power of what makes your garden grow. From that night on, I never sat outside anywhere after dark without a trusty Calcutta Coil fuming discreetly away in my immediate vicinity. And not a single complaint was ever made by man or beast. Well, not until the first time I placed a glowing coil on the windowsill of our bedroom, that is. Ellie was quick to remind me that the merest waft of a nocturnal breeze could well result in the curtains being set on fire. Her way of eliminating the risk was to replace the Calcutta Coil with one of those little plug-in gadgets that heats up and emits anti-bug vapour from a small, insecticide-impregnated lozenge. Like the Calcutta Coil, they're actually just another spin-off from old Maria's burnt-donkey-droppings concept, though less energy efficient, for all their technical superiority. But their night-time bedroom use was a compromise which I was pleased to make in the interests of minimising the fire hazard element of the coil, as envisaged by Ellie.

'Aha,' the more keenly-green among you may well ask, 'but what about the chemical-pollutant threat to the atmosphere posed by those little insecticide-impregnated lozenges?'

Frankly, after all the discomfort and embarrassment I'd suffered during my long quest for deliverance from mosquito bites, I couldn't have cared less. Still, for the sake of maintaining my membership of the Pepe Suau school of equitable environmental awareness, I did balance the use of the little electrically-powered mozzy-scarers by placing – in deference to a rival folk remedy prescribed by old Maria – a potted sweet basil plant on the bedroom windowsill every night as well.

I was sitting on the fence, and I felt perfectly comfortable doing just that. For me, being a lump-free Humpty Dumpty beats being a Quasimodo any day. The trick, though, would be in not having a fall . . .

Whether, as the old almanac predicted, the sun had actually entered Scorpio when the first storm arrived in October, I had no idea, but arrive in October it did, and most welcome it was, too. During the previous week, the weather had been changing for the worse – if you can appreciate why getting progressively warmer should be described in such a negative way. Unlike the pleasantly hot days of late September, when grape-pickers, almond-harvesters and olive-gatherers got on with their urgent work with but occasional short breaks to rest their aching limbs and slake their thirst in whatever shade they could find, mid-October saw the temperatures revert from the balmy of autumn to the almost unbearable of high summer. Or so it seemed.

From early June through August, day-after-day running into week-upon-week of incessant, ever-hotter sunshine had often had me scanning the sky above the valley, in hopes of spying just one little cloud that might drift over the sun and give us a few precious moments of relief from those searing rays. That seldom happened. Bizarre as it may sound to holidaying sun-worshippers, on days like that I actually missed the vagaries of the Scottish climate. In fact, there had been times, when working in the summer fields of Ca's Mayoral, that I had longed for a chill Scotch mist to come seeping through the orchards, so that I could fill my lungs with its freshness and bathe my perspiring skin in its cooling tide. That never happened. Only a couple of times did a freak downpour of monsoon-like rain offer any respite from the glare of the sun, and even then for only a tantalisingly short time.

The climatic conditions we were now experiencing in October weren't *really* as extreme as that, it has to be said. But with the shortening days, the characteristic seasonal dampness of the island air had started to settle on all things roughly horizontal during the hours of darkness. Come dawn, the warmth of the rising sun would cause each dew drop to evaporate and make its own contribution to the humidity that was now increasing with every new day. And it was this sultry quality of the air, combined with a spell of weather that *was* unusually warm for the time of year, which gave the impression that things were returning to the often oppressive conditions that had prevailed during those endless months of summer. They weren't, of course. All that was happening was that Mother Nature was making her preparations to prove the almanac's predictions correct. For everyone knows there's only one thing that will clear the air when the weather has turned stiflingly close and stuffy . . .

The first storm heralded its arrival from the north, the far-off sound of thunder more a mumble than a rumble as it stole between the jagged peaks of the Serra d'es Pinotells and down into the valley over the bald, rocky dome of Ses Penyes mountain. Dusk was falling on what had been the most overbearingly muggy day of late. As evening shadows extended their dark fingers ever further through the clefts and gulleys of thc surrounding mountainsides, the heaviness of the air increased apace. And the sound of the approaching storm crept inexorably closer.

'I'm going to hide under the kitchen table,' Ellie warbled, already panicking at the thought of what might be. Although the storm was still far out at sea, and possibly as distant as the city of Barcelona, over a hundred crow-flying miles away on the mainland of Spain, Ellie's phobic fear of thunder and lightning had already triggered her built-in survival mechanism.

We had been sitting under the beamed *porche* that ran the length of the front of the house, having our usual evening meal with the boys, and muttering complaints about the ambient clamminess, while enjoying a Mallorcan country recipe which had been given to Ellie by Francisca Ferrer. Francisca had also provided the main ingredient, her husband Tomàs's home-grown broad beans, called *habas* in Spanish. Tomàs grew a lot of *habas* – excellent ones, as Francisca was ever proud to declare. She didn't eat them herself, however. She'd once revealed that, as with the eating of the cabbages, the consumption of *las habas* gave her, uhm-ah . . . *el viento* – wind. She spoke with a refreshing frankness. There was only the merest hint of the haughtiness that could so often dominate her manner as she pronounced that we, because of her unfortunate digestive reaction to them, were welcome to as many of Tomàs's excellent *habas* as we wanted. If there was an underlying lack of ungrudging benevolence behind Francisca's offer, Ellie chose to ignore it (at least in front of Francisca), and always accepted her gift of broad beans with a show of smiling gratitude. And why not? Tomàs's beans *were* good, as *is* Francisca's recipe.

To make it, all you have to do is heat some olive oil in a pan, then lightly fry a few diced rashers of bacon, adding a potato, an onion and half a red pepper, all diced as well. When the onion has turned transparent, stir in as many sliced garlic cloves as you think is tactful (three or four is usually enough!), then throw in two or three handfuls of shelled broad beans, before adding about the same amount of chopped tomatoes (tinned ones will do) and a cup of chicken or vegetable stock. Season with a little salt and plenty of freshly-ground black pepper, and simmer until the vegetables are just soft. Before removing from the heat, mix in some herbs of your choice, and a dollop or two of tomato purée to thicken. As you will have guessed, the quantities of the ingredients quoted are by no means critical. The topping of each individual serving with a couple of fried eggs is, however.

That's 'Francisca's Broad Bean Stew'. Try it. It's simple, but scrumptious *and* healthy! A word of warning, though. The 'wind-raising' effect that broad beans visited upon Señora Ferrer is in no way peculiar to her. Of all the pulses, broad beans are, arguably, the most notorious for their ability to produce amazing quantities of gas in the human gut. So, Francisca's recipe may not be one to set before your dinner party guests, unless you're sure they all have open minds about the unavoidably audible results of the flatulence that the high bean content of the dish can generate in some people.

Young Charlie was just such a victim, albeit a perfectly willing one, and, as such, much to his mother's disgust. After one particularly gluttonous feast of his highly-rated broad bean stew, she had caught him in his bedroom attempting to squeeze out the first few bars of 'God Save The Queen' from the business end of his alimentary canal. Her serious threat of forcing him to hand-wash his own underpants soon put paid to such bold musical adventures, however. It hadn't cured him of the physiological condition, of course. Nothing could. But Charlie had since learned to temper his enthusiasm for developing a stage act based on what he described as 'the ability to produce astounding tonal variations on the theme of the extended trouser cough' by perfecting a cunningly-silent version of the same. His mother still disapproved, but I knew it was just a normal 'boy thing', and I actually found his new-found technique quite handy, especially when dining outside in *el aire libre*, as we were tonight. Charlie may not *quite* have been in the brontosaurus league of farting, but after he'd been eating the broad bean stew,

I knew that I could snuff out my trusty Calcutta Coil for at least half an hour, safe in the knowledge that no mosquito would venture near Charlie's selflessly imposed no-fly zone. Admittedly, the ploy did have its obvious drawbacks. Instead of the faint aroma of smouldering autumn leaves given off by the coil, Charlie's equivalent smell, while still essentially organic, was more akin to that of a long-dead rat. But there was invariably a citrus-tinged zephyr wafting through the *porche* from the orchards in the evening, so I found that, as long as I sat upwind of Charlie, the problem barely existed. Into the bargain, an inch or so of Calcutta Coil was being saved, and, as every canny Scotsman recognises, a penny saved is a penny earned. Cooking with Francisca's freebie *habas*, then, made economic sense in more ways than one.

The approaching storm promised more liberal times than usual for Charlie tonight. Not only would his mother's disapproving nostrils be out of range as she cowered in her makeshift lightning shelter in the kitchen, but the sound of the thunder itself would lend him a rare opportunity to let rip with his banned rectal recitals without fear of her hearing them either.

The first peal of thunder to present itself as more a crack than a rumble told us that the storm wasn't too far off now. A brilliant and prolonged flicker of light had preceded it by several seconds, fitfully illuminating the sky above Ses Penyes mountain like some gigantic disco strobe. At the sight of it,

Bonny had retreated indoors to join Ellie under the kitchen table, leaving the boys and me outside to enjoy the forthcoming spectacle on our own. Paradoxically, our compulsive attraction to thunderstorms was just as strong as Ellie's and Bonny's aversion to them. Maybe ours was some kind of extension of the irresistible temptation that drives arsonists to set fire to buildings just so that they can get their kicks by watching the dramatic results. Although none of us would have gone to such destructive lengths as that to feed our variant of the same fascination (it would have been a bit difficult to rustle up a thunderstorm at will in any case!), we had to admit to being hooked on the electrical power of nature in all its visual ferocity. Other more fanciful speculations aside, however, maybe the real reason for this condition was simply that the boys and I didn't have as much common sense as Ellie and the dog. Not, mind you, that we were about to do anything *really* silly, like stand under a tree with our feet in a puddle of water. No, watching the impending show from the relative safety of the open *porche* would be as reckless as we would get. Mother Nature, in turn, was to be both generous and considerate in her response.

Silence greeted her wild offspring's entrance into the amphitheatre of the valley. Minutes of ominous stillness blanketed everything, with not a cricket chirping, not a leaf stirring, not a bullfrog croaking, not a gecko moving a clinging toe on the house wall, not a nervous dog barking in the eerie darkness of the encircling mountains. The explosion when it finally came was both shocking and enthralling in the beauty of its violence. Only a split second separated the lightning from the angry roar of its attendant thunderclap. Great barbed veins of incandescence hovered horizontally over the saw-toothed ridge of Mount Abidala away to the west, their dazzling white light caught in a shuddering freeze-frame that seemed endless.

While the boys cheered, a duet of whimpering struck up somewhere inside the open kitchen door. But Ellie and Bonny needn't have worried. Unlike the previous winter, when a similar storm had seen a lightning strike all but destroy an elegant old eucalyptus tree standing perilously close to that same kitchen door, this time nature had decreed that her awesome spectacle would pass at a distance close enough to impress, though just far enough off to pose no threat to Ca's Mayoral and the other little *fincas* huddled defenceless on the valley floor. And what a spectacle it turned out to be!

Moving steadily southwards, the storm provided a *son et lumière* show above the Tramuntana peaks that outdid in its savage brilliance anything that man might hope to replicate. I had often marvelled at the sumptuously choreographed fireworks displays which mark the end of the annual Edinburgh International Festival; lavish pyrotechnic spectaculars set against the magnificent backdrop of

258

Edinburgh Castle. But none could compare with the extravaganza presently being staged by the sheer stunning might of the elements. It was easy to appreciate now why those venerated poets of ancient Greece and Rome had waxed so lyrical about the power and glory of such Mediterranean tempests as this.

A massive grenade burst of energy marked the start of the climax of the show. An amoebic ball of light, huge and dazzling in the intensity of its brilliance, materialised and hung suspended high above the mountains. Long, writhing tentacles of lightning snaked down from its perimeters, lending it the appearance of a giant Portuguese man o' war, a hellish, heavenly jellyfish, suddenly charged with millions of volts of electricity.

'Good, eh?' gasped Sandy with typical Scots understatement.

But, overly-laconic as his reaction may have seemed at first, he'd actually said it all.

The entire valley was now flooded with a dazzling incandescence that, for the few seconds it lasted, made the rugged rock faces of the mountains stand out in bold relief, every crag and cleavage seeming nearer and more vividly etched than on the brightest of sunny days. Then a mighty tympani roll boomed out, reverberating off those same cliffs in an eruption of ear-splitting decibels. At that moment, I glanced at Charlie gazing awestruck skyward, and I was immediately hit by a whimsical thought. In the midst of such

259

overwhelming clamour, no one, least of all Ellie, would have been any the wiser if he had been simultaneously bum-burping the cannon-fire sequence from Tchaikovsky's *1812 Overture* – which, judging by the grin of pained concentration on his upturned face, he may well have been attempting.

After its grand Mallorcan finale, the storm played out a diminishing series of encores while tracking ever southwards over the sea towards the neighbouring island of Ibiza and the coast of North Africa beyond.

And then came the rain. The wonderful, luscious rain. The refreshing rain that I'd longed for during those interminable days of summer heat. A light wind came down from the north in the storm's wake, a mild reminder of the Tramuntana gales that would buffet the island from time to time during the coming months of winter. But for now, the autumn wind gently drove those welcome raindrops against me as I stepped out of the *porche* and luxuriated in their soft caress. At last the suffocating sultriness of the past week had cleared, and I could breathe easily again, inhaling great lungfuls of fresh air that tasted sweetly of more temperate northern climes.

I thought back to the morning on which I'd marvelled at the quiet beauty of the first sunrise of the true Mallorcan spring. It had been a memorable moment, yet nothing as dramatic as what I'd just witnessed – the arrival of the true

Mallorcan autumn, the violent birth of the season of *winter* spring. Tomorrow would dawn with a new vitality in the air, and with an invigorating feel to the day that would finally render obsolete all those excuses for procrastination I'd employed during the long *mañana* months that had stretched lazily between the two springs of the year.

Tomorrow would be a busy day. Ellie, her confidence restored, would see to that!

CHAPTER 9

FORTUNE FAVOURS THE BOLD

Washed by the rains of the previous night, the landscape of Mallorca glittered in the morning sunshine. The musty smell of warm, moist earth mingled with all the familiar aromas of pine and wild herbs descending from the wooded flanks of the mountains – a heady fusion of nature's scents, made all the more intoxicating by the champagne-like sparkle that now permeated the air. It was one of those glad-to-be-alive mornings that master songwriters used to eulogise over; an 'oh, what a beautiful' morning, on which the corn was as high as an elephant's eye – or might have been, if I'd been any good at growing corn in Mallorca, which I hadn't been! That's another story, but even memories of such embarrassing little farming fluffs couldn't dampen the 'everything's coming up roses' feeling that I was wallowing in as I sat with the boys in the *porche*, soaking up the glories of the morning, and sipping glasses of the orange juice that, for obvious reasons, had become a staple of our diet at Ca's Mayoral.

Even the birds seemed to share the sense of

euphoria that had come with the storm's banishing of the recent mugginess. Sparrows in the huddle of pine trees by the gate suddenly swapped their drowsy, lackadaisical cheeping for long and animated bouts of chattering – spring-like chattering, which suggested that, like their human counterparts of old, Mallorcan sparrows don't have a word for autumn either. Swallows and swifts, not seen in the valley since stopping off on their migratory journey northward earlier in the year, swooped and screeched between the trees of the orchards, hoovering up flies and (I hoped) mosquitos to fuel the remainder of their return trip to winter habitats in Africa. Another spring, to borrow again from those Tin Pan Alley wordsmiths of yesteryear, was bustin' out all over, and I envied that lucky old sun having nothing to do but roll around heaven all day. Effortlessly suppressing tiny pangs of guilt, I closed my eyes and slouched back in my chair to savour the thought.

Bang on cue, Ellie returned at that very moment from a quick shopping trip to Andratx. 'Here!' she said, presenting me with a large plastic bag. 'This is for the inside walls of the house. It's the crack-filler I've been waiting for *you* to get for months. There are four packs in there, and the Ferretería Ca'n Mateu has plenty more in stock now, so you needn't worry about running out!'

On a cursory inspection of the walls of the *almacén*, I could see that the house's spectral

Picasso had been busy since the last time I'd bothered to look at his handiwork, but being a weekend and with four of us on the job, we'd soon have all his hairline engravings in the plasterwork eradicated. That was the theory, anyway. Merely filling cracks without first scuffing out all the loose material that very often borders them is a waste of time, however. If you leave them in situ, those bits of flaky plaster will eventually come loose, taking your recently applied filler with them. So, according to the advice printed on the packet, before starting the repair work, we'd have to take time to scrape firmly along the line of each crack with a pointed tool. And sensible advice it is, because in so doing you widen each crack sufficiently to provide a little V-shaped channel for the filler to be trowelled into and a bigger surface for it to bond with. Again, that's the theory. But what often happens in practice, especially on old walls, is that, in scraping away those little flaky bits, you are also liable to dislodge lumps a centimetre or more deep and as big as the sole of your shoe. In all likelihood, such pieces of crumbly plaster have been attached only weakly to the underlying masonry for years, patiently waiting there for you to come along with your little pointed tool and help them break free at last.

The interior walls of Ca's Mayoral had plenty of those malicious surprises in store for us. Accordingly, the unappealing but relatively minor-looking job that I thought we'd wrap up in next to no time soon took on new and more daunting proportions. All the more so since we were reduced to a team of only three on the first day by old Pep arriving at the door to say that Sandy was urgently required to do some tillage work for a 'client' on a little *finca* away at the top of the valley. I never thought I'd see the day when Sandy scurried off so willingly to fire up that little Barbieri tractor of ours, the two-wheeled diesel 'donkey' which he never failed to remind us he disliked to be seen trudging behind. And I must say that I couldn't blame him for his sudden change of heart.

After only a couple of hours, repairing the cracks in the plaster, essential though the job was, had already turned into one of those tasks you wish you had never started – one of those nightmare undertakings that, the more you work at it, the more it seems you still have to do. Plaster dust and grit is everywhere – in your hair, up your sleeves, in the air, down your neck, up your nose, in your eyes and mouth, and all over the floor. Somehow, it even manages to find its way under the sheets you've spread over the furniture. And, as you soon find out, you've hardly even started the job at this stage!

Once you've 'opened' a crack with your trusty pointed tool, the person behind (in this case Charlie) has to moisten the channel and any bits of exposed masonry with a paint brush dipped in water. Then, the third person in the team (in this case Ellie) has to pack the area thus primed with the filler, which has already had to be mixed from its original powder form into a lump-free and workable paste with *just* the right amount of water. That's the mind-numbing procedure that you know you'll have to follow, crack after crack, wall after wall and room after room.

Then, in all probability, you'll have to start all over again, spreading more filler on top of the first application, which, on drying out, will have sunk some way into the cracks. In the case of the deeper fissures, this process may even have to be repeated twice. When the final layer of filler has been trowelled on and is sitting just proud of the surrounding surface of the wall (it takes hours for each layer to dry sufficiently before the next can be applied), you're ready for the penultimate stage. But don't be lulled into a premature sense of achievement. Sanding down the hardened crack-filler until the repaired area is perfectly flush with the adjacent plasterwork is probably the worst part of the job so far. If you thought the grit and dust that flew about everywhere in the preparatory gouging-out process was irritating, you're in for another unpleasant surprise. The fine white powder that billows out from the wall as the plaster is being buffed down is so invasive that, even if you're wearing goggles and one of those suffocating face masks much favoured by Japanese commuters, your lungs and eyes ultimately feel as if they're being used as plaster-mixing receptacles themselves. To make matters worse, after clinging to the skin of your perspiring face, hands and arms for hours on end, the hardening powder ends up making you feel like an icing sugar dummy waiting to be stuck on top of a wedding cake.

'Wallpaper,' moaned Charlie at the end of the first soul-destroying day. 'Why couldn't you have bought a house with wallpaper on the walls? Then you'd never have seen the poxy cracks!'

Fair point. The fact of the matter is, though, that bare, white-painted walls are the norm inside Mediterranean houses, and not without good reason. I've heard it said that, in such warm and sometimes humid climates, papering walls merely invites infestations of tiny house mites keen to take advantage of the favourable conditions that would then exist for them behind the wallpaper. Whether or not there's any truth in that I don't know. What is certain, however, is that plain, white walls add brightness to the interior of those houses, the older ones especially tending to have small windows purposely built into their thick stone walls in order to keep out as much summer sunlight as possible. What's more, the basic whitewash traditionally used for the purpose is fairly cheap. And white *is* easy to maintain. You simply grab your bucket of whitewash and brush out any scuffs and smudges that inevitably appear from time to time. The same simple procedure would apply when covering up repaired cracks, I reasoned. So, on balance, un-papered white walls did have distinct advantages in a house like ours, annoying cracks notwith-standing.

I explained all this to Charlie, cheering myself up considerably in the process. That, however, turned out to be only wishful thinking on my part. Once again, the practicalities of the matter didn't quite turn out to match the theory. When the fresh whitewash dried on the first crack we'd repaired, it only served to show up just how yellowed and dingy the surrounding paintwork really was. We'd never noticed it before now. And, so far, we'd whitewashed only one meandering patch of many.

'Bugger!' I grunted. 'The whole bloody wall's gonna have to be painted!'

Charlie, looking like Dusty the Miller's appren-tice, took a deep breath. 'Hmm, not good news, Dad,' he sighed, ably echoing his big brother's gift for the classic understatement.

Ellie kept her thoughts to herself, but her mind was clearly at work. Mine was, too. We'd been at the job for a whole day, and we'd only just completed the crack-filling work on one wall of the *almacén*. Only the first room, and still three-quarters of it to go! Then it'd *all* have to be painted – probably two coats – at least. And after that there'd be the kitchen, two living rooms, four bedrooms, two bathrooms and a toilet, to tackle. Two hallways, as well. I felt the wooden spoon of despondency starting to stir around in the pit of my stomach, and not for the first time since we'd bought Ca's Mayoral.

'We'll be at it forever,' I wailed. 'And think of the cost!'

Ellie's response was, on the face of it, hardly sympathetic to someone who imagined he was on the verge of having a nervous breakdown.

'It'll be all for the best,' she stated in a matter-of-fact way. Then, noticing the look of despairing puzzlement crossing my face, she adopted her usual kick-him-when-he's-down tactic by telling me: 'And you can forget your silly old whitewash. After a while it goes all flaky. Rubs off. Makes a mess. No, we'll buy good quality emulsion paint. Vinyl emulsion – the best. Just what the walls need to give them a *proper* facelift.'

'Oh, yeah?' I yodled. 'Well, let's just hire a firm of fancy interior decorators while we're at it, and we can all bugger off on a five-star Caribbean cruise for a month while the work's being done!'

'Good idea, Dad,' grinned Charlie. 'We've got a one-week mid-semester break coming up. Yeah, and another three weeks off school isn't gonna harm the educational prospects of a bright kid like me.'

'Button your lip, Charlie,' I muttered, resisting the temptation to give him a kick in the pants. 'Hobnobbing with those millionaires is giving you ideas beyond my station!'

I turned to Ellie and adopted an air tailored to appeal to her sense of reason. 'Come on, Ellie,' I implored, 'what's the point in us saving money by going through the drudgery of doing all this donkey work ourselves, if we then go and blow a fortune buying the most expensive paint?'

Ellie's deadpan expression didn't change. 'Because it makes sense,' she replied, following up with a characteristic little shrug of her shoulders, a sure sign that she was convinced beyond any argument that she was right.

'You're wrong!'

'No, I'm not.'

'But how the hell can it make sense to spend money that we can't afford to?' I was convinced beyond any argument that *I* was right. It was obvious. 'You don't have any grasp of simple economics – that's your trouble, Ellie.'

'I do. Adding value, it's called.'

'Yeah, yeah, yeah, I see what you're trying to say, but white paint is white paint, and nobody's going to know whether we've used cheap white-wash or expensive vinyl emulsion. Hmmph!' I snorted, appending a little derisory chuckle for good measure. 'Only a woman would see any sense in spending more than's absolutely necessary on a cover-up job like this.'

'And maybe only a woman would see the obvious difference in quality between a white-washed wall and an emulsioned one.' While I was trying to think up a nimble-witted answer to that, Ellie delivered the *coup de grâce* that I instinctively knew she would, and in suitably schoolmarmish tones at that: 'You only get what you pay for, you know.'

'That's right, Dad,' Charlie chipped in. 'Just like genuine Calvin Klein jeans compared to the crap bootleg ones *you* get at Andratx street market.'

Ellie saved Charlie from a certain kick in the pants this time by promptly reminding me of my recent, oft-stated concerns about the long-term viability of our little fruit farm in the face of impending competition from other Mediterranean countries in the European Union. If, as I'd hinted might become the case, we eventually did have to move from Ca's Mayoral to a bigger, potentially more profitable *finca*, Ellie's view was that it made complete sense to make the best possible improvements to our asset now, in order to realise the maximum price for it if or when the time came to sell it on.

'And there's no point in saying we can't afford to do it,' she added, nipping my anticipated objection in the bud. 'We simply can't afford *not* to.'

I could have argued the economic point 'til I was blue in the face, but it would have made no difference. What Ellie said did make sense; she knew it, and she knew that I knew it, too. We had already invested so much of our resources – financial, emotional and physical – in Ca's Mayoral that it would have been foolish indeed not to realise the full potential of every aspect of the property. But I wasn't about to concede defeat without attaching a proviso about the need for a measure of *some* financial prudence. I had my image as head of the family to uphold, after all, particularly in front of Charlie. But Ellie beat me to the punch again.

'Mind you, there's no sense in spending any more on emulsion paint than we need to,' she smiled. 'So, I suggest you call your old pal, Jock "Mr Fixit" Burns, and see what he can do for us.'

I ignored Charlie's knowing little smirk, and declared with all the self-assurance I could muster: 'You took the words right out of my mouth, Ellie.'

Even allowing for the fact that the walls and ceilings in the rest of the house were unlikely to need as much crack-filling work as in the *almacén* (it was a store/workshop, after all, and bore the scars of many years of use as such), we were still faced with a repair and redecoration job that would take us months to complete. The orange harvesting season, by far the busiest time of the year, would soon be upon us, so all this domestic DIY work would have to be fitted in as and when we could find the time. I regarded that as a double blessing, though. Firstly, after only one day, I was already fed up with this wall-patching business. It was obvious that Sandy and Charlie had also become sick of it, in their case right from the very first minute. And I suspected that even Ellie, for all her outward impatience to see the old place spruced up, didn't relish the task confronting us any more than the boys and I did. Spreading the job out, therefore, would serve to keep our periods of disgruntlement reasonably well dispersed.

Secondly, it would also mean that, rather than having to shell out for all of it up front, we'd be able to buy the considerable amount of paint needed in stages. In this latter respect, I hoped that the income from orange sales would eventually finance the interior decoration work as we went along, thus avoiding further unnecessary strain on our already over-stretched bank balance.

The situation we now found ourselves in is one that you don't legislate for when buying a property like Ca's Mayoral. Certainly, we hadn't bargained for it. Maybe that's because we hadn't employed a surveyor or valuator to give the property the once-over in the way that we probably would have if we'd been thinking of purchasing an equivalent place back in the UK. But that just wasn't the way in rural Mallorca. Your eye was your merchant, you did your own haggling over the price, you closed the deal and you took your chances. We'd had no problem with that. Granted, it would have been different if there had been a bank loan involved, but our policy from the outset had been to finance our Mallorcan venture, sink or swim, on what capital of our own we had available. However, that capital had already been dipped into quite a bit more than anticipated in covering essential but unforeseen outlays. Outlays like those involved in bringing the house's antiquated hot water system up-to-date, in renewing the electricity supply cable and internal wiring; in replacing clapped-out domestic appliances; in 'upgrading' the septic tank and ancillary plumbing; and in hiring Pepe Suau to administer his doctoring skills to our trees. Even the need to buy basic items of furniture, large and small, had been greater than we'd expected, having believed, until we actually took possession of the house, that we'd bought it from the Ferrers as 'furnished'.

The cost of crack-filling and house-painting was just one other surprise that we'd have to stump up for. But how many more expensive surprises like this would there be? This was the question I couldn't help asking myself at that moment. Perhaps it was an indication that I was becoming a touch paranoid about the thought of things always seeming to go wrong, just when everything appeared to be coming up roses. Then again, no one could deny that things *had* already gone significantly downhill in the few hours since I'd been sitting in the sunlit *porche*, relishing the promise of the new day, while sipping orange juice with the boys. I allowed myself to think about that – never the best of ideas when you're tired. Despite my better judgement telling me that it would do no good to overreact to this latest disappointing turn of events. I soon felt myself beginning to question once more the wisdom of having embarked on this whole Mallorcan adventure. After all, a millstone round your neck will still weigh you down in the end, no matter how idyllic the surroundings. Much as I wanted to check them, those familiar seeds of self-doubt were beginning to sprout again – ironically as it was, on this first day of 'winter spring'.

Then something happened to remind me of the fable of Robert the Bruce and the spider. Bruce, that great fourteenth-century king of Scotland, battle-weary, alone and being hounded by his enemies, had sought refuge in a cave, there to sink into deep despair about the apparent hopelessness of his situation. He was about to give everything up for lost, when he looked up and noticed a spider hanging from the roof of the cave. It was trying to swing from one position to another in order to anchor its web. Despite trying and failing in its efforts six times, the spider refused to give up, and successfully completed the manoeuvre at the seventh attempt. Seeing this as a favourable omen, Bruce snapped himself out of his negative frame of mind and, sure enough, he emerged from hiding to go on and achieve a heroic victory that would establish him as one of the most legendary figures in Scottish history.

My own uplifting portent was also to feature a spider. It was one of those gangly ones that looks a bit like a daddy-long-legs without wings. I was looking down at the floor of the *almacén*, glumly surveying the mini-desert of plaster dust and grit we had just created, when I noticed him scurrying through the litter, apparently making a beeline for a hole in the corner of the tile skirting.

Bonny noticed him, too. Quick as the spider was, she was on him in the blink of an eye, her puggish

275

face blocking his way as she took a close-up look at what, to her, must have seemed a very odd creature indeed. But the spider was clearly on a mission, and he wasn't about to have his journey interrupted by what, to him, must have seemed a very bad-mannered creature indeed, and a giant one to boot. He jinked this way and that, doing his best to dodge round this sniffing, growling, woofing obstacle. Bonny was a match for all his quick-footed moves, however, and easily barred his way with equally rapid sideways jerks of her head.

Like Robert the Bruce's little friend, my spider had six shots at getting the better of his predicament – all of them unsuccessful. But he didn't quit either, and finally made it at *his* seventh attempt as well. Side-stepping Bonny, he dashed towards his goal in the corner of the room as fast as his eight spindly legs would carry him. His troubles weren't over yet, though. Bounding in hot pursuit, Bonny placed a playful front paw right on top of him. That would be the end of the plucky little fellow, I reckoned. A shame. But, I thought, Bonny probably hadn't wished the spider any harm – just didn't realise the detrimental effect the weight of a sturdy young boxer like herself would have on a spindle-shanked little insect like him, that's all.

Fired by curiosity, Bonny lowered her head, inclined it to one side, pricked up her ears, tentatively lifted her paw and peered under it. The spider was back on his feet so quickly that Bonny, startled, jumped back, let out a yelp and sat down on her hunkers, leaving her quarry to continue his mad dash for the corner unmolested. The spider soon found that he had yet another problem, however. Those quick feet of his now added up to only five, his other three legs having been left behind under Bonny's footprint in the plaster dust. Nonetheless, despite his erratic progress over the floor now looking like the line being taken by two drunken sailors trying to run a three-legged race on an ice rink, the game ex-octoped finally made it to the hole in the corner of the *almacén*.

Witnessing this example of a puny little creature's dour determination to win in the face of such unequal odds, I was immediately inspired, like Robert the Bruce, to give myself a shake and get on with things. Why was I letting myself become so pessimistic anyway? 'Accentuate the positive – eliminate the negative', that's how those songwriters of old had put it, and so far, I'd never found their philosophies to be very wide of the mark. And neither, apparently, had my inspirational spider. 'Latch onto the affirmative,' the old Bing Crosby song said, reminding us of how 'Jonah in the whale, Noah in the ark' had pulled through. 'Spread joy up to the maximum, bring gloom down to the minimum,' the refrain went.

Ellie may have put her point a tad less lyrically, but all the more succinctly for that. Without further ado, I did as she'd suggested and phoned Jock Burns.

'One step ahead – that's what ye've gotta be to get anywhere on this island, by the way.' Jock had just pulled his car into a no-parking zone in one of the most heavily-congested areas of Palma city. 'We'll leave the jam jar right here,' he said, habitually dipping into his well-stocked vocabulary of rhyming slang. 'Handy spot for where we're goin', son.'

I pointed to the signpost on the pavement immediately in front of where we'd stopped. '*Prohibido aparcar*, it says. No parking, right?'

'Ye obviously weren't listenin' to what I just said,' said Jock. 'Just get outta the car and watch and learn, OK!'

'But you'll get a parking ticket – sure as hell!'

'Ye never said a truer word,' Jock muttered. He locked the car, had a swift glance about, then, whistling, casually sauntered over to a car illegally parked next to his and took the parking ticket that was lodged under one of its windscreen wipers. 'Now just walk away and don't look back,' he told me, while placing the ticket under one of the wipers on his own car.

'You'll never get away with that one,' I laughed. 'All the traffic cops need to do is check your car's number against the number on the ticket.'

'Aha, but ye obviously don't understand the thinkin' of the average polisman, son.' Jock allowed himself a smug little chuckle. 'They *don't* think, ye see – otherwise they'd never have joined the polis in the first place. Nah, nah, never pay too much heed to the minor rules and regulations, otherwise ye'll get nowhere on this island.'

We were crossing over Carrer de la Constitució, a busy city centre street overlooked by the imposing building that houses Palma's main post office, dodging our way through the endless stop-start stream of traffic.

'But whoever owns that car is going to get another parking ticket,' I yelled at Jock over the sound of impatiently honking horns and revving engines. 'That'll mean he'll have *two* fines to pay.'

'Two to him, none to me,' Jock shrugged. 'And they say us Scotsmen are mean?'

There was no point in trying to answer that. Instead, I had a quiet laugh to myself, marvelling at Jock's audacity and recalling another money-saving tip he'd once given me, a scam that shared the same quirky reasoning as the parking ticket caper he'd just pulled. 'Never get a puncture mended,' he'd advised me shortly after we'd bought our little Ford Fiesta car from his contact, the shady Enrique, up in the north of the island. 'Just replace the tyre, wheel and all.' When I suggested that, surely, this would be an unnecessary extravagance, Jock pointed out that a fresh tyre *and* wheel for the price of a puncture repair amounted to quite the opposite – an unbelievable bargain, in fact. How his scheme worked was as follows:

If you had a puncture, you just put on the spare wheel in the usual way, phone a certain number, ask for Pablo, mention Jock's name, and leave the car in a prearranged underground car park, one of several in Palma. All you had to do then was tuck an agreed number of one hundred peseta notes behind the front number plate. Chicken feed. Go and have a coffee or do a bit of shopping, and by the time you returned, the deed would be done. As the Ford Fiesta was one of the most common cars on the island, there was bound to be several of them in the parking lot, thereby making the wheel-swapping operation all the easier for his contact, and, consequently, cheaper for me. By the same token, the chances were that we'd get a much better tyre than the one that was being replaced. The same would apply to our little Seat Panda. *No problema*. It was just a matter of transferring your puncture to somebody else. Punctures happen all the time, after all, and if the loser in this particular lark happened to know Pablo's number, the chain would continue and everyone would win, including, presumably, the turn-a-blind-eye car park attendants. I'd never taken Jock up on this proposition, telling myself that the whole idea left too much to be desired ethically. Or maybe it was just that I hadn't had a puncture yet. Time and my conscience (or lack of it) would tell.

As you know, Jock does like his food. It shows, and he isn't ashamed of the fact. Even so, he can be surprisingly fleet of foot when the occasion arises; and what better occasion than when feeling a bit peckish? I was struggling to keep up with him as he cut into a side street called the Carrer Paraires, diagonally opposite the post office. If he'd been wearing a shiny helmet and carrying a hose, everyone would have wondered where the fire was.

'Come on, son,' he yelled over his shoulder, motioning me to hurry. 'Ye've never tasted Franks like the ones in this wee place along here.'

'Franks', I remembered, was short for 'Frank Zappas', Jock's rhyming slang for *tapas*, those renowned Spanish titbits that he found so irresistible. I got the impression that Jock had so many favourite eateries that, even if you blindfolded him and stranded him anywhere on the island, he'd be able to find one of his choice within a couple of minutes, just by letting his nostrils do the work. Without Jock leading me to it, I'd probably never have stumbled upon the Tapas Bar Pica Pica, tucked away as it is behind an unprepossessing facade in a back street that isn't much more than a lane, just one of a honeycomb of similar alleyways that interlink the multitude of plazas and squares in and around the *casco antiguo*, the 'gothic quarter' of Palma city. That said, the smells drifting from Pica Pica's open door as I hurried along behind Jock advertised its presence better than any flashing neon sign could have done. Frying onions, grilling prawns, meat balls bubbling in tomato sauce, chopped liver and sweet peppers stewing in gravy, diced potatoes basking in herby mayonnaise, battered squid rings sizzling in olive oil, garlic mushrooms. All of those wonderful cooking smells of Spain that never fail to tantalise your taste buds through your nose.

As he swept purposefully through the door, Jock was hailed by Antonio, Pica Pica's laid-back proprietor. It was obvious that Jock was a well known customer in this establishment. Antonio was stationed behind the cramped bar, casually serving *tapas* and drinks to a crush of eager clients as though he had all the time in the world. This apparently nonchalant approach to what was clearly a demanding task for anyone to undertake single-handedly turned out to be merely a mark of Antonio's professionalism, however. Typically, the bar counter was glass-fronted, allowing a clear view of the tasty fare of the day laid out behind it, each individual item displayed in one of a neat row of little stainless steel trays. There was a steady demand for everything on show, the anticipation shining in the eyes of the customers bearing ample testament to the quality of the *tapas* on offer. Antonio kept up a steady but unhurried pace, spooning the traditional small portions of food onto saucers, accompanied by a slice or two of crusty bread, a paper napkin and a special *tapas* fork, an ingeniously simple little implement made with one outer prong wider than the rest to act as a built-in knife. Meanwhile, Antonio also managed to serve whatever was being asked for in the way of wine, beer or coffee, and all without keeping anyone waiting for an order for more than a minute or so. This was service of the first order, being administered by a master of his trade. Even without having tasted the food myself yet, I was already beginning to see why Jock had rated it so highly.

The Bar Pica Pica was clearly popular with native Palmesanos, too. Yet it was little more than a corridor, the serving area recessed into one wall, with the floor space available to the public just wide enough to accommodate a few high stools at the counter and a single row of small tables against the opposite wall. The kitchen must have been tucked away at the far end of the bar, for hardly had the imperturbable Antonio exhausted one particular variety of *tapa* than an equally unflappable little woman in cook's overall appeared at a hatch in the wall with a fresh dishful of the same to replace it. Slick.

Jock took me by the shoulders and pointed me in the direction of a table being vacated by two briefcase-toting men in suits. 'Grab that place *pronto*, Pedro. Ye've gotta be quick off the mark if ye want a seat in here.' He set about easing his way through the throng of customers lining the bar, then called over to me, 'And don't worry – ye can leave the orderin' o' the Franks to me, right!'

The arrangement suited me just fine. Who better to choose your food for you than a noted expert, after all? It was round about noon on a pleasantly warm October day, and shafts of sunlight filtered through the blue haze that hung in the air inside Pica Pica. It struck me as a not-unpleasant fog, composed as it was of appetising cooking vapours mixed with a touch of the roasty-toasty cigarette smoke that is a familiar constituent of the atmosphere in such no-frills Spanish bars. In this one, the clientele was predominantly male, as is very often the case. Judging by their attire, they were probably businessmen – shopkeepers and travelling salesmen, swapping trading gossip and discussing orders while sharing a snack and a refreshment to sustain them until lunchtime. The mood was one of animated conviviality, with not a suggestion of anyone being in a hurry to go anywhere or do anything other than what was occupying them right there at that very moment. This was an urban display of the *tranquilo* attitude that we had already grown accustomed to in the countryside, that quintessentially relaxed approach to life that is as much a hallmark of Spanish tradition as are *tapas* themselves.

A *tapa*, to translate the word literally, is a 'top', or a 'cover'. It's said in Spain that the edible *tapas* so popular today evolved from what were originally just small slices of bread which the proprietors of taverns gave to customers as a 'lid' to keep flies out of their drinking vessels. In time, this courtesy was extended to include a little complimentary bite of food to garnish the *tapa* – perhaps only an olive or two, a sliver of sausage, a nibble of ham, or whatever other inexpensive morsel happened to be available. This simple custom developed into the culinary-cum-social institution that *tapas*, and the places that sprang up specifically to serve them, have now become. Essentially, a *tapa* is the ultimate Spanish quick food, but, being Spanish, quick food to be enjoyed at a leisurely pace. It's a little *ración* of the freshlyprepared snack of your choice, to be taken between main meals, whenever your stomach and your fancy for a bit of informal company give you the urge.

The old indoor markets in Spanish towns and cities have had them for ages, and now even recently-built hypermarkets on the outskirts have *tapas* bars on the premises. These are little oases of clamorous calm, where shopping-weary husbands can stand at the counter, recharge their batteries and chew the fat, while their trolley-pushing wives haul the kids around and get on with the business of scouring the aisles and shelves for those essential 'offers of the week'. Not surprisingly, the recent proliferation of such shopping-mall boltholes has been greeted with mixed feelings – your own view depending mainly, I suspect, on what your sex happens to be.

But these days, instead of limiting their intake of *tapas* to a sustaining little titbit, more and more people are ordering a selection of *tapas* for lunch or even dinner. It can be more fun than the old-style three-course meal, simply because of the greater variety of dishes served in *tapa*-sized portions. In a good establishment, for instance, the only restriction on the choice available is the size of your appetite and, correspondingly, the depth of your pocket. In that respect, it's worth noting that, because of their increasingly trendy status, *tapas* bars are no longer the bargain eating places that they once were in Spain – unless, of course, you know which back streets to find the right ones in. Which brings us conveniently back to Jock Burns and the Bar Pica Pica . . .

I could see that Jock had made it through to the counter in double-quick time, and he was now engaged in serious debate with Antonio. Jock's eyes, followed closely by his right index finger, passed slowly over the line-up of palatable sirens tempting him from their lair behind the glass counter. Antonio merely shrugged occasionally and gave a lopsided nod of his head, while simultaneously busying himself with the task of polishing a few wine glasses. Crucial choices were obviously being made by my epicurean chum, and knowing Jock as I did, his inclination would probably have been to order up a goodly portion of every one of the dozen or more different *tapas* to choose from. Antonio's body language, meanwhile, suggested that he'd have no objections if Jock did just that, even if it made him sick. *Hombre*, business is business!

While these delicate negotiations were being conducted, I had ample time to properly take in the details of my new surroundings. My first impression of this being a no-frills establishment had been right. The tables and chairs were of the aluminium 'terrace-furniture' variety, the seats of the chairs cool to the touch of an overheated backside on a warm day, though sufficiently deficient in the comfort zone to discourage you from leaving your refreshed derrière resting on them for too long. This, to be fair, however, would be an essential prerequisite in any eatery of modest proportions depending for its profitability on the quick turnover of as many customers as possible. The floor and walls were tiled – plain and simple ceramic coverings, offering no pretence of anything remotely luxurious, but spotlessly clean and, like the aluminium furniture, easy to keep that way. Obviously, this was a well-run though unashamedly functional little place.

The only concessions to interior ornamentation, apart from Antonio's impressive array of mementos relating to Barcelona Football Club, were a few illustrated tiles, stuck here and there on the wall above the tables. These had slogans offering pithy, proverbial crumbs of advice along the lines of: '*If you are going to tell lies when eating fish, be careful!*'; '*Marry but once, regret a thousand times!*'; and one to cheer the liver of the dedicated tippler: '*To live a healthy life without drinking is not possible!*'

Jock must have noticed me smiling at this latter gem of optimistic reasoning. 'You better believe it, by the way,' he declared with a jerk of his head in the direction of the relevant wall tile. He was arriving back from the bar, balancing an array of little *tapas*-laden plates on his upturned hands and forearms. He gestured with his head again, this time backwards towards the bar. 'I've left the beers on the counter. You go and fetch them while I sort this lot out on the table here.'

By the time I returned with the two *cañas* (glasses of cool draught beer), Jock was already tucking into a helping of what I recognised as *boquerones*, the Spanish name for small anchovies, though not the heavily-salted slivers of the little fish best known in many countries as a decorative component of certain pizza toppings. In Spain, anchovies are eaten in a more natural state, and are so popular and affordable a treat that you'll find them in every supermarket, preserved in little plastic tubs of light olive oil spiked with a dash of vinegar. They're delicious, and their mild taste is the very antithesis of the tongue-stinging sensation imparted by their pizza-adorning cousins. In this instance, fresh *boquerones* had been lightly coated with seasoned flour, flash-fried in hot oil, then served immediately with a few wedges of lemon. Simple, but scrumptious. If you like 'whitebait', the northern European equivalent made with sprats, try *boquerones* Pica Pica-style, and be prepared for a pleasant surprise.

In addition to the *ración* of anchovies, Jock had limited his selection of *tapas* to seven, though

288

whether this could be credited to a sudden rush of self-restraint, or was simply because Antonio had momentarily run out of the others Jock fancied, I don't know. Suffice it to say that the *tapas* he had selected added up to quite a feast, and turned out to be an admirable representation of those that the aromas drifting into the street had conjured up in my mind's taste buds just a few minutes earlier. I thoroughly enjoyed every one – although, having shared each dish with Jock, I wasn't surprised to find myself coming a poor second in the quantity-of-consumption stakes. You don't just need a long spoon to sup with Jock, you need a turbo-charged one as well.

When all of the other plates were bare, one solitary meatball remained before us. Jock downed it and wiped up the last smudges of its gravy with a remnant of bread. 'Aye,' he burped, 'magic as the rest o' the Franks were, you can*not* beat the Carnegies.' He wiped his mouth with his napkin and got to his feet. 'Anyway, we've got paint to buy for you, boy, so let's go. *Nos vamos!*'

Good as his word, Jock had managed to get in touch with a contact who just happened to have a trade-discount arrangement with one of Palma's main paint wholesalers. Also, he was going out of his way to take me there, so that he could use his superior command of the Spanish language to make sure I got what I needed, and at an appropriately reduced price. I'd have been lost in more ways than one without his help today, so the least I could do was offer to pay for the *tapas*.

'No way,' he pooh-poohed. 'I've already taken care o' the Jack and Jill.' He brushed aside my objections as we headed for the door, but I still insisted. 'OK, tell you what,' he eventually sighed, shaking his head in exasperation, 'if it's gonna make ye happy, *you* can buy the fuckin' lunch.'

I paused in the doorway, looked back at the scatter of empty plates on our table, then I glanced at my watch. Just gone one o'clock. Raising a confused eyebrow, I said to Jock, 'But I thought that *was* lunch.'

Jock glanced at *his* watch, chortled softly, then gave me a schoolmasterly pat on the shoulder. It was the sort of mollifying treatment the class dunce would expect to get after he'd just failed a particularly easy exam. 'Naw, naw, naw, son,' Jock crooned. 'Ye're forgettin' where ye are again. This is Mallorca. Nobody even *thinks* about lunch on this island 'til well after two!'

Without Jock, I'd never have found the paint warehouse in a month of Sundays. On leaving the Bar Pica Pica, instead of turning left and heading back to where he'd parked his car, he turned right and hoofed it farther and farther into the city through a confusing maze of streets. Although I assumed he couldn't be hungry so soon after consuming an elephant's sufficiency of *tapas*, Jock set a cracking pace. I was struggling to keep up once again. He had a few other 'business' calls to make in the city as well, he told me when I asked him what his hurry was. Time was money, he reminded me. Fair enough, but my growing concern was that, the farther from his car we tramped, the farther we'd have to carry the heavy tins of paint once we'd bought them. When I put that point to Jock, his response was to inform me that I thought too much. The time to worry about a problem was when a problem arose, and not before – that was Jock's firm opinion. We trudged on, Jock in the lead, the thinker panting along a few paces behind.

Jock cuts quite a dash when in full flight like this, his imposing physique causing oncoming pedestrians of lesser corporal mass to stand aside and let him through. Jock is well aware of this, and he loves it, acknowledging such subordination with flamboyant greetings in mid-Atlantic jive-talk as he sweeps through. I've even known side-stepping old Mallorcan ladies, startled and confused as they were, attempt to return his seemingly-chivalrous salutations verbatim. Salutations like, 'Show me it, baby!'; 'Gee, what a fandango!'; or even, 'Wow, cool castanets, granny!' His awareness of a one-man audience tagging along behind only served to encourage such incurable exhibitionism, and – so far – Jock had got away with it without being handbagged.

On this occasion, he was so fired up with back-handed bonhomie that he even gave the treatment to a policeman marooned on traffic point duty in the middle of a busy intersection. 'Hey, *coño!*' he shouted over from the pavement as we strode on our way. The policeman looked over, his frown of puzzlement revealing that he hadn't a clue who this grinning, waving character was. Jock then proceeded, at the top of his voice, to cheerily ask the cop in Spanish how his wife and kids were, and suggested that he'd meet up with him soon for a drink. All this without breaking his stride. The policeman, obviously fazed, and not wishing to appear ill-mannered to someone he thought that he maybe *should* have recognised, took his mind off the job for just long enough to reply with a nod of his head and a weak smile. The result was a near multiple pile-up. To the sound of horns blaring and brakes screeching, Jock wheeled smartly into an alley and continued on his route march, giggling like a schoolgirl. As his long-suffering wife Meg once told me, when he's in this mood, you have to be prepared to go everywhere twice with Jock – the second time to apologise.

When we eventually arrived in the one-way street where the paint store was located, I imme-diately saw one obvious reason why Jock hadn't brought his car. The narrow thoroughfare was clogged solid – cars and vans parked on both pavements, some even double parked, making it absolutely impossible for other vehicles to get past. Those drivers waiting to get through, mainly van-deliverymen well accustomed to such grid-locks in Palma's backstreets, displayed that uniquely Spanish quality of sangfroid that allows them to sit for several minutes, elbow out of the window, cigar in the corner of the mouth, the only sign of impatience a little drumming of their fingers on the steering wheel. Then, as if being cued by the baton of some heavenly conductor, merry hell breaks loose as all of them, in unison, suddenly start thumping their horn buttons and yelling foul abuse at everyone and no one in particular. This ritual lasts for about half a minute, then silence settles once more upon the traffic jam.

There was something of a jam inside the paint store, too. A line of waiting customers stretched from the door all the way to the counter. Showering pleasantries on them all as he walked purposefully onwards to one of the four men who were serving, Jock then confidently introduced himself as the visiting president of some spurious American paint company or other, and duly demanded to see the manager.

'Confidence, son,' Jock mumbled to me out of the side of his mouth. 'That's what ye need – confidence.'

A minute later, we were not only sitting in the manager's office, but were being offered coffee by him as well. Graciously declining this courtesy, Jock then poured out an ad lib spiel in broken Spanish, delivered in a 'deep-south' American drawl – of sorts. He had obviously borrowed the accent from the cartoon rooster Foghorn Leghorn, punctuated as his patter was with a liberal peppering of fractured phrases, linked with an occasional 'Ah say!', and all ending in 'Boy!'. I'm sure the manager couldn't have understood much more of what Jock was prattling on about than I did, but he smiled patiently all the same. Once Jock was satisfied that he had the poor man suitably confused, he presented him with the trade-discount card his contact had lent him, then grabbed a piece of paper and scribbled down what I noticed was my name and address. Polite farewells were exchanged, and we made our way past that same line of waiting customers we'd passed on our way in only a few minutes before.

'No point in hangin' about like that when ye don't need to,' Jock muttered to me as he smiled his goodbyes to the glum group. 'Life's too fuckin' short, son. Yeah, and you better believe it, by the way.'

With that, we were on the march again, mission accomplished, and apparently retracing, more or less, the route we'd just taken. There was one small complication, however.

'Ehm, not to split hairs or anything,' I hesitantly said to Jock.

'Aye, aye – spit it out then. What's yer problem?'

'The paint.'

'What about the paint?'

'Well, as I say, I don't want to nit-pick or anything, but . . .'

'But what?'

'Well, it's just that . . . it's just that we don't appear to have any.'

Jock gave a self-satisfied little chuckle. 'It'll be at your place tomorrow. Free delivery – fifty percent discount – best o' vinyl emulsion – pay the driver – *no problema*.' He then flashed me one of his winks of near masonic intimacy. 'Hey!' he grinned, 'ye didn't think I'd be daft enough to go to the bother of doin' that big performance in there just to talk myself into helpin' ye lug two fuckin' twenty-litre drums o' paint halfway across Palma, did ye?' He smacked the back of his head, then proudly declared, 'Brass neck – that's what ye need to get anywhere on this island!'

'And you better believe it,' I told myself by way of a slightly bleak benediction to that.

Ten minutes later, I was lost again and trailing along behind Jock like a pup on a string. After a brief visit to a printing works to order tickets for a Saint Andrew's Day celebration he was organising, he had taken a series of zigzag shortcuts from a street I didn't recognise, finally arriving outside a tall building in yet another busy street I'd never clapped eyes on before. This was where his agent had his office, he informed me.

'Agent?'

'Yeah, the guy who books my private gigs – extra to the resident spot at the hotel in Palma Nova, like. You know, weddings, christenings –'

'Bar mitzvahs?' I offered, anticipating the obvious.

'Aye, them as well. Funerals, divorces, anything. They're all nice wee earners, see. So,' he shrugged, 'have keyboards, will travel.'

Another ten minutes later, we were in a lift, descending from the third floor where the musicians' booking agency was located. Jock had concluded his business in customary quick time, and was looking particularly pleased with himself. Several new 'nice wee earners' had just been entered into his engagements diary. There was a mischievous smile on his lips, and an ominous twinkle in his eyes. His bonhomie buzz of earlier had clearly returned – but, I suspected, with a wicked twist. I wasn't wrong . . .

Facing us as the lift doors opened on the ground floor was a priest, accompanied by two nuns. The priest, a pious-looking old gentleman, whose corvine features ideally complimented his long black robes, was wearing true-to-type rimless specs on the end of his nose. To the sound of the plumage-like rustling of starched cloth, he shepherded the nuns aside to let us out. I exited first, returning the demure smiles of the holy sisters with a suitably reverential, '*Muchas gracias, señoras.*' At the same moment, something prompted me to look behind me, and I caught a glimpse of Jock flicking a tiny object into the corner of the lift with his foot. He then discreetly stood on whatever it was and advanced into the lobby, offering the ladies and gentleman of the cloth a genial, '*Vaya con Dios*,' meaning (appropriately enough, as I thought), 'God be with you'. Unfortunately, the moment they entered the lift and pressed the button to close the solid metal doors, the fate of the godly trio was already sealed. Not even the mightiest of divine company could help them now.

As the lift rattled upwards, we could hear a series of chokes and retches echoing down the shaft. There followed an outpouring of Spanish religious phrases, which, in this case, were delivered with such exclamatory potence that they were verging on the blasphemous.

'Holy mother of God!' one nun squealed.

'Jesus, Mary and Joseph!' the other gasped.

'God have mercy on you!' the padre gurgled.

'Oh-h-h-h, spare us, for *Christ's* sake!' the nuns wailed in chorus.

Then, just as the now-panicky voices were ascending out of earshot, we heard the priest roar, 'WHO, IN THE NAME OF THE BLESSED VIRGIN, DROPPED *THAT* ONE?'

I could only try to visualise the ungodly thrust and counter-thrust of accusation and denial that must then have followed inside that ill-fated metal box. I glanced at Jock. He looked as if he was about to explode. His face was purple, the veins on his temples standing out like bloated earthworms, his eyes streaming tears. He was in the grip of one of those fits of laughter that's so overpowering you can't even breathe, never mind produce mirthful vocal sounds. It's all you can do to stop peeing yourself.

'You!' I said, trying to emulate Jock's occasional schoolteacher's tone myself now. 'It was you, wasn't it? It was *you* who dropped one in the lift – just before you got out!'

'Aye,' he wheezed in a sobbing treble, struggling for breath, his chest heaving. 'Yeah, I dropped one right enough.' He reached into his pocket and brought out a blister-pack of little glass phials. 'One o' them!'

I read the zany print on the pack: '*FARTEX-PLUS . . . Stink Bombs for the Connoisseur*'. Jock, it transpired, had confiscated these '*Atomic Pong Pellets*', as they were subtitled, from one of his junior pupils at school. Instead of doing what *might* have been expected from a senior member of staff, he had recognised the practical-joke potential the bombs presented, and, accordingly, had consigned them to his pocket instead of to the dustbin.

'Talk about nuns and priests with dirty habits!' he sniggered, once he'd regained his breath and we were on the hoof again. Beside himself with schoolboy-like glee, he nudged me, the look on his face indicating that another stimulating thought had sprung to mind. 'Yeah,' he declared, only just managing to stem his hysterical tittering for a moment, 'and the beauty of it is this – whoever goes into that lift when it stops isn't

298

gonna know which one of the holy trinity the crappin' culprit is either!'

Jock was still giggling when we eventually emerged from a warren of back alleys into a street that I did recognise. It was what used to be called the Borne (pronounced 'Bornay'), but, with the recent Mallorcanisation of street names, now prides itself with the much grander-sounding title of Es Passeig dels Born. Running inland from Palma's palm-fringed harbour area, the Born follows what was once the bed of La Riera, a capricious seasonal river which had caused many a municipal disaster when in spate, until rerouted four centuries ago to its present course outside the old city walls. The Born is arguably the most striking of Palma's many handsome avenues, a wide boulevard with a magnificent, tree-shaded central promenade running its entire length, from the Plaça de la Reina at the seaward end to the Plaça Rei Juan Carles Primero at the hub of the city's bustling commercial area. Boasting many of Palma's more impressive buildings in the classical Spanish style of architecture, it follows that the Born is also the location of some of the most exclusive and expensive shops in town. It's hardly the sort of neighbourhood in which you'd expect to find a cut-price eating place. But Jock knew of one, and he led me directly to it.

'Half-past two,' he said, without even bothering to look at his watch. 'Time for a spot o' lunch.'

Despite its position directly on the Born, the

Restaurante Yate Rizz has a frontage so incon-spicuous that, if you didn't know it was there, you'd probably walk right on by, concentrating, as you invariably would be, on not being jostled from the narrow pavement into the path of the nose-to-tail procession of traffic racing by. Displayed in a little glass-fronted cabinet by the door was a hand-written card detailing the *menú del día*, the fixed-priced 'menu of the day' which every Spanish restaurant is obliged by law to provide, in addition to any more-expensive *à la carte* fare that may be on offer. In this case, however, the *menú del día* appeared to be *all* that was on offer. But even at that, the management hadn't skimped on choice, with a list of three starters, four main courses and two sweets to pick from. And all this, including wine, for about the price of a bowl of soup in most other restaurants in the vicinity. This, after all, is one of the smartest addresses in Palma, so when you eat out here you expect to be charged accordingly. I wondered what Jock was leading me into.

The interior of the Yate Rizz is small, and not at all luxury-yacht-like, as a rough translation of its name might imply. The general air could best be described, in fact, as one that suggests a history of tender, loving laissez-faire. For, although the décor is on the dingy side of jaded, and the leatherette-covered bench seats look as if they've cushioned a tad too many bottoms in their long lifetime, the atmosphere is inviting and the welcome warm. To Señora Rosita, the quietly-attentive proprietrix, running this modest little eating place with her chef/husband Miquel is obviously a labour of love. Why else, I wondered, would they persist with the task of providing meals at backstreet prices in such a prestigious location as the Passeig dels Born? And their clients clearly weren't concerned about the premise's need of some refurbishment. The room was crowded with people, who, judging by their well-heeled appearance, were probably Yate Rizz regulars who worked in the fashionable shops and the many offices of important civil and commercial organisations nearby. Not by chance, I was to discover, had this little family business become something of an institution in Palma since it was first opened back in 1937.

'Bloody starvin',' Jock grunted as we sat down. 'All that trudgin' about.' He quickly scanned a copy of the menu Rosita had handed him.

'All that trudgin' about' had sharpened my appetite, too, despite having shared that mini-banquet of *tapas* less than a couple of hours earlier. Keeping up with Jock on the hop is one sure-fire way of burning off the calories, and I was now ready, willing and feeling surprisingly able to tackle this 'second lunch' of the day.

As ever, Jock saved me the trouble of deciding what to order. And, true to form, his choice of dishes proved to be faultless. *Escudella Fresca*, a filling soup of field-fresh vegetables, was followed by a main course of *Rauols de Jonquillo*.

Jonquillos, Jock explained, assuming his class-room mien once again, are the small fry of a minuscule fish with the slightly uninviting name of 'transparent goby', or *chanquete* in Spanish. An increasingly rare and, therefore, expensive delicacy, the *jonquillos* had been formed into little pancakes (*rauols*) with a sympathetic blend of herbs and garlic, then shallow fried in olive oil until golden-brown on both sides.

'Sensational,' was the best word that I could think of to describe them.

'*Absolutamente fabulosísimo!*' was the more worthy-sounding compliment Jock beamed up at Señora Rosita when she came to clear away our empty plates. He winked at me, smacked his lips, then, in case I hadn't understood, uttered a somewhat less swashbuckling Scottish equivalent: 'The wee fishies – magic, eh!' Undeniably true as this was, Jock's stomach was soon making its low-satisfaction threshold apparent again. Like moths to a flame, his eyes were drawn to what a group at the next table were eating. 'Hmm,' he sighed, 'mind you, maybe I should have gone for the pork chops instead. Or even the ham omelette there. Chips and everything. Yeah, and those stuffed peppers look fab.'

By this time, I felt about as stuffed as the peppers looked, so Jock's lingering hunger pangs were treated to the bonus of two sweets, his own *flan* (that delicious Spanish version of *crème caramel*), and my fruit salad. He reneged on a coffee and mints, however.

302

'Moderation in all things, son,' he told me, muting a belch behind the palm of his hand. 'Now, let's get the hell outta here. I've got a lot to do before dinnertime!'

I felt almost embarrassed handing Señora Rosita the small amount of money that covered the bill. It was a mark of Jock's considerate nature that he had purposely picked such a value-for-money lunch venue when he knew I'd be paying. After taking so much time and trouble to do me the paint-buying favour, he'd have been entitled to expect a more expensive reciprocation. Instead, he was happy to be treated to a feed that probably cost me less than he'd paid for our *tapas* earlier. And I've no doubt that Jock had had this all neatly worked out long before we'd set out that morning. He'd certainly planned our itinerary methodically, for it was only a short walk round the corner from the Yate Rizz to where he'd left his car, illegally parked, almost three hours earlier. It was still there, complete with the same 'borrowed' parking ticket on the windscreen. With a surreptitious look about, Jock removed the ticket and quickly got into the car.

'What a jammy bugger you are, Jock!' I laughed.

'Fortune favours the brave, son,' he cockily replied, a broad grin of self-satisfaction dimpling his chubby cheeks.

Just then, an attractive but harassed-looking Spanish girl in an open-top Mercedes sports car drove up and prepared to pull into the no-parking place that Jock was pulling out of. He rolled down his window and handed her the parking ticket.

'Have this one on me, honey,' he drawled, reverting to his mid-Atlantic persona. 'And hey, did anybody ever tell ya what a great setta melons ya have there, baby? Wow, talk about a bumper harvest!'

The girl, a total stranger, looked suspiciously at the ticket for a moment, glanced even more suspiciously at Jock, then, the penny finally dropping, replaced her worried frown with a melting smile. She blew Jock a kiss. '*Mmm, muchas gracias, guapo,*' she purred as she steered the Merc towards the pavement. '*Moo-oo-chee-ee-eesimas gracias, eh!*'

Driving away into the stream of traffic, Jock turned to me and smugly declared, 'Like yer man in the song said – spread joy up to the maximum, bring gloom down to the minimum.' He threw his head back and let rip with a blast of laughter. 'Yeah, a sense of humour – that's what ye need to get anywhere on this island, by the way!'

CHAPTER 10

GATHER YE ROSEBUDS WHILE YE MAY

T here isn't a rainy season as such in Mallorca – not, at any rate, in the sense that there's a period when it's guaranteed to be wet for any great length of time. But autumn *is* noted for the inevitability of the occasional storm, and some are liable to be just as spectacular as the one we'd witnessed recently. October, then, is reckoned to be the rainiest month of the year, at least according to the old agricultural almanac, which goes so far as to confidently predict that:

> *'In this month, the rainfall equals or exceeds the evaporation, so that, by the end of the month, there can be a small reserve of water in the soil.'*

This is good news for the farmer, because it means that the time-consuming chore of irrigating the land is almost over for another year.

Yet watering the trees twice daily was a reputedly tedious job that I'd become used to, and had actually grown to like, in a perverse sort of way. The way I saw it was that there wasn't much to complain about in having to sit on a plastic fruit crate in the shade of an orange tree for an hour or two, watching the day go by while a hosepipe does all the work. Admittedly, I did have to drag myself up every so often to move the end of the hose a few paces from the trench round one tree to the trench round another, but that was a hardship I'd forced myself to cope with. I'd even worked out a system whereby I only needed to shift my sit-upon crate once in each block of twenty-five trees, and in this respect, making the effort to make things as effortless as possible was one new challenge I'd ultimately found myself revelling in. So, although easing myself into the *tranquilo* ways of the Mallorcan country folk had been difficult at first, I felt I had made significant progress – albeit *poco a poco*, little by little.

'You should install one of these new-fangled drip-irrigation systems, *amigo*.' This was the opinion of Gabriel, the ever-helpful owner of the Ferretería Capri, along the coast in Peguera. As well as being the owner of this busy hardware store, Gabriel also had a *finca* of his own, down between Andratx town and Port d'Andratx. Coming from a long line of local farmers, he knew what he was talking about in matters agricultural.

I'd been buying some nails and other odds and ends one day, when the topic of irrigation came up during the lengthy chat about this and that which is an inescapable feature of visits to Gabriel's store. He took me out to the pavement, which he used as an overflow display area, and showed me the basics of just such a system as the one he'd recommended – coils of micro-gauge black plastic piping, bundles of little nozzles and a few gate valves. All I'd have to do, Gabriel enthused, was run a network of overhead piping throughout our orchards, provide each tree with a couple of down-pipes with drip nozzles on the end, open the valves and let water pressure and gravity do the rest. *Coño!* he gushed, I'd never have to heave heavy hoses about ever again. The system was totally automatic, he reminded me, *and* it would result in much more efficient use of our precious water than the old-fashioned way I was doing things at present. Raising a finger to stress the point, he added, '*Hombre*, and just think of the other things you can do in all that extra time you will have on your hands.'

Apart from the considerable cost that would be involved in following Gabriel's advice, the idea of modernising one thing in order to release time to do *more* work seemed diametrically opposed to the whole concept of *tranquilo*ness to me. After all, I wasn't exactly flogging myself to death sitting on a fruit crate under an orange tree, as prescribed by my present irrigation method. I put this to Gabriel.

'No, no, no, *amigo!*' he laughed. 'I wasn't talking about saving time to do more *work!*' He gave my shoulder a playful thump, then added, '*Coño*, I was talking about giving you more time to go and sit in bars like everyone else!'

For all that I realised that there was a fair element of tongue-in-cheek in what Gabriel said, I was still relieved to be reassured that the Mallorcan work ethic I'd grown to admire wasn't being totally undermined by technical progress. I thanked Gabriel and told him I'd think seriously about his suggestion – once I'd seen how our finances were shaping up at the end of the forthcoming orange harvest.

Tree-watering during the summer hadn't only given me the opportunity to soak in the placid ambience of the valley, and to savour, undisturbed, the serenity of the surrounding mountains morning and evening, it had also helped me build an ever-closer bond with Bonny, our young dog. Playing with the water as it spouted from the hosepipe had become one of her favourite games, particularly during the hottest weather, so she had proved to be an entertaining companion during those 'lonely' irrigation vigils of mine. We'd known, since buying her as a little puppy ten months earlier, that we'd been lucky in that Bonny possessed all the best features of the boxer breed. She had a gentle disposition, loved fun, and was full of boisterous enthusiasm for life. She could also show a fearless side to her nature when the occasion arose, though not always, at first glance, in her own best interests.

Bonny, still essentially a pup, though a big and muscular one, had a knack of confusing mischief with bravado. She had already got on the wrong side of old Maria by repeatedly stealing her shoes, and while that habit was never likely to earn Bonny any harsher a punishment than a mouthful of threats and a near-miss swipe or two from our feisty old neighbour's hoe, the dislike she had developed for Francisca Ferrer's gang of mangy cats promised repercussions much more detrimental to her personal well-being. These cats were half-wild, mean-tempered, feline bandits; dustbin-raiding strays that Señora Ferrer, incurable animal lover that she was, had adopted over the years. Their deep resentment of us, interlopers in what they still considered to be their home, had been made obvious enough from the day we moved in. The arrival on their patch of a new dog, of all things, had only added further venom to their hostile attitude.

On buying Ca's Mayoral from the Ferrers, we had taken on the job of going over to their weekend *casita* twice daily during the week to feed their herd of cats and two dogs, when they, Tomàs and Francisca, were in their Palma 'residence'. It had seemed like the neighbourly thing to do at the time. However, the cats appeared to appreciate the favour much less than we actually minded doing it. Our arrival with a bucket of food at their den beside the *casita* was always greeted with a cats' chorus of hissing, groaning and malevolent wailing. They'd circle us like a pack of hyenas until the food had been ladled into the lily pond of old plates that Francisca had provided, then, the moment we walked away, they'd converge on the 'kill', snarling and spitting at each other as they greedily devoured it. But, ill-natured though it was, we'd always considered their behaviour fairly understandable. After all, they were only innocent little creatures who'd probably had a rough deal from humans before Francisca had taken them under her wing. The trouble was, though, that Bonny didn't understand these finer points of the matter. To her, they were simply cats, the dog's avowed enemy since time immemorial, and she took obvious pride in demonstrating to us that she regarded them as intruders on *her* patch.

It was a potentially volatile situation, exacerbated by the boys mischievously teaching Bonny to go into instant protect-my-territory mode on hearing them hiss, '*PUSS-SS-SSY CATZ-Z-Z!*' Bonny had come to react to the sound of those two little words as though an alarm switch had been flicked in her brain. One second she'd be sleeping peace- fully in the kitchen, the next she'd be out of the door, galloping over fields, clearing walls like a Grand National winner, heading like a bullet to the back of an outhouse adjoining the Ferrers' place. The shed's mono-pitch roof sloped down towards the wall which separated our two prop- erties, and Bonny knew that it was a habitual sunbathing spot for the cats. There was always likely to be at least a couple of those darned *puss-ss-ssy catz-z-z* dozing up there, and as the gutter of the roof was low enough for Bonny to reach with her front paws, a stand-off between natural adversaries was always the inevitable result. I've seen Bonny facing up to as many as six cats formed into a viciously grinning semi-circle, claws bared and swiping at her face, which she presented as a teasing, close-up, come-and-get-me target. As if this weren't sufficiently fearless (bordering on the foolhardy), Bonny would periodically stop her defiant woofing for a few seconds and take her eyes off the slashing sabres to look round and check that we were watching her performance. Yet, like her fellow exhibitionist Jock Burns, she had somehow managed, so far, to avoid a handbagging – in her case, a potentially bloody one.

A possible contributory factor towards the cats' untypical restraint was that Bonny never showed any intent of actually *harming* them – not that we'd have allowed her to do that, anyway. Nevertheless, as the months passed, we noticed that the size of the cat pack grew smaller and smaller, until only one of the original number remained. We never found out the reason why. Maybe the cats just decided that reverting to their old life of fending for themselves in the wooded wilds of the mountains was more attractive than being continually harassed in 'domesticity' by this canine gate-crasher. Certainly, Francisca Ferrer appeared not to apportion any blame to Bonny

311

for the demise of her group of little hairy disciples. 'Boanee-ee' was still Francisca's *favorita*, now even being awarded pride of place on her habitual 'floating' parades round her *finca* at weekends, her own two mongrel dogs, Robin and his mother Marion, having to be content with sullenly following in Bonny's footsteps, with the sole remaining cat bringing up the rear of this much-diminished procession. It now seemed that, for reasons unknown, the spectacular passing of Princessa, her hapless perambulating parrot, had triggered a sequence of decline in the numbers of Francisca's bizarre little menagerie. For better or for worse, though, replacements would be forthcoming. Of that we were sure!

Not all of our Mallorcan friends and neighbours shared Señora Ferrer's attraction to Bonny, however. Old Maria regarded her as a sneak-thief, Pep mistrusted her in the way that he did all 'mastiffs', and Jordi also gave her a wide berth, not being a 'fang', as he put it, of 'them damn baster bulldogs'. Even the postman and the young chap who called every so often with the bill from Pujol-Serra, the bulk-water-delivery company in Andratx, refused to come into the yard when they saw Bonny there. She had a quirky little habit of meeting visitors at the gate, then taking the finger-tips of one of their hands in her teeth while escorting them to the house. There was nothing malicious about it. She even did the same to us when we came home, and the touch of her teeth was so gentle that it wouldn't have bruised the skin of a grape. Nevertheless, the postman and the water man preferred not to gamble with their full complement of fingers. After Bonny's first welcoming nibble, they'd elected to honk their scooter horns out in the lane, then wait for one of us to appear and take their envelopes through the bars of the gate.

They needn't have worried, although I have to admit that, like all doting dog-owners, I believed Bonny to be much more well-intentioned in her ways than any stranger would be likely to. I didn't blame those two fellows for being cautious, though if they'd witnessed a scene that unfolded one late October day, they would never have doubted Bonny's temperament again.

It was after one of my final tree-irrigating sessions of the season, on a flat-calm evening, when it felt as though the valley had breathed a final sigh of relief for the passing of the oppressive days of summer heat and was contentedly drowsing at last in the soft cradle of autumn. Even Bonny seemed to know that this almost tangible peace should be respected. Instead of her usual rumbustious 'fighting' with the burst plastic football that was her favourite toy, she ambled along quietly beside me as we made our way home over the little fields. After passing through orchards already gloriously spangled with ripening oranges, I stopped for a moment in a place where the low domes of a few younger trees allowed an uninterrupted view of the encircling mountains. Thin threads of wood smoke were spiralling upwards from the forested slopes, marking the location of little hidden *fincas*, in which I could imagine families already sitting round their hearths, as if practising for those chilly nights of winter now being heralded by the shortening days. An owl hooted somewhere in the wooded distance, adding a note of eeriness to the gathering twilight.

The last rays of the setting sun were filtering through the orchard, weaving strange, shadowy patterns on the dusty ochre earth ahead of me. This was a new kind of autumn for me – an autumn that suggested the approaching season of nature's slumber in a way that I was accustomed to observing in the countryside of Scotland, yet that also bore tidings of an awakening of country things. I glanced at a nearby plot in which I had sowed some vegetable seeds just a few days earlier. Already the first tender shoots were venturing into the Mallorcan light, in which, unprotected by glass or plastic, the plants would flourish and grow to maturity during the coming weeks and months. Here was one small reminder, if one were needed, that we were a long way from those frosty Scottish autumns that I knew so well. This was, indeed, the island of winter spring.

We set off again towards the house, its white walls rising above the fruit trees and seeming to blush in the rosy glow of sunset. It was an entrancing snapshot of the Sa Coma valley that had remained essentially unchanged for centuries, save for the television aerial now jutting skywards from our rooftop, and the overhead electricity and telephone cables running over from their poles in the lane. But, I supposed, these were fairly insignificant scenic blemishes compared to the technological 'benefits' they represented.

I was startled by Bonny stopping suddenly and uttering a low growl. She was staring, ears pricked, towards a little gap in the drystone wall that divided our land from old Maria's. It was the same gap that Maria herself normally used when coming over to give us the benefit of her advice on whatever her chosen subject of the day happened to be, but although I could just make out the shape of someone sitting slouched there in the shadows, I could tell that it wasn't her. And so, obviously, could Bonny. This was someone with an outline much more bulky than the one etched by the old woman's slight frame. I saw the hackles rise along Bonny's back. She gave a warning bark and went through the motions of preparing to lunge off towards the shadowy figure.

'Easy, lass,' I whispered, taking hold of her collar. 'Nothing to worry about.'

I doubt that this half-hearted show of bravura instilled any more confidence in Bonny than it did in myself. She took advantage of the security of being held back, anyway, and strained against my hold in fairly convincing fashion, barking ever more bravely all the while.

'*Perdón*, Don Pedro,' the mysterious figure mumbled as we inched nearer. 'I did not mean to intrude. I did not mean to disturb you.'

Bonny immediately relaxed and began to wag her stumpy tail. She recognised the voice as that of Jaume, Maria's elderly son-in-law, who, despite her accusing him of being lazy, was in truth a conscientious manager of her *finca*, a general factotum who stoically did everything asked of him. The immaculate condition of Maria's fruit trees and the neatly-tilled state of her land were proof enough of Jaume's dedicated efforts, for all that they may have been undertaken at a 'steadier' pace than his pernickety old mother-in-law would have liked.

A big, portly fellow with an avuncular air about him, Jaume, now officially retired, had spent all of his working life as a waiter in one of Palma's swankiest hotels, and he freely admitted (though not in front of Maria!) that he disliked farming. Moreover, I suspected that he regarded it as a slightly demeaning activity for a gentleman of his former *profesión*. But, son of the valley that he was, he knew enough about local agricultural practices to have discreetly kept me right on the odd occasion that I'd asked his advice. Though still maintaining the circumspect manner of the old-style silver service waiter, Jaume's temperament was essentially a jovial one, and his gentle sense of humour was responsible for his having bestowed upon me the mock-lordly appellation of

'Don Pedro' the first time we met. He now employed the term as a matter of course, and I'd taken quite a shine to its status-enhancing sound, waggish though I realised Jaume's use of it was.

But there was something oddly downbeat about Jaume's demeanour this evening. Gone was the usual effusive ring to his greeting, and although his bowed head made it impossible to catch the look on his face, I could tell that something was amiss. Even when I reached his side, he didn't look up, but just sat there on the heap of fallen stones, his shoulders hunched forwards, one hand covering his eyes and stroking his forehead. Bonny, too, must have sensed that all was not well. Instead of barging forward to revel in the fuss of welcome that Jaume habitually lavished on her, she sat down a few feet away, gazing at him, her head tilted inquiringly.

'Ehm . . . *todo* . . . *todo va bien*, Jaume?' I said haltingly, realising after I'd come out with it that to ask if everything was OK had been a pretty clumsy opener. It was plain to see that everything was far from being OK.

Jaume didn't answer at first, but sniffed loudly a few times, removed his glasses, then reached into his pocket and brought out a handkerchief, which he used to dab his eyes. 'No,' he eventually replied, his voice breaking, his head still lowered, '*todo no va bien, amigo.*'

Bonny let out a little whimper of concern and cocked her head to the other side.

I didn't know what to say, far less what to do. Although I'd passed the time of day with Jaume often enough and was truly fond of him as a neighbour, I knew that I was still a relative stranger in his world. As much as I wanted to offer him comfort in his obvious distress, the risk of appearing forward held me back. I found myself in the grip of that inherent Scottish trait of emotional inhibition, of finding it difficult to be demonstrative enough to break the ice in sensitive situations such as this. The best I managed was to ask Jaume, totally superfluously in the light of what he had already told me, if there was something wrong.

He sat silently, staring at the ground, his fingers playing nervously with his lips as he fought to control whatever dark feelings were consuming him. My first thoughts were that something had happened to old Maria – that perhaps the grim reaper, whose scythe of finality she'd disdainfully avoided for so long, had finally cut her down. There was a note of real concern in the way I spoke her name to Jaume. I had already come to regard the old woman, crotchety ways, quirky foibles and all, as affectionately as if she had been my own grandmother. She was as much a feature of the valley, diminutive in stature though she was, as those towering, timeless mountains that now looked down on the sad little scene into which Bonny and I had been drawn.

To my relief, however, it transpired that my

318

anxieties were unfounded, for Jaume assured me after a while that it wasn't Maria who was the source of his grief. Looking up at me at last, he inhaled deeply, then let out a long sigh that seemed to dispel some of his anguish, at least for the moment. Even in the half-light of evening, I could see that the old fellow's eyes were red and puffy, his cheeks moist from recently shed tears. Visibly girding his willpower in an effort to put a brave face on things, he managed to pull himself together for long enough to explain that he and his wife had only returned a few hours ago from the mainland, where they had been visiting their son José, a soldier in the Spanish army. On arriving back in Mallorca, they had driven directly from the airport to the valley, their spirits high after spending several days delighting in the company of their two little granddaughters. But their euphoria was to be short-lived. When they turned off the lane, they noticed a car in the distinctive green-and-white livery of the Guardia Civil parked outside the gate of their *finca*.

Their immediate reaction, like mine, had been that some misfortune had befallen old Maria – a robbery, perhaps, or even a mugging. Nowhere was safe from such crimes these days, after all. But it was Maria herself who'd greeted them at the gate, and while she appeared less than her usual sprightly self, they could see that she was unharmed. And, unusually for her, though ominously for him, it was to Jaume, not her daughter, that Maria spoke first.

He was to prepare himself for a shock, she told him. One of the two policemen, who had been standing a few tactful paces behind the old woman, had then come forward to advise him that he was required to go with them to identify two bodies in the morgue at their Palma headquarters.

I noticed a little shudder ripple through Jaume's body as he paused to blow his nose and rub his eyes. He swallowed hard, fighting back the tears, finding it difficult to go on. Even if I'd been able to think of comforting words to say at that moment, I knew within myself that they'd have been inadequate. All I could do was stand there in inept silence and let Jaume take his own time to struggle with his emotions. It was only then I noticed that Bonny had moved closer to him, and was sitting at his feet, staring up at him, a pleading look on that expressive boxer face of hers. It was almost as if she was willing him not to be so unhappy. She gave another little whimper, catching Jaume's attention. With a sad smile, he laid his hand lightly on the top of her head.

'*Qué muchacha tan buena,*' he murmured. 'There's a good girl.'

It was a touching little cameo, and I couldn't help but be moved by it. Bonny's spontaneous show of sympathy also seemed to restore Jaume's composure sufficiently for him to continue his account of the evening's traumatic events. On the journey to Palma, the police had told him that, the previous day, two people had been found dead in a suburban apartment. The evidence suggested that they had been suffocated in their sleep by fumes from a faulty gas-fired water heater. I felt a shiver run up my spine as I recalled having read a report of this very incident in the *Majorca Daily Bulletin* that morning. According to the report, such tragic accidents, though relatively rare, had become a worrying occurrence in a country where so many households now depended on bottled gas. *Butano* canisters were a convenient and economic source of fuel, but all too often the gas appliances they were connected to were not given essential safety checks at regular intervals. The results, as in this case, could well be fatal.

Jaume lowered his eyes again, a hand raised to cover his trembling lips.

'It was my sister – my only sister. And her daughter – my niece Catalina. They were my flesh and blood, as dear to me as my own son and grandchildren.'

He spoke almost inaudibly, in a voice thick with grief. I could tell that he was trying his utmost not to break down, but after a moment or two his shoulders started to heave, and he buried his face in his hands.

'I could not let my wife and her mother see me like this,' he wept. 'A man should not be seen to shed tears.' He glanced up at me fleetingly and said, 'I am sorry, *amigo* – I had to tell someone, and I hope you will forgive . . .' His voice trailed away and he covered his face again, his pent-up sorrow finally erupting into spasms of silent sobbing.

I wanted to put my arm round his shoulders and to ruffle his grey, curly locks in the way you would when comforting a child. I wanted to tell him, as he had told me when I was in a state of despair on first learning of the poor health of our fruit trees, that, no matter how bleak things seemed at present, everything would be all right in time. But, once again, words failed me and self-consciousness stood in my way.

It was then that Bonny reminded me that dogs are not afflicted by such pitiful human inhibitions. Despite her immaturity, she seemed to instinctively realise that Jaume needed consoling, and she didn't hesitate to offer succour in the only way she knew. She snuggled into his side and rested her chin on his knee, gently licking the hand that he lowered to stroke her. Without need for words, she was saying more in these spontaneous little acts of understanding than I could have done with all the 'superior' means of expression at my disposal. I walked away with a lump in my throat, leaving Jaume in the care of Bonny's soothing companionship, and feeling humbled by this poignant example of a dog's unquestioning and selfless devotion to man – even to a relative stranger.

I felt somehow flattered that Jaume had chosen to unburden himself to me at a time of family bereavement, while at the same time ashamed that

I'd had to rely on a young dog to respond adequately. I had seen a rare quality of kindness in Bonny that was to manifest itself in many other ways during her life, though I'm sure that Francisca Ferrer's scattered *puss-ss-ssy catz-z-z* would always view her character in a very different light.

Unfortunately, not listed among Bonny's attributes was the ability to wield a paint brush. So, applying the white vinyl emulsion to the *almacén* walls was one task that had to be left to the humans of the household, and I fancy that Bonny was more than happy to lie out in the sun while we got on with the work indoors. But, with four of us on the job, the required two coats of paint were soon enough slapped on, and we were able to stand back and admire our handiwork at last.

'Seems too smart a place to use as a workroom now,' said Sandy, a glint of inspiration in his eyes. 'In fact, I reckon it'd make a better games room. I mean, how often do we use it to store fruit in, anyway?'

'He has a point there,' I said to Ellie. 'The way we do things, the fruit's sorted in the field as it's picked, and if we ever need to keep it overnight, we normally just stack the crates under the *porche*. Let's face it, this big *almacén* has hardly been used since we came here. A waste of good space, really.'

Charlie was quick to concur. 'Yeah, that's right,

Mum. We could have a snooker table and everything. Just like the O'Briens.'

'Nice try, Charlie,' Ellie replied, feet firmly on the ground, as ever. 'You forget that we haven't exactly got the luxury of the O'Briens' bank balance to dip into, however.'

Sandy wasted no time in contradicting that observation. 'A three-quarter-size snooker table won't cost that much. You occasionally see them advertised in the *Daily Bulletin* – people packing up and leaving the island – glad to grab at least a little *dinero* for the thing, rather than cough up fortunes to have it shipped out. They're heavy, you know – slate beds and all that.'

Ellie still didn't look convinced, so I reckoned it was time to feed her some of her own medicine. 'Adding value to the property,' I said. 'According to you, that's the name of the game, and converting this into a games room would do just that.'

'And a bar,' Charlie chipped in. 'We could build a bar over in the corner there.'

The whole concept was beginning to appeal to me more and more. 'And just think of the fun we'd get out of it, Ellie,' I urged. 'Fun for the boys, stuck out in the sticks here with the long winter nights approaching. It'd be really good for them – and us. Family unity and all that.'

'And with his own bar,' Sandy quipped, 'there'd be no need for Dad to go to the pub any more.'

'Absolutely,' Charlie enthused, 'and he could

even start his own brewery. Plenty room for that in here as well. Yeah, and another thing –'

Ellie held up her hands. 'OK, OK, OK – you've got me persuaded. We'll turn it into a games room, *if* you can do it on the cheap yourselves without hiring any tradesmen, and on one important condition.'

'What's that?' the boys and I inquired in unison.

'You are *not* starting your own brewery! I've only just managed to get the whiff of Francisca Ferrer's cats and dogs out of here, so I'm not about to have the place stinking of fermenting horse pee. I know what home-brew smells like.'

I said touché to that, while Sandy and Charlie dashed off to rummage in the dustbin for back copies of the *Majorca Daily Bulletin*.

Unwitting though it had probably been, that off-the-cuff suggestion of Sandy's became the turning point in our attitude towards our new life at Ca's Mayoral. Until then, we had given priority to being as frugal as we could in our outlay on the property, spending no more than was absolutely necessary on anything that wasn't directly related to the improvement of the orchards. Even Ellie's insistence that we should redecorate the house had been tempered by the proviso that the paint be bought at a discount. It was an outlook born of the dread of running out of cash before we had established (we hoped!) a worthwhile income by restoring the fruit farm to a state of optimum productivity. This cautious approach was sound enough in principle, but sticking to it chapter and verse had blinded us to the fact that, by investing carefully in non-agricultural improvements as well, we would not only be adding further value to Ca's Mayoral as a whole, but would also be maximising our enjoyment of living there. While not entirely having locked ourselves into an all-work-and-no-play way of life, our primary concern so far had been to keep our noses to the grindstone, trying to make ends meet, while conserving what capital we had for the proverbial rainy day. Sandy's inspired suggestion for converting the *almacén* into a games room had suddenly opened our eyes to the fact that it's possible to be just *too* cautious at times, with a risk of that very canniness being detrimental to the entire venture in the long term. As Jock Burns might have philosophised, why worry about a rainy day until one comes along? This was Mallorca, after all – the sunshine capital of Europe, so fling your umbrella away and make the most of it!

Perhaps, in a more sombre way, my recent chance meeting with Jaume had sparked similar feelings in me. 'Gather ye rosebuds while ye may' would be the proverbial version of the way I was now starting to look at things. We had dedicated our energies and limited financial resources almost exclusively to the farm since arriving on the island almost a year ago, and there was little more we could do to improve its cropping potential now, except to continue the regime of attentive husbandry that we had settled into. With more than a little help from our neighbours and, of course, Pepe Suau the tree maestro, we had survived, without serious mishap, our initiation into a hitherto unfamiliar way of farming. We had served the first year of our apprenticeship, had learned much, and had proven to everyone that we were serious about the fairly daunting task we'd taken on, and were determined to see it through to the best of our abilities. Much of what lay ahead for us now depended on luck, good or bad, so the time was right for shaking off the shackles of uncertainty about the wisdom of having taken such a gamble with our lives. In any case, there had never been any possibility of clawing back the dice that we'd thrown the day we decided to pack up and move to Mallorca, so why not now make the final commitment of chucking our entire stash into the pot? It wasn't a case of casting financial caution *totally* to the wind (our Scottishness would never have allowed that!), but rather a matter of ratcheting up the courage of our existing convictions, and, if fortune favoured us, having a damned good time doing it.

And so began what was to prove the most fulfilling period of our lives at Ca's Mayoral to date. It was also to prove the busiest. With the irrigation season over, the orchards had to be cleared for the last time of the garlands of weeds that continually grew in great profusion in the watering channels around every tree on the farm. Hundreds of them. Then it was a matter of ploughing the land, before cultivating and grading it to provide level and safe underfoot conditions for the hectic orange-picking season ahead. Sandy and I were only too pleased to share this field work, leaving Ellie the unenviable task of getting on with the crack-filling and painting of walls inside the house, aided and abetted by a less than enthusiastic Charlie at weekends. I'd never known Charlie appear so keen to sit in his room and 'study' on Saturday and Sunday mornings before, but trying to pull that lame excuse on Ellie elicited the reaction it deserved. If he wanted to enjoy the improvements that were being made to the house, not least of which would be the games room he had so zealously pushed for, he'd have to do his bit like the rest of us. And so, albeit reluctantly, he did.

Now that our somewhat overprotective attitude towards our bank balance had been relaxed slightly, suggestions for other lifestyle upgrades in and around the house were soon being keenly bandied about at the breakfast table. Each night's sleep seemed to nurture further ideas, the most fanciful (and potentially expensive) coming, not surprisingly, from Charlie. The effects of his mixing with the multi-millionaire O'Briens were becoming ever more apparent in Charlie's material aspirations. His highfalutin plans for items like his own private jacuzzi in the corner of his bedroom were summarily knocked on the head, however. As Sandy dryly observed, a sudden craving for a personal hydro-spa was rich coming from someone with such an avowed aversion to soap and water as Charlie.

An idea which did meet with universal approval, though, was one put forward by Ellie herself. A barbecue area. Not too exciting a proposition on the face of it, admittedly, but the way Ellie envisaged her proposal taking shape was attractively ingenious – transforming, as it would, a garden blemish into a spectacular feature, and with the minimum of outlay, at that.

The old wall, which ran along the laneside boundary of the farm nearest the house, stood a good three metres high, and had been constructed, no one knew how many centuries earlier, to carry mountain water along a channel built into its top to the ancient mill which the Ferrers had recently converted into their weekend *casita*. The wall was built of random rubble, unfussily faced with a dressing of honey-hued mortar, long since cracked and cleft by the combined effects of searing summer heat and flash winter rainstorms. But these imperfections only added to its rugged beauty. Swathes of ivy clambered all the way up the riven surface here and there, then tumbled back down in lush billows of variegated green and gold, interwoven with the flowers of wild roses climbing over from the other side. It was a gem of rustic Mediterranean charm, picture-postcard pretty in its unmanicured simplicity. Except for one thing . . .

In the most obvious spot, exactly where a path from the house emerged through the grove of pine trees that filled a wedge of land running up to the gate, an indentation at the base of the wall had been used as a rubbish-burning pit by the former owners of Ca's Mayoral. The evidence was an ugly fan of ingrained soot, spreading upwards and permanently tarnishing the wall's craggy face. Since there was no obvious way of removing the blemish, except by chipping away the affected area of age-old mortar, and thereby disfiguring the wall even more, Ellie's idea was to make a feature of the offending black smudge itself:

'Just build a big, chunky barbecue out of matching stone hard against the wall, with the grid for the fire placed directly under the sooty bit. A few wall lanterns dotted about, some discreet uplights at the bases of the pine trees – knock together a rustic wooden table and benches, and bingo! – this scruffy spot will be transformed into a really amazing place for outdoor eating on summer nights. Simple!'

Inspired as Ellie's concept certainly was, making it a reality would be anything but simple. Underground power cables would have to be run over from the house, the little clearing in the pine trees where she envisaged placing the table and benches would have to be paved, and the actual building of the barbecue itself would take some careful planning before a single stone was laid. Obtaining the stone, however, wouldn't present *too* much of a problem.

The ubiquitous *marès*, those biscuit-coloured sandstone blocks that have long been used to build everything in Mallorca, from humble pigsties to Sa Seu, Palma's magnificent fourteenth century Gothic cathedral, are still widely quarried on the island. One of the main sources can be seen quite clearly from the road to the town of Llucmajor, which bypasses the bustling resort of El Arenal east of Palma. The *marès* are cut from the bedrock with edges as clean as bricks of butter, making the quarries appear from above like volcanic craters in Legoland. We'd use relatively slim slabs to pave the dining area and access pathways, and also to form the basis of the barbecue construction itself. And if we bought directly from the quarry, the cost would be kept to a minimum. Getting rough rocks of a matching colour to give the barbecue the rustic look that Ellie envisaged was a different matter, though. For that, we'd have to rely on the Mallorcan countryside, and on the surrounding mountains in particular.

It was Frederick Chopin, the celebrated Polish pianist and composer, who, after spending the winter of 1838/9 in Mallorca, said that 'the roads [on the island] are made by the torrents and repaired by the landslides'. Although no one could fairly claim that to be the case today, torrential rain, when it happens, does create landslides in the mountains, and it was the rocks carried down by those that we were interested in finding now.

Sandy and I set out on an expedition one fine day after just such a storm, he driving the Ford Fiesta, I following behind in our Seat Panda. With the back seats in each little car folded down, we'd be able to load up with a reasonable amount of stones per trip – once we'd located a suitable source.

We took the road that corkscrews up and over the northern flanks of the Sierra Garrafa towards the village of Capdella. I'd seen this mountain road blocked by landslides before, so our hopes were high that there would be at least a small rockfall somewhere by the side of it on this occasion. As the road winds its way through a wide, undulating pass halfway to its highest point at the Col de Sa Grua, you drive between field after field of symmetrical rows of vines, planted in the 1980s by one of Mallorca's newer wine producers, Bodegas Santa Catarina, and located in perhaps the most dramatic setting of any vineyard on the island. I promised myself a tasting tour of their state-of-the-art winery one of those days! Sandy, indicating that something had caught his eye, pulled the Fiesta onto a flat shoulder of scrubby grass just a few hundred metres further on.

We were in one of those little mountain valleys so typical of Mallorca, where pine and evergreen oak cover the rising slopes on one side of the road, the land falling gently away on the other to where a lonely farmstead sits amid little fields of rough pasture, sheltered from winter winds by silver-green copses of wild olive. Just ahead and to the left of where we had parked, a small scree could be seen spilling out between the stout trunks of a huddle of carob trees, the fresh, red soil clinging to every stone a legacy of the mountainside from which it had been recently washed. We were in luck.

Getting out of the car, I immediately noticed an unlikely smell mingling with those familiar resinous scents of the forest and the accompanying mustiness of damp earth that always follows rain. It was the smell of hot tar. More typically, though, the only sounds to disturb the stillness of the mountain air were the wistful warblings of an unseen finch, and the tinny clanking of sheep bells. Without speaking, Sandy and I stood drinking in the serenity of our surroundings for a few moments, breathing in the soothing calm of it all. Just then, we heard the sound of men laughing. It seemed to be coming from the direction of a little dirt track that cut through the woods right there beside us.

'Probably some local shepherds,' I said. 'Maybe we'd better check with them before we take any of these stones, just in case we're trespassing on someone's land.'

As we made our way along the curving track, we could hear the men chatting happily in *mallorquín*. We also noticed that the smell of tar was getting stronger. The path eventually opened into a small clearing, where three men appeared to be having a lunch break. But they weren't shepherds, and their lunch wasn't of the usual packed variety that you'd expect to be eaten by men working in the mountains. These were roadmen, sturdy Mallorcans all, and they were having themselves a barbecue – but a barbecue with a difference!

Their flatbed truck was parked in the middle of the glade, as far away as possible from the surrounding trees and bushes. And the reason for the vehicle being thus positioned was clearly the glowing brazier on its deck. We could see, however, that the tar-melting tub had been removed, and a big cooking pot set in its place.

'Weh-*ep!*' one of the men shouted when he noticed us standing at the edge of the clearing. He immediately beckoned us, a broad grin on his face. '*Ay-y-y-y, ven aquí, hombres!* Come and join us!'

He was holding a bottle of wine in one hand, a dead hen in the other. With no hand left to shake ours with, he simply told us that his name was Felip, and introduced his two colleagues as Tomeu and Francesc. Antoni, the fourth member of his crew, was in the woods 'on a mission', he informed us, but would be back soon. Felip handed us a couple of empty jam jars from inside the cab of the truck, then poured us a generous measure of wine apiece. He went on to tell us that they were workers employed by the municipal council to go round the countryside doing routine road maintenance, including filling in cracks and potholes. Hence the brazier and tar bucket.

So, what was the reason for the celebration, I asked with a nod in the direction of the wine bottle and cooking pot.

'Celebration?' Felip queried, his chums joining him in a little chuckle. 'There is no celebration, *tío*. We are preparing to cook our lunch in the usual way, that's all.' He gestured towards the brazier, then added with a wry smile, 'If our employers supply us with a source of heat to work with, it would be a sin to waste it during our rest periods, no?'

There was logic in that, I thought to myself, wondering why the same notion had never occurred to Felip's counterparts in Britain, who were traditionally content to settle for a more passive workaday lunch of a few pre-made sandwiches, a packet of crisps and a bottle of Coke.

In contrast, Felip informed us that on today's menu would be *fideus*, the Mallorcan equivalent of thin vermicelli pasta, cooked with whatever ingredients the mountain had provided. As snails were an essential component of the recipe, Tomeu and Francesc had collected sufficient for their purposes after the recent rain – always the best time to find plenty of the little tabby-shelled fellows 'taking a stroll' up the stalks of the wild fennel that can be found growing in profusion by the mountain roadsides. The snails, Tomeu explained, were now in the pot, simmering in salted water on a bed of that same fennel from which they had been gathered.

A single crack of gunfire rang out from somewhere in the woods.

'Ah,' beamed Felip, 'that will now be *fideus amb conill* – *fideus* with rabbit. *Perfecto!*' He threw the hen to Francesc. 'Here, *amigo* – pluck that. We can roast it now that we do not need it for the pot.'

A stocky figure carrying a rifle, a dead rabbit and a small basket emerged from the cover of the surrounding trees.

'Antoni!' the three roadmen shouted in chorus, their faces wreathed in smiles.

'*Coño!*' Felip yelled at him, 'I see another suicidal creature of the forest has thrown himself in front of your bullet, eh!' Husky laughter reverberated round the glade.

Antoni pulled a self-congratulatory smirk, then ambled over to the truck and emptied the contents of his basket onto its deck. He pointed proudly to about a dozen amber-coloured mushrooms. '*Setas*,' he said, 'the first I have found this season.' He then lifted up a handful of accompanying greenery. 'And,' he nonchalantly added, 'some wild garlic, a bunch of thyme and a few capers for a touch of extra flavour.'

His mates instantly voiced their praise of his efforts. *Hombre*, this was going to be a lunch to remember!

Felip then turned to Sandy and me. 'You are

welcome to share our lunch with us, *muchachos*, if you have not already eaten. We do not get many visitors to our open-air restaurant here. Besides,' he winked, 'it would appear that the mountain has provided us with a little too much for just four bellies today.'

Thanking him for his kind invitation, I declined all the same, explaining that we'd only come into the mountains on a quick rock-collecting trip.

Felip shot me a look that left me in no doubt that he thought I need look no further for rocks than inside my own head. *'Rocks?'* he queried in a disbelieving falsetto. 'You have come all the way up the mountain just to carry *rocks* all the way back down?' He took me by the elbow and sat me down on the bottom step of the truck's cab. 'Sit there and be *tranquilo*, my friend. The rest will do you good.' He then exchanged a few words in *mallorquín* with his companions – words which I didn't understand, though I gathered from the chortles they induced that they hadn't been said in endorsement of my intelligence.

The laid-back Antoni glanced over at Sandy, who was standing at the opposite side of the truck, holding his jam jar of wine and looking a touch mesmerised by proceedings. 'Oy, *chico!*' the little hunter-gatherer called out to him. 'Do you know how to skin a rabbit?' Sandy's nod of affirmation saw the rabbit suddenly airborne and flying towards him. *'Bueno,'* Antoni grunted, 'rip the clothes off that one before he goes for a swim with the snails!'

Felip must have noticed me looking first at the rabbit, then at a sign nailed to a tree at the entrance to the clearing. Very common in the wilder country areas of Spain, the sign is in the form of a small square, divided diagonally in black and white, with the words *'Coto Privado de Caza'* ('Private Hunting Ground') printed below it. Felip raised his shoulders in the expected 'it's-no-big-deal' kind of way, and casually put it to me: 'How can any man, no matter how much land he has, claim that he *owns* even one wild rabbit?'

The hitherto taciturn Francesc declared his absolute agreement, then added, as if to reinforce the validity of their conviction, that they had come by the hen via the same 'law of providence'. He related how the stupid creature had crossed the road in front of them as they drove past a farm further down the mountain. That type of dangerous habit can only lead to one consequence; the hen would ultimately be run over and killed. By stopping and wringing its neck today, he reasoned, they had merely advanced the inevitable – *and* saved the hen from being squashed beyond use for the pot.

Felip nodded his support, flashed me an impish smile, then said, *'Coño*, if a fig falls from someone's tree when you are walking under it, you open your mouth, no?'

While these chaps had obviously massaged my recently adopted 'gather ye rosebuds' dictum to suit their own immediate ends, I couldn't help but admire their way of thinking. It was an outlook that would be hard to condemn – unless, of course, you happened to be the owners of the *Coto Privado de Caza* and the hen. But such debatable details weren't about to spoil lunch for Felip and his team of road-repairing stalwarts. The rabbit, duly skinned and chopped into bite-size chunks, was added to the pot with the other ingredients that the forest had provided. And while all this was stewing away gently, the hen had a long metal poker (its coating of solidified tar first bashed off against a rock) inserted scewer-fashion via its nether regions, and was spit-roasted against the red-hot charcoal embers at the base of the brazier.

The tantalising smells soon wafting around the clearing would have done credit to the kitchens of any five-star restaurant. And Felip couldn't have been more attentive to the task in hand had he been the head chef of such a fine establishment – regularly checking and adjusting the seasoning of the stock, while prodding the rabbit chunks for tenderness. When he was satisfied that the right moment had come, he instructed Francesc to fetch the packet of dried *fideus*, to break them into short lengths and immerse them in the bubbling liquid. A few more minutes of stirring and simmering had the pasta cooked to what Felip considered to be *al dente* perfection. The resultant steaming stew was then emptied into a big earthenware *greixonera*, which, once placed on a convenient tree stump, served as a communal eating dish for everyone.

I've had *fideus amb conill*, a popular item in many Mallorcan eateries, several times since then, but I can say in all honesty that I've never enjoyed the dish as much as on that autumn afternoon in the lee of Sa Grua Mountain. Perhaps it was the sylvan magic of the forest clearing, the background music of birdsong and sheep bells, or the invigorating scents of the mountain itself. Perhaps it was the company and ungrudging hospitality of our chance hosts, the knowledge that we had sampled, for the first time, a meal prepared *in situ* from ingredients gleaned from the surrounding countryside (with a little help from the gods of falling figs!), or maybe it was the tarry tang of the accompanying charcoal-roasted chicken. Perhaps it was simply a combination of all these things. I'm not sure, and to try and analyse why such impromptu occasions turn out to be so special is a pointless exercise, anyway. They happen so rarely that the best thing to do, if you're lucky enough to stumble into one, is simply to enjoy your good fortune and be thankful for it.

Sandy and I certainly felt a warm glow of bonhomie enveloping us as we drove away from Felip and his merry men later that afternoon, after they'd spent what should have been their post-lunch siesta sharing another bottle of their wine with us and unhurriedly chatting, as is the Mallorcan country way, about this, that, everything, and nothing in particular.

'Where are all the stones you went to collect?' Ellie demanded when we eventually arrived back in the Ca's Mayoral yard, the backs of both of our cars patently empty. 'And you've been drinking, Sandy! I can tell by the silly grin on your face. You're your father's double!'

Bonny, sensitive as ever to such predictable human outbursts, took Sandy's fingertips in her teeth and led him gently away towards the house, and safely out of range of whatever strife might be about to erupt back in the yard.

'Ellie, I would *never* encourage Sandy to drink too much,' I protested.

'Who said he needed any encouragement? Like I said, he's your double!'

The truth was that neither Sandy nor I had partaken of anything remotely approaching a law-breaking quantity of alcohol. Those 'silly grins' on our faces were merely a reflection of the feeling of goodwill imbued by the outcome of our fortuitous rendezvous with the municipal roadmen. I knew, however, that any attempt at explaining this to Ellie would be futile. Where, indeed, were the stones we had gone to collect all those hours before? The immediate arrival of Felip's truck in the yard could not have been better timed.

'I thought you were only going to build a barbecue!' Ellie gasped.

There was an undisguised note of smugness in my voice as I told her: 'The words gift-horse and mouth come to mind, my dear.'

'But – but there are enough stones on that truck to build a . . . a . . . a . . .'

I gave her shoulder a calming pat. 'Don't worry, I'm sure you'll think of something soon enough. Meanwhile, just content yourself in the knowledge that, as rocky as these rosebuds and figs may seem, they were gathered with our mouths wide open.'

Ellie looked me up and down in a way that suggested I'd just discharged from my person an odour evocative of a retreating skunk.

'Now I *know* you've had too much to drink!' she muttered. Rolling her eyes heavenward, she turned on her heel and marched resolutely off.

I was left standing there scratching my head, while a chorus of knowing chuckles emerged from the cab of the truck.

'Do not concern yourself, *amigo*,' Felip called to me through his driver's window. 'We have a saying: "He who can understand the mind of a woman has the secret of turning a mule turd into a nugget of gold."'

'Amen to that,' I thought, and started unloading the rocks.

EPILOGUE

PEACE IN THE VALLEY

As October drifts towards November, you wake up one morning, push open the shutters, and suddenly realise that Mallorca has changed. Even in the depths of the countryside, far from the tourist bustle of the coast, you sense a feeling of relief, and can almost see a smile of contentment on the face of the landscape. It's as if the very fibre of the island knows that the last of the hordes of holidaymakers who have descended on it during the past six months have now finally departed. Once more Mallorca can relax and can revert to being its old self, *la illa de calma*, 'the island of peace'.

For us, now that we were approaching the end of our first year in the valley, it was a time for reflection, a time to be grateful for the many good things that had come our way, and a time to laugh at those mistakes we'd made while taking our first, faltering steps in our new life. I suppose it's always easy to see the funny side of any mishap through the moderating vision of hindsight, but we had been truly lucky in that none of the pitfalls and minor disasters that we had encountered had done us any serious harm, or had created any irreversible setbacks. We were a year older and, if not a year wiser, then certainly a year more accustomed to the ways of our adopted homeland.

Even Ellie's linguistic gaffes in Spanish were becoming more rare, much to the disappointment of those of us who enjoy having a good giggle at someone else's faux pas. I personally hoped that she would still come out with priceless blunders like those that had involved her asking the butcher for a penis instead of a chicken, ordering a waiter's testicles when she meant rabbit, and wishing a haemorrhoidal fishmonger a happy new arsehole instead of New Year. And to her credit, Ellie always managed to laugh about these little 'slips of the tongue' herself – once she'd banished her blushes, that is.

For myself, the apparent waning of the mosquitos' interest in taking my blood to nurture future generations of tiny misery makers had me guardedly rejoicing. Could it be that, after a year of eating a Mallorcan diet, my Scottish blood had become sufficiently 'unexotic' to be no longer attractive to the local mozzies? I certainly hoped so, and it did seem that way. On the other hand, it could just have been that the incidence of *all* insects was on the decline due to the onset of cooler weather. I'd find out come spring, but for the present, I was bravely weaning myself from dependence on my trusty Calcutta Coils and plug-in chemical bug repellents, and enjoying the new

344

sense of freedom that came with it. I was also enjoying, most of the time, the feeling of relaxed fatalism that had come with our decision to adopt an all-or-nothing approach to making a go of things at Ca's Mayoral. I think we all were.

I mentioned this to Ellie one evening when we were wandering through the orchards, checking on the ripening progress of the oranges, and looking forward to fulfilling the first orders which we hoped would come in from the fruit merchants any day now.

'Well,' she said, 'until we made that decision, I don't think we'd *really* cut the old ties with the place that had been our home for so long. There was always the thought that, if we protected our nest egg, we could always cut our losses by bailing out and going back if things turned really bad for us here. But that way of thinking only created its own kind of pressure. Now that it's officially sink-or-swim time, I reckon we're all having fun staying afloat.'

'Yeah, even as a non-swimmer, I'm glad I chucked my water wings away.'

Although I said that in a devil-may-care way, I couldn't help crossing my fingers behind my back. Everything now rode on the income that would be derived from those very orange trees that we were strolling through now. But Ellie was right; doing things by half measures would only have postponed the evil day if our business as orange farmers did go pear-shaped. And whatever the situation turned out to be by springtime, we'd be far better off with a property whose potential we'd completely fulfilled, than finding ourselves sitting on a nest egg that, if the worst did come to the worst, wouldn't sustain us for very long, anyway. I uncrossed my fingers and donned my mental flippers. As a born worryguts, I knew that this would be a process I'd repeat ad nauseam during the coming months. The main thing, though, would be to outwardly accentuate the positive – at least in front of the family.

Since the adoption of the barbecue-building idea, improvement work inside the house had been left increasingly to Ellie; the consensus of opinion, at least between the boys and myself, being that 'heavier' outdoor tasks should take precedence while the weather remained good. The truth of the matter was that this was nothing but a blatant excuse for abandoning Ellie to the boring, but 'lighter', work of interior decoration. But she didn't seem to mind. It was better, in her view, to have all hands to their chosen pumps than to none at all. And in any case, she maintained, she could get on better with the scraping, filling and painting chores without having three moaning males constantly getting in her way. We agreed wholeheartedly and left her to it.

Despite every spare moment being devoted to creating the barbecue area, it'd still be a month or two before everything was complete. The underground cables had now been laid, though, and the various lights and lanterns installed. A start had also been made to slabbing over the 'dining' area, so things were beginning to take shape, and the transformation of what had previously been an eyesore was already looking good.

Even the surplus stones that Felip and his boys had kindly delivered were being put to good use in the creation of extra little features, which Ellie (as I knew she would) had dreamed up before the roadmen's truck had even left the yard that afternoon. A little rockery would look good in that corner, she'd decided – yes, and another one over there. Then there would be drystone retaining walls to set off some of the new pathways. Oh, and maybe, if there were enough stones left over, she could even get me to build some sort of water feature underneath the walnut tree by the west terrace. It would be, she thought, 'nice and restful' to sit there listening to the cool water tinkling over the stones of an evening. I agreed, although it was beginning to look as though it'd be a long time before I'd manage to find a minute to sit and be 'nice and restful' anywhere. Once Ellie got an idea into her head, it usually had to be implemented yesterday.

So, it was with even more pleasure than usual that I'd grabbed the opportunity to take this evening's leisurely orange-inspecting saunter over the farm with her. More welcome still was the sight of the orange trees, showing ever more evidence of the benefit of Pepe Suau's skilled surgery and the ensuing care that we'd taken over their feeding and watering. Just as Pepe had predicted, their rejuvenation after years of neglect had been swift, and although the trees may not yet have been carrying quite as many fruits, there was still a gratifyingly heavy crop weighing down their branches, with individual oranges looking far plumper and healthier than those of a year ago. The outlook for the harvest was promising, and we could have hoped for no more at that point in time.

A series of flickering lights drew our attention back towards the house, a couple of fields away.

Ellie clutched my arm. 'Tell me that wasn't lightning,' she whimpered. 'I wouldn't want to be caught out here under the trees in a thunderstorm. My worst nightmare!'

I patted her hand. 'Nah,' I laughed, 'just Sandy trying to connect up the barbecue lights to the mains, that's all. No need to worry.'

'*Sandy*? Elec*tri*city?' Ellie had gone all pop-eyed. 'He'll *kill* himself!'

'No chance. He's a dab hand at all that wiring stuff. Knows a helluva lot more about it than I do. That's why I left him to get on with it.'

Ellie shot me a look of shocked disbelief. 'You did *what*? But he's only eighteen! Too young to die!'

I shrugged my shoulders. 'Still knows a helluva lot more about all that electrical stuff than I do.' I paused while Ellie worked herself towards a state of foaming-at-the-mouth maternal protectiveness, then blandly added, 'Besides, he's got Charlie to keep him right if he's not sure about which wire's which.'

A shrill shout of '*HOLA!*' rang out just in time to prevent Ellie from having a fit, and saving me from having to admit that I'd actually hired Juan the Andratx electrician to do the tricky mains-connection work, his visit cunningly timed to coincide with our little wander through the orchards that evening.

'*HOLA!*' called the voice again, more urgently this time. We recognised the piping soprano of old Maria, but had to peer through the twilight shadows to see where she was hailing us from.

'There,' I said to Ellie, 'over there by our well, in the corner of the next field. She sounds a bit worked up. Better go over and see if there's anything wrong.'

'I need your permission to do something,' Maria shouted to us as we approached. '*Es importante!*'

'What on earth would Maria need to ask *our* permission for?' Ellie muttered. 'I wouldn't have thought she's asked anyone's permission for anything she's done in her entire life.'

'Men!' Maria growled the moment we reached her. Her little black eyes ablaze with fury, she was looking at Ellie, ignoring me totally. 'I have been waiting for that swine for over thirty years, and now he turns up and treats me like this! *Bastardo!*'

We stood leaning against the stone parapet of the well while Maria started to pour out her tale of woe, a love story promising to be painful in the depth of its pathos. Who could this cad have been, we wondered, and what had he done to upset Maria like this? She didn't leave us wondering for long . . .

Bartolomé Martí was an old flame of Maria's, who, like many before him, had left Andratx to go and seek his fortune in Argentina when still a young man. Maria had then lost contact with him, and had all but forgotten about him until he returned home for a brief visit thirty years ago. The embers of their feelings for each other could easily have been re-kindled when they met again then, but as Maria's husband had only recently passed away, such a liaison would have been regarded in the community as highly improper. Also, Bartolomé, a doggedly ambitious man, felt that he still had much work to do back in Argentina in order to reach the goals he had set himself. But, he promised Maria, he would return to her one day, a rich man capable of giving her things she had never dreamed of during her cloistered life in the valley.

'To cut a long story short,' said Maria, 'I never heard from him again until a few weeks ago, when he sent me a postcard saying that he would be arriving back in Mallorca today.' That, she divulged, was when she had retrieved from her bathroom cabinet the mug in which she had submerged her false teeth more than twenty years ago. It was only the top set, she pointed out, the bottom ones having been lost in the intervening period. But, she added with a little smirk of pride, after all that time sitting in a peroxide solution, those upper dentures glittered like little pearls.

Politeness prevented me from telling her that they were so glittery, in fact, that they'd nearly dazzled us blind the first time we saw her coyly trying them out. I recalled that old Pep, too, had been fazed almost to the point of emigration by the sight of them.

Maria's eyes glinted with rage again as she hissed, 'And what do you think that *bastardo* Bartolomé said to me when he turned up at my *finca* a few minutes ago? He told me that he already has a wife and seven children in Argentina, but for old time's sake, he would like to treat me to a dirty weekend in Ibiza!'

Ellie and I tensed as we made a supreme effort not to snigger. Fortunately, Maria was now probably too far up on her high horse to have noticed, anyway.

'What kind of a woman does he think I am?' she snapped, thumping the ground with her hoe. 'A weekend?' she squeaked. 'Pah! I have had constipation for longer!' She wagged a bony finger at us, her expression deadly serious. Then, leaning forward, she lowered her voice to a quivering croak and declared, 'I am a woman of principle, an upholder of the values of the old days. When I give myself to a man, it is for life – *not* for a weekend!'

Much as I respected Maria's rectitude, I couldn't

help but feel that someone more cynical than I might be of the opinion that, at over ninety years of age, her differentiating between 'for life' and 'a weekend' could be regarded as tempting providence a mite too recklessly. But, knowing her as I did, I was confident our indestructible old *vecina* would be around to thump her hoe for more weekends than she could wag a finger at yet.

She dipped into the pocket of her long black frock and pulled out her pearly white false teeth. 'And that is why, good neighbours, I must ask your permission to throw these down your well. It is the deepest in the area, and so the best place for them.'

There was nothing to say to that, so Ellie and I made a simultaneous 'be our guest' gesture. As the discarded dentures plopped into the water far below, Maria brushed her hands together, flashed us one of her infectious 'two-up-three-down' smiles, then turned to shuffle off, calling back to Ellie: 'Never again, *Señora de Escocia*, will I waste valuable time saving myself for any man!'

Darkness falls quickly in the valley, dusk limited to the few minutes it takes the sun to dip behind the pine-fringed ridges of Abidala Mountain in the west, so Ellie and I were glad of the bright glow which suddenly spread out from the far end of the house as we picked our way homeward through the trees.

'Looks like the wiring-up exercise has gone well,'

I commented. 'And not one scream of death by electrocution. Told you Sandy and Charlie knew what they were about.'

'The blind leading the blind,' was Ellie's dry response. 'Remind me to say a prayer of thanks to Saint Sparky when I go to bed tonight.'

The sound of what I took to be Juan the electrician's van rattling off down the lane told me that all had gone according to plan. As far as Ellie was concerned, the boys' and my undertaking to do everything without paying for professional assistance was still intact, and I felt that the fib I'd told her to uphold it on this occasion was justified on the grounds of safety alone. The results, when I saw them, vindicated the deception even more, however. What had previously been a dark, uninviting area of the garden at night had been transformed into a place of stunning beauty. Soft light from lanterns on the wall threw the stonework into rugged relief, etching intricate, three-dimensional patterns that wandered randomly between the spreading veils of ivy. That scruffy old wall had been turned into a sculpture to delight the eye. Even the sooty smudge that had been the catalyst for the whole exercise appeared surprisingly attractive – a bold brushstroke now forming the focal point in a picture of unadorned natural charm.

'But wait 'til you see this,' grinned Charlie, throwing a switch on the house wall. 'Magic, or what?'

The little green floodlights that we had concealed here and there in the surrounding grove of pines did indeed add a magic touch to the scene, their pastel glow spreading up through the branches and creating yet another dramatic dimension in what was well on the way to becoming something of a jewel in Ca's Mayoral's unpretentious crown. And it was already easy to see that the modest cost of setting this scene would be more than justified in the considerably higher value that such an asset would ultimately add to the property.

The project having been her brainchild, Ellie was understandably pleased with herself, and it showed. To much squirming and mumbled objection, she gave the boys hugs of congratulation for their contribution to a good job shaping up to being well done.

'I've got an idea,' she beamed. 'I know the barbecue area's still far from being finished, but I think we should eat out here tonight – just to kind of celebrate the switching-on of the lights. Well, if they can make a fuss about such events in Oxford Street in London and Times Square in New York, why shouldn't we throw our own little party here?'

The word 'party' did it. The old worktable and four rickety chairs were quickly carried out from the *almacén*, and a makeshift barbecue cobbled together from the remains of a rusty bucket with a piece of wire mesh laid on top. It worked a treat.

Sardines never tasted so good. Ellie had bought the little fish straight from one of the boats down at Port d'Andratx earlier in the day, and if there's a better way to eat sardines than when they're sea-fresh and cooked in the open air over a charcoal grill, then I've still to discover it. A sprinkling of salt, the juice of lemons plucked from a nearby tree while the fish are sizzling away, a bowl of homemade tomato *salsa* on the side, and you have a feast fit for a king. I've heard it said that the best place of all to eat sardines is on the beach where the fishermen have landed them, and where the tang of the sea and the sound of the waves add the perfect accompaniment. Maybe so, but for me, there could have been no greater pleasure than to be sitting in our softly-lit grove that autumn evening, shielded from the outside world by the mellow warmth of the old wall, the air heavy with the scent of pine mingling with the wood smoke from the old bucket. At that moment, with all the family gathered round the table and Bonny lying contentedly at our feet, I wouldn't have exchanged that simple little corner of the Ca's Mayoral garden for all the manicured opulence of the O'Brien's mansion. And if that's the nearest I ever get to feeling like a millionaire, then that'll do for me.

The old chair creaked as I sat back and sipped my wine, my mood as mellow as the lanternlight on the wall. I looked up through the canopy of pine branches to the moonless sky, in which those

355

almost touchable Mediterranean stars trembled and glinted in a velvet cushion of deepest purple. My thoughts returned momentarily to Scotland, where dusk today would have seen flocks of rooks tumbling and swirling in the chilly skyscape like pieces of burnt paper blowing in the wind as they made their way to their roosts in the now leafless woods. I recalled the plaintive call of wild geese that would now be echoing through the frosty darkness above our old home, heralding the arrival of thousands of the great birds from their summer breeding grounds on the far fringes of the Arctic Circle. As if to remind me of how our lives had changed, a nightingale's liquid song rose up from a thicket down by the dry bed of the *torrente*, near the well where Ellie and I had witnessed old Maria marking her 'life-changing' decision an hour or so ago. Even the nightingale's fluting cascades of song were a sign that he'd soon be faced with change, too, heading south, just as we had done a year earlier, although the little bird would be following the swallows to an even farther destination, somewhere in the winter warmth of tropical Africa.

For us less venturesome migrants left behind in Mallorca, the coming few months would bring an abundance of pleasantly-temperate days, with associated cloudless nights on which, as the old almanac predicted, the cold would start to nip. But I was looking forward to it. Unlike the previous winter, when our arrival in the valley had been greeted by a freak snowfall and we hadn't even one stick of fuel for the fire, we now had a huge pile of wood that was the legacy of Pepe Suau's dramatic pruning of our orchards. I counted us fortunate indeed to be faced with a winter of choice between the aromatic subtleties of logs cut from the branches of orange, lemon, apricot, pomegranate, quince, persimmon and all the other exotic fruit trees on the *finca*.

Now that the apprehensions that had coloured our first year on the island were being replaced by a keen appetite for whatever lay ahead, there was a welcome atmosphere of optimism at Ca's Mayoral. And the satisfaction that I could see would be derived from completing previously unthought-of *dolce vita* projects like the barbecue area was no more than a natural extension of this.

Tomorrow we would drive up the spectacular corniche road that weaves its northerly way along the Tramuntana mountainsides high above the sea, our destination the pretty old town of Sóller, where, according to a newspaper ad that the boys had finally found, a snooker table 'just right' for the proposed games room was for sale. En route, there would be the workshop of Juan Juan the *carpintero* man for me to visit in Andratx. Ellie had noticed some old *persiana* shutters stacked outside his door – 'just right', she thought, for stripping down to the original wood and using to form the basis of the games room bar that Charlie had so brilliantly suggested. It was also Charlie who, after the last of the grilled sardines had been

357

devoured, reminded me of the suggestion that I, a non-swimmer of all people, had made one oppressively hot and humid August evening – the suggestion that the building of a swimming pool before next summer wouldn't just be a good idea, but an absolute necessity. I'd even predated, some-what rashly as it now seemed to me in the relative cool of autumn, Ellie's maxim that such an invest-ment would add considerably more value to the property than the cost of its construction. She was quick to pick up on Charlie's reminder now.

'It's well over two months since you promised me you'd start getting quotes for a pool the very next day,' she told me. 'That's a lot of *mañanas*, even by your adopted Sa Coma valley standards.'

Visions of impending red figures on our bank statements loomed before me. I poured myself another glass of wine, then, crossing my fingers under the table, smiled calmly and said, 'You're absolutely right. As soon as we get back from Sóller tomorrow, I'll go into Andratx and talk to Toni Ensenyat the builder about an estimate.'

Ellie shook her head. 'I've got an even better idea. Toni's place is only just along the street from Juan Juan's, so I think you should go and see him *before* we go to Sóller as well. Oh, and by the way,' she went on, a pertinent afterthought obviously having popped into her head, 'just in case you get waylaid by your chum Jordi like that day you went to buy the Proplast crack-filler, this time *I'll* come with you!'

'And so will we!' the boys promptly declared.

Clearly, I had finally run out of *mañanas*. My sighs getting heavier as the wine bottle got lighter, I raised my glass and resignedly proposed a toast: 'Here's to family decisions.'

'*Viva* democracy!' said Sandy.

'*Viva* swimming pools!' grinned Charlie. 'And yachts and speedboats and Mercedes sports cars!'

Charlie worried me.

Ellie smiled in that 'look for the best in everything' way of hers. 'But most of all,' she said, clinking glasses, 'here's to our future here.'

'*Viva* the future!' we all chanted. 'And *viva* Mallorca!'